UNDERSTANDING POLICE HUMAN RELATIONS

by
Dilip K. Das

The Scarecrow Press, Inc.
Metuchen, N.J., & London
1987

The author gratefully acknowledges permission to reprint the following materials previously published by him:

Excerpts from "Police and Community in America: Influences from Across the Atlantic," Police Studies, Vol. 9, No. 3 (Fall 1986). Used by permission of Anderson Publishing Co. (John Jay College of Criminal Justice, New York).

Excerpts from "Handling Urban Disorders: Are the Lessons Learned from Past Police Practices Incorporated in State-Mandated Recruit Training?" Police Studies (Fall 1984). Used by permission of Anderson Publishing Co. (John Jay College of Criminal Justice, New York).

"Some Issues in Police Human Relations Training," reproduced from the Journal of Police Science and Administration, Vol. 12, No. 4 (December 1984), pp. 412-424, with permission of the International Association of Chiefs of Police, P.O. Box 6010, 13 Firstfield Road, Gaithersburg, MD 20878.

Library of Congress Cataloging-in-Publication Data

Das, Dilip K., 1941–
    Understanding police human relations.

    Bibliography: p.
    Includes index.
    1. Police psychology.   2. Police training.
I. Title.
HV7936.P75D37   1987   363.2'01'9   87-4734
ISBN 0-8108-1994-5

This book is dedicated to the memory of
my wife, Tripti, who expired on our way
to America in 1978, and to my children,
Trideep and Mintie.

CONTENTS

LIST OF TABLES AND FIGURES

Table

Figure

ACKNOWLEDGMENTS

My heartiest thanks are due to all writers and publishers for allowing me to make use of their ideas and words.

This book is a product of my Ph.D. dissertation at Sam Houston State University, Huntsville, Texas. I am grateful to Dr. Larry T. Hoover, who chaired the Dissertation Committee, and the members, Dr. Victor G. Strecher, Dr. Marilyn D. Moore, and Professor Jerry D. Dowling for their insightful comments on the subject of the book.

In connection with the research on police human relations, I had invaluable assistance from all Peace Officer Standards and Training (POST) Commissions in the country as well as the National Association of State Directors of Law Enforcement Training (NASDLET), the national coordinating body of mandated training programs. I am most grateful to the Executive Directors, the Training Coordinators, and many other officials who supplied me with course materials, responded to my numerous telephone queries, and supported me in every possible way. These officials are indeed helpful, dedicated, and competent professionals.

I owe a debt of gratitude to Dr. Robert J. Fischer, Chair, Department of Law Enforcement Administration at Western Illinois University, for his unfailing help and support in this work. In his capacity as the Director of Criminal Justice Research Center at the University, Dr. Steven M. Cox has always been available for assistance and counseling in connection with the book. I am also grateful to Elaine Derry and Elaine Vanni, who had to put up with a lot of the burden I placed on them with endless correspondence with the training authorities. Dr. Michael H. Hazlett, my colleague, generously offered me his skills, time, and scholarship in doing the statistical analyses used in the book.

Finally, Carelin Gingerich deserves sincerest thanks for her excellent secretarial support in the preparation of the manuscript. Without Carie's help this book would have never seen the light of day.

INTRODUCTION

Asking Jesus to exercise "authority" over the sickness that paralyzed his servant, the centurion said (Matthew 8):

> I am personally under authority and have soldiers under me. To one I say, "Go!" and he goes; to another, "Come!" and he comes; and to my slave, "Do this!" and he does it.

The Indian police, which I joined as an assistant superintendent of police (lieutenant) in 1965, was founded on a solid structure of "authority" as rigid as that described by Matthew in the Bible. It served as an impregnable fortress of colonial power. The British trained their colonial bureaucrats to be intensely loyal to the imperial masters, the higher echelons of that steelframe of bureaucracy were filled by officers from Britain, and the Indians manned the subordinate positions. A strong arm of that bureaucracy was the police with the mandate to defend the interests of the empire at all costs.

I came to the police almost two decades after India's independence with a Master's degree in English literature. Humanism, liberal thinking, and the idealistic values that literature generated were probably some of the first sacrifices at the altar of the new career. Policing seemed to demand an ability to live with insensitivity. Four centuries ago, while musing on what made a good police officer, Shakespeare's Dogberry in Much Ado About Nothing said:

> You are thought here to be the most senseless and fit man for the constable of the watch; therefore bear you the lantern. This is your charge: you shall comprehend all vagrom men; you are to bid any man stand, in the prince's name.

Anyone devoid of finer senses and ready to obey a superior's commands could be an excellent candidate for a policeman's job! This I learned soon after joining the Indian Police.

The sense of disillusionment became more pronounced during the late 1960s and early 1970s when all over the world there was an upsurge of students. My literary fire must have turned into ashes because I learned to look upon those young, impetuous, and bright youths as subversive, irresponsible, and mindless. Again, I could understand my metamorphosis in the words of another Shakespearian police officer, namely, Constable Dull in Love's Labour's Lost:

> I'll make one in a dance, or so;
> or I will play
> On the tabor to the Worthies,
> and let them dance the hay.

Policing taught me to look at people through the master's eyes, the perspective of the ruler. Instinctively I seemed to have realized that to survive was to play to the tune of the establishment. I was not different from Constable Dull who was proud of being able to play to the "Worthies."

During the tumultuous 1970s, I decided to tour several European countries to observe how the police were handling the unique phenomenon of youth revolts. To me it was a pilgrimage, a mission to understand how the police worked in the world's most affluent and liberal societies. What I saw made me more uneasy about my occupation of policing. Although the British police seemed to have exercised restraints, there were signs of open battles between students and police in France, Germany, Italy, Holland, and the rest of Europe, including Scandinavia. Everywhere in the continent the police aroused hostile reaction from many segments of the population by their handling of youth protests. Anger, hostility, and hatred against the police were written large in every campus across Europe. To some the police seemed to have caused more problems than the troublesome youths they were trying to contain.

I witnessed in those societies the same hostility and antipathy against the police that I experienced in India. As a matter of fact, when my Indian experience was reinforced by the European exposure, a stronger feeling was driven home that policing was the Cinderella of professions. It was the curiosity to explore my disillusionment that led me to join the Criminal Justice graduate program at Michigan State University after fifteen years of policing in India. A year later the same urge took me to Sam Houston State University for a Ph.D. in criminal justice, and then to Western Illinois University to teach law enforcement.

Twenty years spent in active police work in India, studying policing as a student, and teaching law enforcement in the United States have not changed the impressions of the police I acquired as a young officer in India. True, the Indian police were founded by the British to defend their colonial interests. Based on the Irish model, the police were trained to identify themselves with the rulers, although this has never been police philosophy in Britain nor in other Western democracies. However, my personal experience in those countries did not alter the image of the police in my heart. Even in the land of the Bill of Rights, police brutality, discrimination, corruption, politicalization, and so on, have been part of the police tradition over the last 150 years. Notwithstanding the geographical, cultural, and political differences, the police in India, their counterparts in Europe, and American police shared many traits.

My experience is a personal testimony to the existence of a universal core of Cinderella-like qualities in policing. No doubt such characteristics differ in intensity from one society to another as the police are products of the societies they come from. However, nowhere are the police able to escape the inevitable consequences of the occupation. Hence, alienation, authoritarianism, cynicism, and other negative features in the police transcend the boundaries of time and space. Self-righteousness, the public posture of being defenders of justice, and a nagging uncertainty about themselves have been pursuing the police throughout history. "Simple Constable" Elbow's words in Shakespeare's Measure for Measure bear a contemporary relevance:

> If it please your honor, I am the poor duke's constable, and my name is Elbow. I do lean upon justice, sir, and do bring in here before your good honor two notorious benefactors.

Elbow seems to echo the allegedly self-righteous attitude of American police. They, too, brought the Mapps, Mirandas,

and many such people to the court, but the United States
Supreme Court maintained that they were probably not "leaning
upon justice."

Finally the experience in America, as well as in the
other parts of the world including India, demonstrates that
education and training are the only means to change the
police. In a negative sense training enabled the British to
enthuse millions of bureaucrats to defend the Colonial interests,
which insured for the empire that the Indian police manned
by Indians would prosecute the Indian freedom fighters, including Gandhi, for asking the alien masters to quit India.
The improvement of American police is certainly attributable
to increased training and education. Many observers of comparative policing (Fosdick, 1969; Smith, 1960; Bayley, 1976;
and Berkeley, 1969) have admired the superiority of police
training in Europe as well as Japan. According to them, the
secret of those successful police forces is their training. The
remedy for restoring Cinderella to her beauty and grace,
therefore, seems to lie in effective police education and training. Exactly what is effective, however, has not yet been
spelled out. Nevertheless, it cannot be denied that the police
need to be sensitive to people's hopes, aspirations, and sentiments. In order to achieve this understanding, they seem
to be in the need of more human rather than technological
training.

It is important, therefore, to explore what is police
human relations and examine whether it can be a means of
improving policing. In spite of all the technological advance-
ments, American police have not been able to solve the crime
problem. It is also widely recognized that the police alone
are not responsible for their ineffectiveness against crime.
After all, they are only a part of the larger system of criminal
justice. However, the police have been traditionally looked
upon as an agency for keeping the peace and rendering service in response to public demands. Without neglecting crime
work, probably it is pragmatic for them to "try to achieve
excellence in the delivery of service not directly related to
crime control" (Das, 1985, p. 384). In their study of the
unique attributes of excellent companies, Peters and Waterman
have found that such companies "stick to their knitting"
(1982, pp. 13-15, 295, 299) which they explain as a quality
in outstanding organizations of sticking "very close to their
central skills." Excellent companies invest their energy and

resources in businesses in which they can use their expertise
to the best advantage without having to leave their base.

Policing is people business and people want the police
to maintain the peace as well as be available for all kinds of
service. According to McNee (1983, p. 243), the last commissioner of the London Metropolitan Police, the "appropriate
measure" of police efficiency as well as effectiveness is "public
satisfaction with its police force." Turk says that (1981,
p. 123) an ideal of "mutual civility" fostered in "a civil police,"
as well as a civil citizenry, can be the most effective remedy
against police deviance. So the police need to develop skills
and values as human relations experts. Excellent companies
regard profit as "a natural by-product of doing something
well" (Peters and Waterman, 1982, p. 284). In the same
spirit the police should bear in mind that their success in human relations may contribute to their effectiveness in crime
control. What is police human relations will be the subject
matter of the chapters that follow.

References

Bayley, D. H. (1976). Forces of order. Berkeley: University of California.

_____. (1977). Police and society. Beverly Hills, CA:
Sage Publications.

Berkeley, G. (1969). The democratic policeman. Boston:
Beacon Press.

Das, D. K. (1985). What can the police learn from "excellent
companies"? Journal of Criminal Justice, 13(4), 381-386.

Fosdick, R. B. (1920). American police systems. New York:
The Century Co. (reprint 1969). Montclair, N.J.: Patterson
Smith.

McNee, D. (1983). McNee's law. London: Collins Publishers.

Peters, T. J., & Waterman, R. H., Jr. (1982). In search of
excellence: lessons from America's best run companies.

Smith, B. (1960). Police systems in the United States. New York: Harper & Row.

Turk, A. T. (1981). Organizational deviance and political policing. In C. D. Shearing (ed.), Organizational police deviance. Toronto: Butterworth.

Chapter 1

HUMANE ROOTS OF AMERICAN POLICE

Human relations is so abstract a subject that it is difficult to present it in precise and objective terms. Understanding it in the context of policing is equally challenging. It may be understood as lack of authoritarianism, absence of corruption, service attitude, good public relations, and in many other ways which essentially signify value-oriented qualities desirable for the police. However, the list of such worthwhile attributes is likely to be endless and, therefore, a discussion on police human relations can be unwieldy. In view of such a disconcerting possibility, it is proposed to adopt here a historical perspective to analyze the roots of police human relations which will involve an examination of the nature of the formative forces of American police. It is hoped that an approach of this nature will provide more tangible insights into the nature of police human relations.

In analyzing the formative forces it is seen that the police in this country were envisioned to be anchored in a few basic values and ideals. The sources of these value-shaping influences are primarily three: the Bill of Rights, the Metropolitan Model of 1829, and the service tradition of American police. Each of these historical landmarks has made its unique contribution to the philosophy, moral character, and idealistic underpinnings of American police. These value-oriented dimensions can be regarded as the basic constructs of police human relations in America.

While referring to the ideals that American police can find in the Bill of Rights, it is noted that this historical document does not even mention the word, "police." However, the idealistic roots are clearly visible in its many references to the exacting standards of policing. In this country the government is committed to "insure domestic tranquility" for promoting "general welfare" and, more importantly, securing "the blessings of liberty." For achieving these cherished goals the Bill of Rights, as Becker and Whitehouse (1979, p. 11) maintain, deals with "the conduct of the enforcement of laws by police organizations and police personnel." Proper respect for the rights of citizens and the appreciation of official restraints have been emphasized through the concepts of probable cause, due process, self-incrimination, excessive bail, excessive fine, cruel and unusual punishment, and other procedural guarantees.

It can be said that the Bill of Rights echoes the ideals enshrined in Western civilization concerning the humane exercise of coercive authority by the State. It embodies some of the most refined ideas of the Enlightenment thinkers like Montesquieu, Rousseau, Voltaire, and Beccaria. According to Walker (1980, p. 44), "Enlightenment ideas about human rights" provided the basis for the American revolution and found most eloquent expression in the Declaration of Independence. He explains:

> The U.S. Constitution embodied the ideas of Locke, Montesquieu, Beccaria, and others that liberty could be best served by defining and limiting the powers of government. The Bill of Rights contained in the first ten amendments to the Constitution defined specific limitation upon government authority. The Fourth, Fifth, Sixth, and Eighth Amendments became the cornerstones of individual liberty with respect to the criminal process.

These guarantees "proved to be an irreducible touchstone defining the parameters of the criminal process."

The norms of policing outlined in the Bill of Rights seem to be echoing (Bittner, 1980, p. 17) the "aspiration of Western society to abolish violence and install peace as a stable and permanent condition of everyday life." These guidelines and directions, based on rational principles of Enlightenment, seem to embody the belief that in modern, policed societies (Silver, 1967, p. 13) the police personify "the values of the center." With their "organizationally defined missions," they make these values "palpable in daily life." Procedural restraints contained in the provisions of the Bill of Rights invite law enforcement agents "to spell out and

examine the fundamental assumptions of our system of social
control" (Skolnick & Woodworth, 1967, p. 136). As stated
in Lisenba v. California, the police must be fully sensitive
and completely attuned to the "fundamental fairness essential
to the very concept of justice." According to Eldefonso and
Coffey (1981, p. 23), police officers must be appreciative of
the spirit of American legal philosophy. They say:

> The law enforcement officer must look not only to
> the Constitution and the Bill of Rights for the pro-
> tection of the individual, but to the penumbras, or
> shades, of the Bill of Rights as well to guide his or
> her action in order to guarantee the rights of the
> criminally accused.

Enshrined in the Bill of Rights is the direction for the
police concerning how to treat those whom they govern, as
well as how to govern themselves. As the most visible form
of coercive governmental authority, the police in the public
mind are synonymous with government itself. The government
needs legitimate power, as Madison (Gabriel, 1954, p. 75)
mentioned, to "enable" themselves "to control the governed."
However, government also needs "to control itself." This can
be achieved through "auxiliary precautions" like the flexible
and dynamic ideals set forth in this American Magna Carta,
namely, the Bill of Rights. Its validity and contemporaneity
for police conduct is perennial. "Due Process" will remain an
eternal yardstick for just and fair police action. Justice Frank-
furter stated in Rochin v. California that there was no "formal
exactitude or fixity of meaning in the due process clause."
It is not constrained by "a fixed technical context" as it is
applicable in "a continuing process." In the words of this
famous jurist, the police should be able to appreciate as follows:

> In each case, "due process of law" requires an eval-
> uation based on a disinterested inquiry pursued in
> the spirit of science, on a balanced order of facts
> exactly and fairly stated, on a detailed consideration
> of conflicting claims.

These precepts of police conduct are also uniformly
valid in every part of the country. A police officer, wher-
ever he or she may be, must be aware that (Klotter & Kanovitz, 1985, p. 35) "limitations in exercising these powers have

been placed on the states by the specific provisions of the
Constitution and by court decisions." Thus, transcending
all constraints of time, place, and situation, the Bill of Rights
has set forth before American police a clear and unimpeachable
set of higher values of law. Hall (1982, p. 212) explains
that "a variety of humane values limits the efficiency of purely
logical adjudication and the discovery of the truth."

Entrusted with such noble purpose and sensitive responsibilities, the police are expected to be permeated with right
understanding and appreciation of law. It is obvious that such
ideals cannot be internalized by practitioners of the craft of
policing trained only in the mechanics of their trade. Implicit
in those values is the police need for wisdom and enlightenment to be able to act in accordance with the principles based
on humane concerns.

The English Impact

Another major influence in the growth of American police
is Sir Robert Peel's Metropolitan model. This historical development has been so profusely documented that much of the
discussion in this section will be basically a restatement of the
well-recognized and established position. Nevertheless, this
influence will be analyzed here in order to reiterate the humane nature of the English model and its importance as the
prototype of American police. While the Bill of Rights con-
tains the Enlightenment ideology for policing to be grounded
on the higher values of law, this model across the Atlantic
draws attention to the need for police adherence to democratic
and moral principles which contributed to the humane basis
of Peel's innovation.

Fosdick (1969, p. 82) commented that the failure of the
existing American police system led to the importation of the
British model. According to Miller (1977, p. X), "1830 marks
the first full year of operation of the London police, and the
beginning of a decade in New York marked by social disorder
and increasing discussion of adopting a London-model police
force." He adds that by 1845 "Americans adopted the general
structure of the London force." Richardson (1974, p. 17)
says that the idea of "a salaried, bureaucratic, uniformed
police" was "borrowed" from England. It was from that country that America imported the concept of "a policed society

in which the community creates an agency responsible for im-
posing order and discipline."

Lane (1967, pp. 34-35) mentions that the mayor of Boston wanted the city police to follow "the system of London."
According to Monkkonen (1981, p. 38), the Metropolitan police
were "the model for the United States police system." Manning
(1977, pp. 98-100) comments that American police were "based
upon the principles enunciated by Sir Robert Peel," and Radelet (1980, p. 5) adds that within a decade after 1844 when
Peel's model was adopted in New York, "the main features of
the London Metropolitan Police were firmly established in this
country." Booth (1962, p. 8) observes that the police systems of England and the United States share fundamentally
common features as both were established on "the Anglo-Saxon
principle that each community is responsible for preserving
its own law and order," and the police are subject to "democratic control." As a matter of fact, it has been argued
(Sherman, 1983, p. 147) that not only American cities but the
whole of Western Europe "eventually moved toward this civilian
police model" started by Peel.

In regard to the nature of English police, some argue
that it was burgeoise instrument for the protection of class
interests. Harring (1983, p. 13) maintains:

> Marx clearly understood the police to perform a critical
> function in the reproduction of capital; namely, the
> repression and disciplining of the working class.
> Friedrich Engels fully shared this understanding. For
> example, he saw a constant relationship between the
> number of arrests in Manchester and the number of
> bales of cotton consumed in city mills. These obser-
> vations were made with reference to 18th and 19th
> century Britain.

Monkkonen (198, p. 42) points out the class nature of the
police was inevitable in the very genesis of the preventive
police that Peel popularized. It necessitated the identification
of a "crime-producing dangerous class" responsible for producing "the criminal behavior." He does not say that "the
new police was originally created with a purposeful class control function" but implies that "class control resulted from
their efforts to prevent crime, one of the major reasons for
creating the new police." According to him, "the goal of class

control followed as an unintended consequence of the new idea
of preventing crime."

Numerous authorities regard the Metropolitan Police as
a democratic, people-oriented institution. Charles Reith (1956,
pp. 140-142) notes that the members of the force were asked
to cultivate "mild manners" and be "respectful" and "civil" to
the public in order to earn popular respect and support.
As a matter of fact, "approval, respect, and affection of the
public" were the goals police officers were asked to work for.
Lyman (1964, p. 152) comments that since "it was essential
that the police win public acceptance," Peel insisted on "the
selection of personnel" as one of the "important" tasks for
the Joint Commissioners. He felt that "retired, noncommission-
ed army officers with good character certificates" would be
"suitable" for recruitment. He firmly believed that "the moral
character of the police be above suspicion."

According to Critchley (1967, p. 52), the new force was
reared "as a democratic body, in tune with the people, understanding the people, belonging to the people and drawing its
strength from the people." Banton (1964, pp. 223, 231, 237,
239) observes that English officers were trained to regard
themselves "as public servants under the law" without ap-
propriating to themselves the authority to act "as representa-
tives of the law" that American officers tend to do. He elaborates that English police officers have traditionally imbibed
certain "sacred" qualities like a "clearly established" role, a
sense of "moral rectitude," "invulnerability to public criticism,"
and so on. Commenting on the influence of English police on
the English character, Gorer (1955, p. 337) says:

> I would like to suggest that, increasingly during the
> past century, the English policeman has been for his
> fellow-citizens not only an object of respect but also
> a model of ideal male character, self-controlled, pos-
> sessing more strength than he has to call into use
> except in gravest emergency, fair and impartial,
> serving the abstraction of Peace and Justice rather
> than any personal allegiance or sectional advantage.

Stead (1977, pp. 76-81) argues that Peel did not intend
to create a "new style, more respectable watchman" through
the Metropolitan Police Act of 1829. He sought to link the
"New Police" with the spirit and halo of an age-old tradition.

The Act "laid down that the new police were to hold the most
ancient of England's public offices: the office of constable."
Thus, with vision and imagination, Peel brought to bear the
impact of hallowed common law tradition on the newly created
force.   These "fit and able men" were ushered in as officers,
"with all such Powers, Authorities, Privileges, and Advantages" as could be derived from the "Common Law of the Realm."
It was made clear that the new functionary was not to be
viewed as a domestic mercenary.   His was a unique status with
the "power to encroach upon the liberty of the subject" which
was by no means compatible with "the status of any military
rank, even the highest."

     Tobias (1975, p. 96) comments that "the special nature
of the police of Great Britain lies in the fact that it springs
from common-law roots."   It represents "the community policing
itself" and British police were not, like the police in France,
"the heir of the 'police of the prince' of the Roman Empire,
tracing its descent through feudal times, and standing armies
to the gendarmeries of continental despots."   According to
Brogden (1982, pp. 170-173), "the particular style of policing
practiced in mainland Britain" would not be possible without
popular approval and consent.   He adds that it symbolizes
a "concrete ideology, a major and substantive view of the
relation between civil society and police apparatus."   Historically, Brogden points out, the British police officer was con-
ceived as a "citizen-in-uniform," deriving authority from "traditional common law, rather than from statute," and engaging
in preventive policing through an active involvement "in the
social life of the community."

     Moral and democratic attributes of the British police
have been noted widely by American scholars.   It has been
found (Jackson, 1985, p. 137) that "the peculiar relationship
between the British police and the public" is viewed even today by a vast majority of police leaders in that country "as
one of consent--not threat, as one of comity--not enmity, as
a nonadversarial relationship with the public at large."   Manning (1977, p. 98) comments that the Metropolitan police upon
which American police were "initially designed" were charged
with the responsibility of preventing "crime without resorting
to repressive legal sanctioning."   Theirs was a mandate to
enable civil administration to "avoid military intervention in
domestic disturbances."   According to Reppetto (1978, p.
303) Peel's police enjoyed a "moral consensus ... in carrying

out their role as moral preceptors." It was a model that embodied democratic policing with the unique "advantage of close
contact with the public." Allan Silver (1967, pp. 14-15) maintains that the Metropolitan police acted "as the official representative of moral order in daily life." They constituted a
"continual pervasive moral display ... pervasive moral assent
... the extension of moral community."

Rubinstein (1973, p. 10) argues that Jeremy Bentham,
Patrick Colquhoun, Edwin Chadwick, and Henry Fielding--
"the principal originators of the idea of centralized police"--
were of the opinion that a well-organized police force would
ultimately "eliminate most crime." Their success would encourage Parliament to treat prisoners in a humane fashion and
eliminate harsh punishments which were imposed for even
petty crimes. It was clear to the architects of the Metropolitan
police that the New Police were "a civilian force" and their
military structure was to "inspire the men." Rubinstein adds
that "the ethical, moral, and value-laden principles connected
with the growth and development" of the police in England
were deeply "mingled with the roots of American police."

Based on the English model with its central core in
democratic principles and moral authority, American police
were to be committed to these values as a part of their philosophy. These are attributes that imply a humane nature of
policing. On the basis of this explanation, democratic principles and moral authority can be considered an important
dimension of police human relations in America.

The Service Tradition

The practice of responding to the calls for service from
the public is viewed by Shane (1980, p. 195) as a unique
feature of the Anglo-American police tradition. He observes
that "the police are an integral though not necessarily an
acknowledged part of the support system of society" in ad-
vanced societies like those in England and America. They
are regarded as "natural allies of human delivery system."
In Britain the tradition of police as a service agency can be
traced to the early history of the Metropolitan model. According to Critchley's Peel, Rowan and Mayne (1977, p. 83)
they were able to "mold" the new police into "the hybrid between a force and a service that has been the outstanding

characteristic of the British police." In regard to development
of policing as an urban service, Monkkonen (1981, p. 55) observes that in the last half of the nineteenth century, American police represented "an important and dramatic change in
the nature of urban life." "American urban administrations,"
he continues, "began to provide a growing range of rational-
ized services--police, fire, health and sewage--which previously had been provided on an entrepreneurial basis by various
organizations."

    Closely linked with this development was the growing
demand for the police to attend to an enormous range of miscellaneous responsibilities. Such a diversified role implicitly
called for police ability to be of service to the people. According to Charles Reith (1956, p. 321), the pressure for
service functions was so heavy that Rowan and Mayne had to
issue a warning that "they would not undertake any duties
of any kind that were not conferred on them by law." However, a variety of factors including constant availability,
ability to use force, militaristic organizational response, and
so on, tended to place the police at the center of all miscellaneous duties. Among service tasks the Metropolitan police
handled included, as Reith records, fire fighting, maintenance
and control of sanitation, issue and control of licenses of all
kinds, inspection of dilapidated buildings, relief of destination,
regulation of weights and measures, collection of taxes, re-
moval of road obstacles, and delivery of postal matters in
outlying areas. They were also responsible for clearing mud
from pavements, suspension of the making of slides by boys
in winter and suppression of top-spinning and hoop-trundling
in streets by children. The police enforced rules against the
use of pavements by smokers, sandwich-board carriers,
sweeps, and bakers. They also prohibited ringing of bells
by muffin-men. Maitland (1974, p. 114) noted that the English Parliament had found the police, "this disciplined force
... handy for many purposes." Steedman (1984, p. 53)
describes this development in the Victorian age:

> The police act of 1856 broke new administrative
> ground by empowering magistrates to oblige the police
> to perform work other than that involved in keeping
> the peace .... The police were expected to perform
> traditional functions of county government, functions
> that involved the mediation of local statutory bodies
> of fairly recent creation, and administrative functions

thrown directly on the police by central legislation in
the 1870's.

On this side of the Atlantic the ever-increasing service
role of the police had always been growing in dimensions.
Wilson (1978, p. 31) mentions that order maintenance for the
watchman walking the beat included everything from "removing
obstructions on streets and keeping pigs from running loose,"
to handling "many situations that had nothing to do with enforcing the law." Lane (1967, p. 17) observed that Boston
police attended to "the care of the streets, the care of the
vaults, and whatever else affects the health, security, and
comfort of the city." In 1920, Fosdick (reprint 1969, pp. 211-
212) complained that the police were employed for "all sorts
of governmental purposes ... made a sort of catch-all for such
miscellaneous duties as cannot easily be accommodated elsewhere." In the early part of the present century, Haller
(1975, p. 321) observes, "the police were involved" in taking
"injured persons to the hospital," family disputes, recovering
lost children, and "the innumerable services that have always
constituted most police work." Goldstein (1977, p. 307) advocates that "ultimate objective of all efforts to improve police
is to increase their capacity to deliver high-quality services
to the citizenry.

Apart from the formal development of the police as
an urban service agency and their responsibilities for an endless range of miscellaneous work which were entrusted to them
through urban administrative arrangement, there was yet
another side to the police service role. This developed as a
result of consumers' demands. As the cities became anony-
mous conglomerations of masses of people, the police were
responding to more and more demands for intervention in
private lives. The constable, the patrol officer--the watchman's descendant--became a "philosopher, guide, and friend"
(Cumming et al., 1965, p. 276).

Various empirical studies conducted by American scholars
(Cumming et al., 1965, p. 279; Reiss 1971, p. 75; and Wilson,
1978, p. 19) have substantiated that citizens' demands for
service constitute an undeniable element of the police role in
society. In their study Cumming, et al, found that about
50% of calls to the police related to a wide range of service
requests concerning health matters, children's problems, incapacitated persons, nuisances, disputes, violence, protection,

missing persons, and youth's behavior. Reiss observed that
83 percent of all calls received by the Chicago police were
concerning noncriminal incidents including disturbances, sick
and injured persons, and miscellaneous events. In his study
of the Syracuse Police Department Wilson (1978, p. 19) found
that nearly 38 percent of the calls to the police were service-
related involving accidents, illnesses, animals, persons in need
of assistance, drunk persons, and so on. Approximately another 30 percent of the calls asking for police help involved
family troubles, assaults, fights, and troublesome neighbors.
Pope (1981, p. 35) states that "in England, too, the service
demands on the police are greater than those for law enforcement." In Facts about the Metropolitan Police (The Metropolitan Police, 1984, p. 4), it is maintained that "few people,
when considering the police, would think of them in terms of
social workers." However, it adds, that "the first Commissioners made it clear" that it was the duty of every police officer
"to help members of the public" and "look upon himself as the
servant and the guardian of the general public." The Metropolitan Police have asked the rank and file to bear in mind
that the calls for service are due to their "reputation" and
"the confidence the public have in them."

     Whitehouse (1978, p. 14) comments that demands for
service have "apparently been present as long as there have
been municipal police departments." Fosdick (1920, reprint,
1969, p. 373), who was an extremely ardent advocate of
strengthening the law enforcement role of the police, admits
that "police work cannot be isolated from other welfare agencies." He explains:

          Policemen on beat probably come more intimately into
          contact with the life of the people than any other class
          of men and their wide opportunities for observation
          can be harnessed to various forms of constructive
          social work.

Radelet (1980, p. 219) argues that the weaker sections of
society have come to depend on the service functions of the
police and the alleged practice of inadequate "services in
inner-city neighborhoods" is viewed by minorities "as the
worst form of racial discrimination." Betz (1985, p. 186)
observes that "the poor and dispossessed have more problems
and less skills in solving them." They, therefore, need that
"the police provide social service." Rubinstein (1973, p. 348),

also, speaks about the people who need services from the
police: they are the ones with "woeful tales of wayward
mates and children," "momentarily angry persons," and "the
poor and the wayward."

As a matter of fact, experience tends to show that all
sections of society look for service from the police. In England, Brogden (1982, p. 206) recalls, the Victorian police
forces bore "responsibilities such as the provision of winter
relief, the pursuit of smallpox suspects, the inspection of
common lodging houses," and so on. But today "the police
institution is perceived by all social strata as the ultimate
safety net" and the police "obviously do play a broad service
role." According to Bittner (1985, p. 313), "there is scarcely
a human predicament imaginable for which police aid has not
been solicited and obtained at one time or another." He
(1974, p. 40) argues that the most important task of the
police is "service" and not "the perennial pursuit of Willie
Sutton." He adds that the policeman is likely to miss "his
true vocation" if he neglects to "follow the footsteps of Florence Nightingale."

Interpreting the reasons for demands for service from
the police that have evolved historically, Manning (1977,
pp. 99-100) states that public services of varied nature were
"central to accumulated police obligations." Services that
people were expected to do for each other were, as it were,
"symbolically" transmitted to the police as people's agents.
He says:

> The police were designed to respond to citizen demands
> and requirements for service as much because this
> represented prevention or deterrence of the sources
> of crime as because the police were intended to act
> symbolically as one citizen would to another in time
> of need.

Manning adds that "the symbolic centrality of police action as
standing for collective concern of people, one for another,
cannot and should not be underestimated."

Conclusion

Many evils that beset the modern American police have

been traced to history. Locke (1982, p. 17) maintains that
"political interference and police corruption" are inextricably
connected with the origins of the police in America. He says
that many other issues including that of "respect and support
for police officers" have been in the forefront of public debate
"since the mid-nineteenth century." Walker (1983, p. 2) refers to various historical problems that have been pursuing
American police including "corruption and inefficiency." According to him, "the police are the prisoners of the past ...
ancient problems linger on ... affect the public image of American police." Discussing the "historical roots of police behavior," Haller (1975, pp. 303, 323) mentions that many negative traits like violence, subculture, politicalization, and the
like are due to "the historically entrenched police orientations."

However, historical roots also link American police to a
few ennobling sources which provide the basis for idealistic
underpinnings. These are higher values of law, democratic
and moral principles, and willingness and skills for service
to the people. History can serve as the rockbed of principles
for the development of an institution and the rich past seems
to be a source of inspiration for the police in England. In
asking his officers to follow "the policing principles of the
Metropolitan Police," the present Commissioner (1985, p. 6)
says:

> I have served contentedly under the wise counsel of
> the "Primary Objects of the Police," the ringing tones
> created by Sir Richard Mayne, Commissioner in 1829
> ... the principles which should govern policing if,
> against many conflicting pressures, it is to blend its
> traditionally British character with the new require-
> ments of a vibrant society.

In a similar manner the Bill of Rights which echoes some
of the finest ideals that flowered during the Age of Enlightenment, can serve as the guide to American police. In numerous
cases in which the Supreme Court of the United States has
dwelt on the need of police appreciation of the spirit of law,
it has reaffirmed the inseparable connection between law enforcement and the Bill of Rights. Over the last half century,
the nation's highest court has demonstrated in Brown v.
Mississippi, Spano v. New York, Miranda v. Arizona, and
many other cases that the provisions in this document embody
the acid test of propriety in police action. In interpreting the

Bill of Rights jurists have found many noble sentiments for
the police to imbibe:

(1) Justice Brandeis:

In a government of laws, existence of the government will be imperiled if it fails to observe the law
scrupulously. Our government is the potent, the
omnipresent teacher. For good or ill, it teaches
the whole people by its example (Olmstead v. United
States, 1928).

(2) Chief Justice Warren:

The methods we employ in the enforcement of our
criminal law have aptly been called the measures by
which the quality of our civilization may be judged
(Coppedge v. U.S., 1962).

(3) Justice Goldberg:

If law is not made more than a policeman's night-
stick, American society will be destroyed (Niederhoffer, & Blumberg, 1985, p. iv).

These words provide ample proof that law enforcement must
be measured by the yardstick of the highest standards of legal
rectitude. This provides a dimension to police human relations
reaffirming that it should be based on an appreciation of the
higher values of law.

The historical links between the Metropolitan police
model and the police in America are inseparable. The English
model as against that of France or Germany, appealed to
America because of the democratic principles and moral authority which are its basic attributes. In his account of the
police forces in Europe, Fosdick (1915, reprint 1969, pp. 22,
87) states that the "extraordinary power" of the German police
was "difficult to comprehend when looked at from the point
of view of English institutions and conceptions." He (1920,
reprint 1969, p. 87) also notes that in France there were
various obstacles to "local autonomy in police matters ... the
principle of home rule in police matters is, to a large extent,
nullified in France." The French police system, Emsley (1983,
p. 163) explains, thrived on "the traditions of la police gen-
erale, of the military nature of policing and policeman."

However, "such elements were discouraged, or at least played
down, in English police forces." Moreover, in continental
Europe where legal system derived from the traditions of
Roman law (Opolot, 1981, pp. 36, 82-83), "the tendency was
to identify police and administration as one." However, under
common law in England, "a sharp distinction was maintained
between police and administrative functions." In the English
system a police officer "possessed only the powers of every
other citizen." Unlike the police forces on the continent,
Stead (1977, p. 76) maintains, English police had "none of
the aggressive authority of the military, none of the insidious-
ness of the spy, none of the petty fogging impudence of the
minor civil servant."

"In the best sense of the term," Glueck (1974,
p. 61) argues, "police work, in the Continental city, is a profession practiced by men of education, training, and dedica-
tion." Mueller (1974, p. xii) notes that Europe had "professional but inadequately democratized police forces," and it is,
therefore, logical that "America's not so professional" but "more
democratic police forces" found the English model more suitable. It had a democratic image, a characteristic of being the
people's police, and had an element of moral authority. These
attributes are described by an erstwhile Commissioner of the
Metropolitan police as follows (Mark, 1977, p. 56):

> The only power we possess is the power to inconven-
> ience by bringing people before the courts, and even
> then we are at risk if we use that power improperly
> or unfairly. The fact that the British police are
> answerable to the law, that we act on behalf of the
> community and not under the mantle of government,
> makes us the least powerful, the most accountable and
> therefore, the most acceptable police in the world.

Terrill (1984, p. 17) corroborates Mark's observation adding
that the police in England are "citizens who happen to be
in uniform." Becker (1973, pp. 68-69), too, mentions that
"the concept of big arrests seldom enters into the philosophy
of the Constable." They are concerned with the humble but
basic tasks of "prevention and protection." Above all, they
are also concerned with "the proper police image" only which,
they know, can generate the "public respect" needed for the
performance of their duties. Thus, democratic principles
and the moral authority that derives from them should be
important aspects of police human relations in America.

Since their inception the police had to attend to a variety of miscellaneous tasks for various reasons. However, in the Anglo-American context miscellaneous bureaucratic functions ceased a long time ago to be police responsibilities in the manner these existed in the Roman Law countries. Nevertheless, the police in England, as well as in America, have always been required to respond to a wide range of requests for help from citizens. In many cases these are from the underprivileged sections of society. This traditional heritage of being a helper and a friend of all people demands an attitude of service on the part of a police officer. These requests involve crisis intervantion, conflict resolution, taking care of alcoholics and handling numerous problems that need psychological as well as various other appropriate skills. It is necessary that police officers are equipped with attitudinal and professional resources for effective handling of service requests. This is an equally important side of police human relations.

As noted above, research has shown that a patrol officer spends most of his or her time in service calls. Service functions, Brown (1985, p. 21) argues, have assumed considerable significance since it is through such involvement that the police are expected "to meet the public safety and quality of life needs of local communities." As pointed out earlier "excellent companies" (Peters & Waterman, 1982, p. 295) "stick to their knitting" which refers to the practice of such companies to build their strategy "on some central skill or strength." According to the authors, "Organizations that branch out somewhat, yet still stick very close to their central skill, outperform all others." Police departments need to regard service tasks as responsibilities that call for their "central skill." It appears that through service tasks they can probably better measure their achievement in terms of tangible results and client satisfaction. These tasks are not as elusive and uncontrollable as law enforcement. It is true that in spite of low achievement, law enforcement will continue to be an important concern for the police. However, proper attention to service tasks will probably enable the police to meet the needs of consumers in a more practical way.

In brief, the humane roots of American police can be traced to a tripartite traditon. Embodied in the Bill of Rights is a message that the police must seek an appreciation of the higher values of law. The Peelian model borrowed by American

police underscores the concerns for moral authority and democratic principles. Another feature of Anglo-American police
tradition, the service role, signifies the need for helping attitudes and skills for service. It is through careful nourishment of these roots that the police in America can find their
true mission. These are to be regarded as the three most
important dimensions of human relations for the police in
America, and the model it presents can be called a historical
model of police human relations.

References

Banton, M. (1964). The policeman in the community. New
    York: Basic Books.

Bard, M. (1973). The role of law enforcement in the helping
    system. In J. R. Snibbe & H. M. Snibbe (eds.), The
    urban policeman in transition: a psychological and socio-
    logical review. Springfield, IL: Charles C. Thomas.

Becker, H. K. (1973). Police systems of Europe. Spring-
    field, IL: Charles C. Thomas.

_____, & Whitehouse, J. E. (1979). Police of America.
    Springfield, IL: Charles E. Thomas.

Betz, J. (1985). Police violence. In F. A. Elliston & M.
    Feldberg (eds.), Moral issues in police work. Totawa,
    NJ: Rowman and Allenheld.

Bittner, E. (1974). Florence Nightingale in pursuit of Willie
    Sutton: a theory of police. In H. Jacob (ed.), The po-
    tential for reform of criminal justice. Beverly Hills, CA:
    Sage Publications.

_____. (1980). The functions of the police in modern
    society. Cambridge, MA: Oelgeschlager, Gunn, & Jain.

_____. (1985). Maintaining peace on skidrow. In W. C.
    Terry III (ed.), Policing society: an occupational view.
    New York: Wiley.

Booth, D. A. (1962). In S. G. Chapman (ed.), The police
    heritage in England and America. East Lansing: Michigan
    State University.

Brogden, M. (1982). The police: autonomy and consent. London: Academic Press.

Brown, L. P. (1985). A future direction for police operations. The Police Chief, 52(6), 21-25.

Coppedge v. United States, 82 U.S. 438 (1962).

Critchley, T. A. (1967). A history of police in England and Wales, 900-1966. London: Constable.

_____. (1977). Peel, Rowan, and Mayne: the British model of urban police. In P. J. Stead (ed.), Pioneers in policing. Montclair, NJ: Patterson Smith.

Cumming, E., Cumming, I., & Edell, L. (1965). Policeman as philosopher, guide, and friend. Social Problems, 12(2), 276-286.

Eldefonso, E. B., & Coffey, A. R. (1981). Criminal law. New York: Harper and Row.

Emsley, C. (1983). Policing and its context 1750-1870. New York: Schocken Books.

Fosdick, R. B. (1915, reprint 1969). European police systems. Montclair, NJ: Patterson Smith.

_____. (1920, reprint 1969). American police systems. Montclair, NJ: Patterson Smith.

Gabriel, R. H. (1954). Hamilton, Madison, and Jay on the Constitution: selections from the federalist papers. New York: Bobbs-Merrill.

Glueck, S. (1974). Continental police practice. Springfield, IL: Charles C. Thomas.

Goldberg, A. (1976). In A. Niederhoffer, & A. Blumberg (eds.), The ambivalent force. Hinsdale, IL: Dryden Press.

Goldstein, H. (1977). Policing a free society. Cambridge, MA: Ballinger.

Gorer, G. (1955). Exploring English Character. New York: Criterion Books.

Hall, J. (1982). Law, social science and criminal theory. Littleton, CO: Rothman.

Haller, M. H. (1976). Historical roots of police behavior: Chicago, 1890-1925. Law & Society Review, 10(1), 303-324.

Harring, S. L. (1983). Policing a class society. New Brunswick, NJ: Rutgers University Press.

Jackson, D. W. (1985). "Public police thyself!" Deadly force and public disorder, two crises in British community policing. Police Studies, 8(3), 132-148.

Klotter, J. C., & Kanovitz, J. R. (1985). Constitutional law. Cincinnati, OH: Anderson.

Lane, R. (1967). Policing the city: Boston 1822-1885. Cambridge, MA: Harvard University Press.

Lisenba v. California, 314 U.S. 219 (1941).

Locke, H. G. (1982). The evolution of contemporary police service. In B. L. Garmire (ed.), Local government police management. Washington, DC: International City Management Association.

Lyman, J. L. (1964). The Metropolitan police act of 1829: an analysis of certain events influencing the passage and character of the Metropolitan Police Act in England. The Journal of Criminal Law, Crimonology and Police Science, 55(1), 141-154.

Maitland, F. W. (1974). Justice and police. New York: AMS Press.

Manning, P. K. (1977). Police work: the social organization of policing. Cambridge, MA: MIT Press.

Mark, R. (1977). Policing a perplexed society. London: Allen and Unwin.

The Metropolitan Police. Community Relations Branch and Public Information Department. (1984). Facts about the Metropolitan police. London: New Scotland Yard.

Miller, W. R. (1977). Cops and bobbies: police authority in New York and London, 1830-1870. Chicago: University of Chicago Press.

Mueller, G. O. W. (1974). In S. Glueck (ed.), Continental police practices. Springfield, IL: Charles C. Thomas.

Monkkonen, E. H. (1981). Police in urban America 1860-1920. New York: Cambridge University Press.

Niederhoffer, E., & Blumberg, A. (1985). The ambivalent force. Hinsdale, IL: Dryden Press.

Olmstead v. United States, 277 U.S. 438. (1928).

Opolot, J. S. E. (1981). World legal traditions and institution. Jonesboro, TN: Pilgrimage, Inc.

Peters, T. J., & Waterman, R. H. (1982). In search of excellence: lessons from America's best run companies. New York: Warner Books.

Pope, D. W. (1981). Preventive policing in the community. In D. W. Pope & N. L. Weiner (eds.), Modern policing. London: Croom Helm.

Radelet, L. A. (1980). The police and the community. New York: Macmillan.

Reiss, A. J., Jr. (1971). The police and the public. New Haven, CT: Yale University Press.

Reith, C. (1956). A new study of police history. Edinburgh: Oliver and Boyd.

Reppetto, T. A. (1978). The blue parade. New York: The Free Press.

Richardson, J. F. (1974). Urban police in the United States. Port Washington, NY: Kennikat Press.

Rochin v. California, 342 U.S. 165 (1952).

Rubinstein, J. (1973). City police. New York: Farrar, Straus and Giroux.

Shane, P. G. (1980). Police and people: a comparison of five countries. St. Louis, MO: Mosby.

Sheman, L. W. (1983). Patrol strategies for police. In J. Q. Wilson (Ed.), Crime and public policy. San Francisco, CA: Institute for Contemporary Studies.

Silver, A. (1967). The demand for order in civil society: a review of some themes in the history of urban crime, police, and riot. In D. J. Bordua (ed.), The police: six sociological essays. New York: Wiley.

Skolnick, J. H., & Woodworth, R. J. (1967). Bureaucracy, information and social control: a study of a moral detail. In D. J. Bordua (ed.), The police: six sociological essays. New York: Wiley.

Stead, P. J. (1977). The new police. In D. H. Bayley (ed.), Police and society. Beverly Hills, CA: Sage Publications.

Steedman, C. (1984). Policing the Victorian community. London: Routledge and Kegan Paul.

Terrill, R. J. (1984). World criminal justice systems: a survey. Cincinnati, OH: Anderson Publishing.

Tobias, J. J. (1975). Police and public in the United Kingdom. In G. L. Mosse (ed.), Police forces in history. Beverly Hills, CA: Sage Publications.

Walker, S. (1980). Popular justice. New York: Oxford University Press.

_____. (1983). The police in America. New York: McGraw-Hill.

Weiner, N. L. (1981). Policing in America. In D. W. Pope & N. L. Weiner (eds.), Modern policing. London: Croom Helm.

Whitehouse, J. E. (1978). Historical perspectives on the police-community service functions. In P. F. Cromwell & G. Keefer (eds.), Police-community relations: selected readings. St. Paul, MN: West Publishing.

Wilson, J. Q. (1969). What makes a better police officer? The Atlantic, 223, 1-10.

_____. (1978). Varieties of police behavior. Cambridge, MA: Harvard University Press.

Chapter 2

NEED FOR TRAINING TO IMPLEMENT THE
HISTORICAL MODEL OF POLICE
HUMAN RELATIONS

Appreciation of the higher values of law, moral authority and democratic principles, and proper attitude as well as skills for service were seen as the basic tenets of the historical model of police human relations in America. But police training in the country was not utilized as a vehicle for building the police on this model and, therefore, it remained a pious hope. Moreover, the absence of such training did not become an urgent public concern till the turbulent 60s which pathetically brought to light many problems and failures of American police. Public criticism regarding police handling of riots and Warren court's numerous pronouncements on police violations of civil rights showed that recruit training in this country was inadequate to make the historical model a reality.

The Metropolitan Police Example

As against this indifference in America, the near religious zeal for training during the formative years of the Metropolitan Police comes as a sharp contrast. Rowan and Mayne, the first commissioners of the "new police," firmly believed that an effective way to build an excellent force was to train the personnel regarding humane conduct. They were particularly sensitive to the fact that there was widespread opposition to "Peel's Bloody Murderers" (O'Byrne, 1981, p. 13). In order to neutralize hostility and antagonism against the constables, they exhorted them to behave with dignity and compassion. With constant care, never-failing vigilance and ceaseless efforts, the commissioners succeeded in acquiring for the "force approval, respect, and affection of the public" (Reith, 1956, p. 140).

Numerous "general instructions" were issued by them highlighting the importance of simple qualities to be practiced by the police officers (Reith, 1956, pp. 141-142). Some of these were the following:

(1) Overlooking ridicule, silly expressions, or ignorant remarks.

(2) Good temper and discretion.

(3) Abjuring of undue violence and harsh language to individuals in custody.

(4) Calm and proper manner, scrupulous civility, and proper control of temper.

(5) Avoidance of insolence, incivility, and interference.

(6) Mild manners and never-failing respectful attitudes.

Strict and detailed attention to such simple precepts brought ample rewards to the Metropolitan Police. It helped them become an object of national pride and their contribution to national life was widely acclaimed.

Simple people-centered principles followed by the leaders of the "new police" strikingly resembled those which were found in excellent American companies studied by Peters and Waterman Jr. (1982, pp. 13, 51, 251, 284). According to these authors, such companies were guided more by "wisdom" than intellect and they kept things "simple." So did the architects of the Metropolitan Police who believed that "a broad, uplifting, shared culture" could be a source of inspiration to the people in an organization. Peel, Rowan, and Mayne were obsessed with "training, continuous self improvement" like the excellent companies. They, too, felt that they needed to state their values "in qualitative rather than quantitative terms."

Peel's nine principles (Davis, 1973, pp. 113-121) are identical to qualitative terms preferred by excellent companies. These principles symbolized "wisdom" concerning humane values and morals:

1. The basic mission of the police was to prevent crime and disorder without having to resort to repressive measures like military force and severe punishment.

2. The ability of the police to perform their duties depended upon public approval and their ability to earn public respect.

3. The police should ensure that the public cooperate voluntarily in the observance of the law.

4. Public cooperation diminished the need for the use of physical force and coercion by the police.

5. Impartial law enforcement, constant service and friendship to everyone, and ready sacrifice in protecting and preserving life were the most important ideals for the police.

6. The police should use only the minimum degree of physical force as the last resort for achieving their objectives.

7. The police should be fully aware of the age-old tradition that the police were the public and the public were the police.

8. The police should never seem to usurp the powers of the judiciary.

9. Police efficiency consisted of the absence of crime and disorder, not the ostensible police efforts against them.

State of Police Training in America

Unfortunately in this country, the historical model of police human relations, as indicated earlier, had only a remote possibility of being inculcated by police officers. This was so primarily because police training in this country has traditionally been a neglected area and until fairly recently there was no reference to human-relations training. According to Walker (1977, pp. 3, 11), American police were "the creatures of partisan politics" since their inception. Police work was not regarded as a professional "career," but it was "a form of casual labor." No need for "special training" for police responsibilities was felt by politicians and others who were at the helm of police affairs.

Walker mentions that with "a few notable exceptions," the absence of training was the rule at the beginning of the

century. According to Haller (1976, p. 303), there was no
police training in Chicago in 1900 although the department had
about 3,225 officers. Before joining the street they received
a "speech from a high-ranking officer, ... a hickory club, a
whistle, and a key to the call box." This was not very different from the situation described by a metropolitan chief
to the Wickersham commission (1931, p. 66):

> I say to him that now he is a policeman, I hope he
> will be a credit to the force. I tell him he doesn't
> need anybody to tell him how to enforce the law, that
> all he needs to do is to go out on the street and keep
> his eyes open. I say: "you know the ten command-
> ments, and you go out on your beat, and you see
> somebody violating one of those ten commandments,
> you can be pretty sure he is violating some law."

Haller (1976, p. 306) further comments that in the 1920s police
training schools "became institutionalized and all recruits were
required to attend." However, the training consisted of
"close-order drill," "revolver and other weapons training,"
"departmental rules," "laws and ordinances," and "tours of
courts and specialized divisions." Haller points out that a
study done in 1929 found police training generally inadequate.
Elsewhere, too, the situation in regard to recruit training was
not at all encouraging. According to Fosdick (1920, reprint
1969, 298), a few cities like New York, Philadelphia, Detroit,
Cleveland, St. Louis, Cincinnati, Newark, Louisville, and
Berkeley maintained that there was "need for thorough-going
instruction." However, a much larger number of cities did
not consider "text books," "classes of instruction," "written
tests" as important. In those cities police recruits received
"a little preliminary practice in patrol in company with an
older officer" and a little bit of "so-called instruction."

It is regrettable that the quality of police training was
rather universally poor and useless. In 1909, however, New
York (Saunders, 1975, p. 139) started a police academy.
Even after the initiation of formal training, Richardson (1970,
p. 68) argues, a rookie's education came from being "indoctri-
nated by the veterans and molded by his contacts with the
public." Training was haphazard, amateurish, and impromptu.
Following the disastrous riots at the Astor theater in 1849,
which the police handled miserably, it was felt that they
needed instruction "in the school of the soldier." As riots

became more frequent, the police were given more and more
training in "infantry tactics and drill." But the police officers
"resented" military training. Endorsing Fosdick's views on
military training for the police, Berkeley (1969, p. 74) mentions that such training could turn an officer into "a good
cog." Moreover, military training led to an indifferent attitude to the public. In fact, in the drill field "cordiality and
sympathy" are not regarded as the most important virtues.
Fogelson (1977, p. 83) records that in 1912 the New York
City School for Recruits, although "reputedly the nation's
finest," suffered from poor quality of instruction, lack of
supervision, and improper curriculum. He (1977, pp. 103-
104) adds that generally the police academies were poor and
instructors were not qualified at all. Students were not
tested and no record was kept.

    According to Fogelson, by 1930 large-scale academies
were operated by some departments. These were an "improvement" over the training establishments that existed earlier
in the period. During this decade, Gammage (1963, pp. 11-
12) recalls, the Pennsylvania State Police Academy started
pioneering work in the area of recruit training. Among the
variety of courses taught at the academy, there were law,
cavalry drill and horsemanship, drill dismounted, boxing,
wrestling, jujitsu, swimming, rifle and pistol shooting, and
handling of machine guns and tear gas. Nevertheless, Gammage observed that this type of training was not capable of
producing police professionals because of the wrong emphasis.
The recruit training was basically characterized by rigorous
military discipline, long working hours and ritualistic adherence to rules and regulations. In spite of all these deficien-
cies, the recognition of the importance of police training was
a significant development. In the 1930s, Saunders (1975,
p. 135) maintains the F.B.I. was able to generate "national
attention to the need for training in all agencies."

    In the 1940s police training started breaking new ground.
As a result of 1943 riots there was a new urgency on strengthening the "police community-relations movement" (Walker,
1977, pp. 124, 163) which brought together "progressive-
minded police administrators and race-relations experts in
allied fields." Walker notes that in this decade "training programs had become established features of most departments."
Smith (1960, pp. 132,282) acknowledges that by the 1940s
a "veritable revolution in police attitudes" to training had

taken place. Now it was regarded as essential for the police.
According to him, the training programs of the Pennsylvania
State Police, New York City Police Department, the New York
State Police, and a few other places were generally satisfact-
ory. Smith, however, points out that the general quality of
the existing programs was rather "uneven and with all but a
few ... distinctly inferior." He regrets that there were
states which did not have a "single training unit worthy of
the name." In numerous states "police schools" were conducted on a "casual basis" for "uncertain periods" with no visible
impact on "the general level of police service." Smaller forces
were not capable of supporting "training of any kind." Larger departments could not operate training facilities regularly
because of the "irregular and unpredictable intervals" of recruitment.

Nevertheless, police training continued to expand in all
directions. During the late 1950s (Wilson, 1963, pp. 166-170),
Chicago Police Department required 455 hours of training out
of which 265 hours were earmarked for criminal law, field
procedures, investigation, and physical training and skills.
In Wilson's (1963, p. 170) program for Chicago recruits, the
subjects and the time allotted for what can broadly be described as human-relations aspects of police work were as
follows:

Basic Sociology	4 hours
Basic Psychology	5 hours
Abnormal Psychology	5 hours
Human Relations	2 hours
Police Minority Group Relations	2 hours
Police-Press Public Relations	2 hours
Ethics	1 hour
Handling Mentally Disturbed	1 hour
Total	22 hours

This constituted only about 5 percent of the total recruit
training hours. It is a reflection on the state of affairs that
even in a city like Chicago, where 20 years later there would
be a black mayor, the time earmarked for police minority relations was only 2 out of 455 hours. Compared to this, physical training and skills alone were taught for 79 hours.

In brief, American police training till the 30s was rather

perfunctory. In the 1940s training for police officers was
gaining momentum and by the late 1950s, it had become more
widespread and elaborate. Nevertheless, the content of training programs did not lay emphasis on building the police on
the basis of the historical model, namely, respect for the
higher values of law, moral authority, and ethical principles
as well as service attitude and skills.

Developments of the 1960s

In spite of the inadequate attention to the historical
model, American police functioned without major challenge till
the 1960s. However, that decade witnessed certain novel and
highly disruptive situations that dismayed the police as well
as made society painfully aware of their problems. The 1960s
were marked by "massive civil disorder" (Wilson, 1985, p.
260), a veritable "due process revolution" (Graham, 1970)
initiated by the United States Supreme Court, and serious
concerns with professionalization of the police. According to
Wilson (1985, p. 239), numerous happenings that took place
in the 1960s facilitated "an institutionalization in all parts of
society of the natural desire of youth for freedom." Regarding the impact of those years, Rumbaut and Bittner (1979,
p. 241) comment that in that period the police found themselves "in the crucible" and confronted with "the crisis of
legitimacy." So powerful was the impact of the challenges
that it shaped our "contemporary conceptions of the police
and the problems of policing." According to Rumbaut and
Bittner, these upheavals were to make the police more responsive to the time. They added that "large-scale research and
planning efforts were initiated--to a great extent, if not
wholly--as the consequence of inquiries that expressed dis-
content with the police." Earle (1973, p. 10) sums up those
momentous developments with a brief statement that "during
the 60s, the task of policing was transformed in dimensions
rather than degree." The major developments of the decade
pointed to the need for policing based on humane ideals incorporated in the historical model.

Controversial police intervention in large-scale unrest,
and frightening challenges faced by them from significant
sections of society, necessitated searching inquiries regarding
the role of the police. According to respectable scholars and
learned commissions, insensible police behavior intensified the

aggressiveness and virulence of protestors. The President's
Commission on Campus Unrest (1970, p. 26) observed that
the police offensives drove "vast numbers of indignant students
and faculty" to make a common cause with those who protested.
It added that "strong feelings of generational loyalty were
aroused as students watched their classmates being dragged
off limp, resisting, and sometimes bloodied, to jails."

According to Skolnick (1969, p. 262), the police betrayed
a lack of perceptive understanding of the social upheavals
in maintaining that the campus disturbances were engineered
by youths of subversive ideological persuasions. He illustrates
his observation by referring to the evidence of the then
F.B.I. Chief, J. Edgar Hoover, before the National Commission
on the Causes and Prevention of Violence. In his testimony
Hoover indicated that the student unrest was the work of Com-
munists. He said:

> Communists are in the forefront of civil rights, anti-
> war, and student demonstrations, many of which
> ultimately become disorderly and erupt into violence.
> As an example, Betina Apthekar Kurzwell, 24 year old
> member of the Communist National Committee, was a
> leading organizer of the "Free Speech" demonstration
> on the campus of the University of California at Berkeley
> in the fall of 1964.

"Abrasive relationships" of the police with certain groups were
attributed as one of the causes of the social unrest (National
Advisory Commission on Civil Disorders, 1968, p. 157). According to Bordua (1967, p. x), "training and discipline could
have helped the police to reduce avoidable provocations in
the 60s."

Police behavior in the course of numerous protest movements showed that the appreciation of the higher values of the
law did not seem to be a part of their philosophy. What can
be inferred from the observations of Skolnick, Bordua, and
the Commissions is that the police were hardly sensitive to the
broad implications of the First Amendment that the people had
the right "peaceably to assemble and to petition the Government for a redress of grievances." Violent and panicky police
reaction also seemed to indicate that the police were not really
"understanding the people" (Critchley, 1967, p. 52). Such

behavior also highlighted the absence in the police of democratic and moral responsibility for developing sensitivity to
people's feelings and sentiments.

The 1960s were marked by a liberal Supreme Court,
presided over by Chief Justice Earl Warren (1962, 369 U.S.
438) who believed that "the methods we employ in the enforcement of our criminal law" were "the measures by which the
quality of our civilization" could be judged.

Graham (1970, pp. 5, 149-150) says that the Warren
Court's interpretations of the Bill of Rights imposed "a tighter
rein on the police" and reflected the judiciary's reactions to
the years of police malpractices. Prior to the Court's ruling
on exclusionary rule, claims Graham, the Baltimore police
conducted a 19-day manhunt in pursuit of two Negro brothers
who were suspected of killing a police sergeant in a liquor
store holdup. In this particular operation, squads of patrolmen, armed with shotguns and clad in bulletproof vests, were
reportedly found to be prowling certain black neighborhoods,
and searching numerous homes on the suspicion that the
wanted persons might have taken shelter inside. In this
connection Graham refers to the records of the U.S. Court
of Appeals for the Fourth Circuit which included the following
account:

> At 2:00 a.m., a search party led by the lieutenant
> knocked on the door, and Mrs. Lankford awakened
> by the knock, opened the door. The officers entered
> the house and began their search.... The husband
> was awakened in his second floor bedroom by two
> flashlights shining in his face and found four men
> with shotguns in his room. They questioned him,
> while other officers searched the remaining rooms, in-
> cluding the children's bedrooms, and left.

In the cases involving violation of individual rights,
the Warren court underlined the need for treatment based on
the higher values of law for the Mapps, Mirandas, Escobedos,
and others like them. In all these stories the Supreme Court
found a streak of police overzealousness that called for conduct based on the spirit of law. In brief, the due process
revolution reaffirmed the need for appreciation of the higher
values of law by law enforcement officers. Never before was
the country's highest court so directly involved in routine

police operations. In a sustained drive to ground police conduct in the Bill of Rights, the Warren Court delved into typical areas in which the police had been found traditionally indifferent to proper respect for law. So these cases involved
everyday law enforcement matters like searches, interrogation,
need for counsel, and so on.

Along with these novel developments, there took place
in the 1960s a more pronounced quest for police professionalism.
According to Richardson (1974, p. 154), professionalism symbolized an effort to enable the police to handle effectively "the
sensitive human relations" demands. It was combined with an
avowed concern to build meaningful police and citizen relations
on a "high code of ethics." Regoli (1976, pp. 1, 5) interpreted the rise of professionalism as a means for the police
to gain public confidence through an ideological change in
their status and higher standards of education, selection, and
training. He pointed out that those dedicated to ideals of
professionalism preferred to view themselves not "as cops but
rather as specialists in human relations." Morton Bard (1973,
pp. 408-411) advocated that, as a professional, the policeman's
primary role was that of a helper. He maintained that law
enforcement was a "participating profession in a helping system." Bard held that law enforcement could not achieve
"maturation" and "responsibility" unless efforts were made to
"maximize the potential of the police as acknowledged members
of a helping profession." In this decade professionalism forti-
fied the ideals of spirit of service and skills for service. Although historically the police have been rendering services
of all sorts, it was through the developments of the nature
narrated above that the new concept of the police as a helping
profession started emerging seriously. As helping professionals they were expected to develop right attitudes as well
as skills for a helping career. These developments gave a
new status to police service functions.

Movement Toward Human-Relations Training

The controversies and debates regarding the police role
in handling the riots of the 60s, the momentous decisions of
the Supreme Court of the United States, and the new perspective that the police were helping professionals naturally
drew attention to the state of police training. In the early
part of this century (Gammage, 1963, pp. 5-6), there was no

public concern for giving the police the right kind of training
in order to prevent their becoming a social problem. He
maintained that "until 1915, any suggestion that a policeman
needed formal training would have been received with amazement and doubt." Upon the completion of a brief period of
training on the street, "the new man was assumed to be a
finished product, capable of enforcing the law." Now it started
to be emphasized that training was an effective means of in-
stilling values and ideals in police officers. In the Task Force
Report: The Police (1967, p. 37), it was held that training
"should be viewed as a vital and indispensable process" for
the performance of the "highly sensitive" police tasks. Further, police training was regarded as the most important vehicle to "elicit a commitment on the part of a police officer to
the importance of fairness as well as effectiveness in the
exercise of his authority." It was said:

> He should be provided with a basis for understanding
> the various forms of deviant behavior with which he
> must deal. And, he should be acquainted with the
> various alternatives and resources that are available
> to him, in addition to the criminal process, for dealing
> with the infinite variety of situations which he is
> likely to confront in his daily work.

As a matter of fact, by the late 50s new strides were
initiated in the hitherto neglected area of police training. In
1959 New York and California created training commissions with
state-wide jurisdictions to enforce state-mandated minimum
basic programs. These training bodies, popularly known as
Peace Officer Standards and Training Commissions (POST
commissions) assumed responsibilities in those states for issuing
certification, which constituted the authority granted by a
state to a person to act as a police officer. According to
Leonard and More (1974, p. 159), the New York Municipal
Police Training Council Act of 1959 provided for the establishment of a council to "formulate and put into operation a manda-
tory police training program." For the execution of the program (Gammage, 1963, pp. 41-42), the Act provided that the
abovementioned Council could make recommendations to the
Governor on many important matters concerning police training
including approval of police training schools, minimum courses
of study, attendance requirements, certification of instructors,
and content of the minimum basic training courses.

The work of POST commissions, which currently pre-
scribed and supervised basic police training courses in all
states, developed throughout the 1960s. In 1970 the Directors
of the State Law Enforcement Training commissions formed a
national association, known as the National Association of State
Directors of Law Enforcement Training (NASDLET). This was
an important achievement, as the new body became a coordinating agency for state-mandated police training, which was
strongly recommended by the National Advisory Commission on
Criminal Justice Standards and Goals. The Commission's (1973,
p. 334) recommendations were as follows:

> Every state, by 1975, should enact legislation estab-
> lishing a state commission empowered to develop and
> enforce state minimum mandatory standards for the
> selection of police officers. This legislation should
> provide that the commission represent local govern-
> ment.

This is one of the few standards promulgated by the 1973
Commission which has been realized.

Mandated law enforcement training is one of the useful
innovations of the recent days. Compared to the situation in
the early 1900s when no formal training was required for police
officers, compulsory basic training for all recruits is indeed
a big leap forward. All POST commissions in the country are
legislatively entrusted with the responsibility of ensuring that
no one is certified to act as a police officer until the mandated
basic minimum requirements of training are met. They are
also required to prescribe course content, performance objectives, and minimum duration of the basic training programs
in all states. Catlin and Hoover (1973, p. 347) comment on
the contribution of these commissions as follows:

> There is currently an intensive effort to improve the
> quality and quantity of police training in the United
> States. A particular type of agency has emerged and
> taken a leadership role in providing such improved
> and expanded training. This is the State Law Enforce-
> ment Training commission, also commonly referred to
> as Commission on Police Officer Standards and Training.

Included in the minimum basic programs are courses on
police human relations. In order to understand human relations

for American police it is considered necessary to look at the content, duration, emphases, and other related issues in state-mandated training in this area. It is hoped that an inquiry of this nature will enable us to determine what is regarded nationally as human relations for the police in this country. In the course of our inquiry we will examine whether state-mandated human-relations training is grounded on the historical model discussed earlier. Further, on the basis of the courses taught to police recruits, it will be analyzed if there is another model of police human relations in contemporary society.

Conclusion

The historical model of police human relations continued only as a concept since police training remained a neglected area in America. In contrast to this pitiable situation, there had always been a great emphasis on police training in England since the days of Peel's Metropolitan Police. However, the historical negligence of police training in America did not become a widespread national concern till the 60s. Many disturbing developments of the decade were responsible for enlargement of police training including a renewed emphasis on police human relations. It was during this time that the work of the POST commissions expanded continuously and mandated training became a reality.

References

Bard, M. (1973). The role of law enforcement in the helping system. In J. R. Snibbe & H. M. Snibbe (eds.), The urban policeman in transition: a psychological and sociological review. Springfield, IL: Charles C. Thomas.

Berkeley, G. E. (1969). The democratic policeman. Boston: Beacon Press.

Bordua, D. J. (1967). Preface. In David J. Bordua (ed.), The police: six sociological essays. New York: Wiley.

Catlin, D., & Hoover, L. T. (1973). Role of law enforcement training commissions in the United States. Journal of Criminal Justice, 1, (4), 347-352.

Coppedge v. United States, 82 U.S. 438 (1962).

Critchley, T. A. (1967). A history of police in England and Wales, 900-1966. London: Constable.

Davis, E. M. (1973). Professional police principles. In E. Eldefonso (ed.), Readings in criminal justice. Beverly Hills, CA: Glencoe Press.

Earle, H. H. (1972). Police recruit training: stress v non-stress. Springfield, IL: Charles C. Thomas.

Fogelson, R. M. (1977). Big-city police. Cambridge, MA: Harvard University Press.

Fosdick, R. B. (1920, reprint 1969). American police systems. Montclair, NJ: Patterson Smith.

Gammage, A. Z. (1963). Police training in the United States. Springfield, IL: Charles C. Thomas.

Graham, F. P. (1970). The due process revolution. Rochelle Park, NJ: Hayden Book Company.

Haller, M. H. (1976). Historical roots of police behavior: Chicago, 1890-1925. Law & Society Review, 10(2), 303-325.

Leonard, V. A., & More, H. W. (1974). Police organization and management. Mineola, NY: Foundation Press.

National Advisory Commission on Criminal Justice Standards and Goals. (1973). Police. Washington, DC: U.S. Government Printing Office.

National Advisory Commission on Civil Disorders. (1967). Report. Washington, DC: Government Printing Office.

National Commission on Law Observance and Enforcement. (1931). No. 14: report on police. Washington, DC: U.S. Government Printing Office.

O'Byrne, Michael. (1981). In David Watts Pope and Norman L. Weiner (eds.), Modern policing. London: Crook Helm.

Peters, T. J., & Waterman, R. H., Jr. In search of excellence: lessons from America's best run companies. New
York: Warner Books.

President's Commission on Campus Unrest. (1970). The report. Washington, DC: U. S. Government Printing Office.

President's Commission on Law Enforcement and the Administration of Justice. (1970). Task force report: the police.
Washington, DC: U.S. Government Printing Office.

Regoli, R. M. (1976). Police in America: a study of cynicism. Washington, DC: University Press of America.

Richardson, J. F. (1970). The New York police. New York:
Oxford University Press.

_____. (1974). Urban police in the United States.
Port Washington, NY: Kennikat Press

Rumbaut, R. G., & Bittner, E. (1979). Changing conceptions of the police role: a sociological review. In N.
Morris & M. Tonry (eds.), Crime and justice: an annual
review of research, Vol. I. Chicago: University of
Chicago Press.

Saunders, C. B., Jr. (1970). Upgrading the American
police. Washington, DC: The Brookings Institute.

Skolnick, J. H. (1969). The politics of protest. New York:
Simon and Schuster.

Smith, B. (1960). Police systems in the United States.
New York: Harper and Row.

Walker, S. (1977). A critical history of police reform.
Lexington, MA: Heath.

Wilson, J. Q. (1985). Thinking about crime. New York:
Vintage Books.

Wilson, O. W. (1963). Police Administration. New York:
McGraw-Hill.

Chapter 3

CONSENSUS MODEL OF POLICE HUMAN RELATIONS

For understanding police human relations, an analysis of the roots of American police has been presented. It was noted that those humane roots failed to thrive because of the lack of police training in this country. The factors leading to the emergence of police human-relations training have also been discussed. This chapter will be utilized for presenting one important contemporary nature of police human relations through the discussion of a model identified in the mandated programs as the consensus model of human relations.

Gathering Data

The methods of descriptive research were found appropriate for this study since it sought to explore the contemporary practices and emerging trends. According to Best (1981, p. 25), descriptive research serves a very useful purpose if it is used for recording a course of action. He argues as follows:

> Descriptive research describes what is. It involves the description, recording, analysis, and interpretation of conditions that exist. It involves some type of comparison or contrasts and attempts to discover relationships between existing nonmanipulated variables.

Descriptive research aims at identifying all aspects of a specific problem. Borg and Gall (1979, pp. 38-39) maintain that the purpose of such research is "to collect information that permits us to describe the characteristics of persons, an educational process, or an institution." They identify some questions that are appropriate for descriptive research:

Studies dealing with the following questions, for example, are descriptive: (1) What playground is
available in intercity elementary schools? (2) How
many calories are provided in typical school lunch programs? (3) What is the amount and specific nature
of clinical training received by persons currently employed in federally supported mental health clinics?
(4) What specific verbal strategies are used by elementary school teachers to respond to incorrect pupil
answers during recitation and discussion lessons?

This study for understanding police human relations is
exploratory in nature. Its purposes are to define police human
relations as it emerges from state-mandated training on human
relations, compare it to the historical model, and offer recommendations to police leaders and policymakers. Hence, the
techniques of descriptive research are particularly applicable.
Van Dalen (1979, p. 342) maintains that "descriptive researchers do the pioneer spade work" and primarily their "data are
qualitative rather than quantitative." In a work of this nature,
Van Dalen argues, "broad generalizations" are difficult to es-
tablish since "descriptive data can mirror only particular aspects of specific events or conditions in a given setting."

The data in the study came primarily from two sources,
namely: (a) written documents and (b) telephonic conversa-
tions. The written documents received from the POST commissions were the human-relations training curricula primarily
consisting of (a) course content, (b) course goal, and (c)
performance objectives. Course content was usually presented
in an outline format, and it described many points of a topic.
Course goal was a statement of what the course sought to
achieve in the long run. Performance objectives related to the
immediate outcome of the course and its directly intended impact on the trainee.

The POST commissions were requested through a letter
in March 1983 to send descriptive materials concerning the
police human-relations courses in their mandated programs.
In order to elaborate on what was meant by human-relations
courses, they were told that some of the relevant topics would
be these:

• Police role in a democracy

- Crowd behavior
- Community or citizen relations
- Minority relations
- Minority or ethnic subculture
- Communication skills
- Perception skills
- Crisis intervention
- Battered women
- Dealing with variant behavior
- Handling stress
- Police ethics

Without an account of the three dimensions of police human relations found in the historical model, the above-mentioned guideline was intended to convey to the POST commissions the likely topics associated with police human relations. They were, however, also requested to send descriptive material of any other courses included by them within the mandated human-relations offerings. By August 1983, descriptive materials were received from 38 states. However, it was not clear whether the participating states indeed sent materials pertaining to what they considered as human-relations courses, since in some cases they seemed to have forwarded any material falling within the 12 areas specified in the original letter. Moreover, not all states indicated clearly the block of instruction within which a particular course was included and taught. By "block of instruction" we meant segments into which a particular training curriculum is divided like patrol, law, investigation, and so on.

In January 1985, the POST commissions were again contacted through a letter (Appendix C) to specifically state whether the courses they forwarded for the study were regarded by them as human-relations topics. They were, therefore, asked (Das, personal communication, January 23, 1985) as follows:

> When I wrote to you in 1983, I mentioned that human-relations training was likely to cover topics like these:

> Police Ethics, Communication Skills, Crowd Behavior,
> Handling Stress, Minority Relations, Battered Women,
> Police Role in a Democracy, Community or Citizen Re-
> lations, Minority or Ethnic Subculture, Crisis Inter-
> vention, Perception Skills, and Dealing with Variant
> Behavior. In response, you sent me material on many
> similar courses mandated in your state (please see en-
> closure). It is, not, however, correct to assume that
> all these courses are actually in your human-relations
> block of instruction since some of those are also taught
> in other blocks of instruction.... I need to determine
> precisely the offerings (subjects/topics) you view as
> human-relations courses and the time allotted for each.
> Kindly insert the information in the enclosed table.

As a result of the new survey, all the 38 states which par-
ticipated in the project in 1983 sent a list of courses they included within human-relations training. Letters were also
sent to nonparticipating states which were 12. All these states
responded this time.

The second source of data, namely the telephone contacts, was necessary because a large number of states did not
respond to the initial request for materials made through
letters. Interestingly, these telephonic contacts afforded opportunities for discussion with a number of important POST
commission officials regarding their concepts of police human-
relations training.

Consensus Mode of Police Human Relations

As a result of the letter and the telephone requests,
50 curricula or course outlines were received. A list of human-
relations courses can be seen in Appendix A. For the appreciation of the essential ingredients of these courses, each
course was broken down into basic elements through the examination of the accompanying materials (Appendix B). These
steps were undertaken to identify the true nature of the
courses, determine whether some topics were more widely
taught than others, and prepare a list of nationally most widely
utilized police human-relations subjects. It was found possible
to do so and the popular courses were identified. These
courses were included within what would be described as the
consensus model of police human relations. Additionally, the

common elements of the courses in this model were put together separately. This is the core of police human relations as it emerges from an examination of the state-mandated courses in America.

Included in the consensus model was Police Ethics taught by 39 states in one form or the other. While most of the states taught it as a full course, some included ethics as part of a larger course. Among the states falling into the latter category were Kansas (Police Professionalism), Massachusetts (Environment of Policing), Oregon (Law Enforcement Profession), and South Carolina (Dealing with Victims and the Public). Since all these were courses concerning ethics, morality and professional values, the topic encompassing them could be called Ethical Ideals and Values.

Another topic that needed to be included in the consensus model was handling persons with abnormal behavior like mental illness, mental retardation, drug and alcohol related problems and so on. This topic was taught by 37 states. Again, some states offered this course as part of a larger topic. In Minnesota, for example, it was taught within a course entitled, Dealing with People, while abnormal behavior was discussed in a Florida course called Human Problems and Services. In Washington police trainees were taught about this aspect of their work in a course listed as Crisis Intervention. Since these courses were in regard to the handling of various kinds of abnormal personalities, they were grouped within a topic which could be described as Dimensions of Variant Behavior.

A third category of courses dealing with crises, conflicts, and death notifications which was taught by 34 states deserved an important position in the consensus model. While most states taught crisis intervention and conflict management as full-fledged courses, some came to notice for including instruction on these subjects within some larger courses. In Kansas, Crisis Management was included within a comprehensive course entitled Family Disturbance and Crisis Intervention. Since courses taught in this area were connected with police training in managing crises and conflicts, these could be described as Crisis Management courses.

The courses on community relations, including all aspects of police relationships with the community, which were taught by 30 states, formed another topic in the model under discussion. Most states taught community relations as full courses, but some even included instruction on this area within other courses. In North Carolina, for example, community relations was included within a course entitled, Dealing with Victims and the Public. In Mississippi it was taught as part of a course described as Human Relations. Since these courses covered various aspects of community relations, they were more suitably described as All Aspects of Community Relations.

Among the courses requiring inclusion in the consensus model were those dealing with wife battering, child abuse, domestic disputes, and many other family-related offerings taught by 24 states in their human-relations segment of instruction. While many offered full courses on this topic, some taught these subjects within other courses. Washington included all events in domestic settings in Disturbance Calls. This topic formed part of one larger course, namely, Family Disturbance and Crisis Intervention in Kansas. Since the courses taught in this segment of human-relations training pertained to family and domestic occurrences, they could be given the title, Family and Domestic Disorders.

Law Enforcement Stress, an area of human-relations training in 24 states, was an important topic in the above-mentioned model. It dealt mostly with stress and connected developments to which police officers were found most vulnerable. These courses were normally taught as simply Police Stress or Stress Management. Some states included stress as an element of another course. Iowa, for example, taught it in a course entitled, Psychology for Law Enforcement, Self-Understanding and Handling Stress.

There can be included within the consensus model courses dealing broadly with police need for understanding people's attitudes and prejudices which were taught in 23 states. These courses were on psychological aspects of police citizen encounters. One such course was Citizen Evaluation in California, which deals with the necessity of police sensitivity that they were constantly evaluated by citizens. Some of the similar courses were Building Respect for the Police (Louisiana), Police Image (Mississippi), Police Authoritarianism and Discretion (Kentucky), Perception of Human Behavior (Maine), and Officer/Violator Relationship (Utah). All these courses were primarily designed to teach the police trainee to be

sensitive to the feelings, impressions, and reactions of people
in general. Indiana taught a course entitled, Police Psychology, which has now been changed to Introduction to Human Behavior. Florida offered a course, namely, Human Behavior,
for teaching principles of human behavior including the psychological factors affecting behavior. Again, in some states
this was a topic taught as a full course while in others understanding human behavior was included in other courses.
States that included instruction on this topic within courses
with varying titles were Iowa (Psychology for Law Enforcement, Self-understanding, and Handling Stress) and Mississippi (Human Relations). These courses could be conveniently
grouped under the label, Understanding Human Behavior.

Among the states, 22 were offering courses on communication skills which was a topic included in the model under
review. While mostly these courses bore the title, Communication Skills, some offered them under more specific names.
New Jersey had courses entitled Telephone Communication and
Oral Communication. North Carolina included communication
skills as one aspect of their course, Dealing with Victims and
the Public.

Another 22 states provided instruction in a topic discussed within the consensus model, namely, group behavior,
riot control, civil disorders, and other related matters. These
courses could be classified under a title called Group Behavior.
While the topic was normally offered as full courses, it was
included as part of some other courses, too. In Ohio, for
example, it was taught as a part of a comprehensive course
entitled Human Relations.

The final topic within the consensus model was a segment of human-relations training emphasized in 19 states.
These were courses highlighting the need for special relationships of the police with groups like ethnic minorities, the
press, female citizens, youths, and so on. Since these courses were on police dealings with special groups, these could
be termed as Relations with Special Groups.

Thus, the topics which were widely used nationally in
human-relations training were these:

(1) Ethical Ideals and Values

(2) Dimensions of Variant Behavior

(3) Crisis Management

(4) Community Relations

(5) Family and Domestic Disorders

(6) Stress

(7) Understanding Human Behavior

(8) Communication Skills

(9) Group Behavior

(10) Relations with Special Groups

It was to be noted further that these topics constituted the consensus model of police human-relations training in the U.S.A. The model embodied the core area of consensus in the otherwise diverse and varied police human-relations cours-es. These core courses were evaluated against the three dimensions of human relations which constituted the historical model.

The courses taught in the consensus model did not specifically include instruction on the appreciation of the higher values of law. Many reasons can be found for this ab-sence. It was observed by the American Bar Association (1973, pp. 205-209) that police training was "generally sim-plistic, unimaginative, and of little real value to the officer." It was added that the courses on legal implications of search and seizure were, for example, handled rather mechanically. Hence, without a discussion of the ethical and constitutional concerns in the Supreme Court's decisions, officers were asked not to violate <u>Chimel</u> for the sake of ensuring conviction. The academies made short shrift of the significance of the <u>Miranda</u> decision and generally training was used for teaching "respect" and adjusting to "semi-military aspects of police operations." This practice seems to be continuing even today.

Many states offered brief courses on constitutional law. Such states were California (Constitutional Rights Law), Con-necticut (U.S. Constitution), Georgia (Constitutional Law), Missouri (Constitutional Law), New York (Constitutional Law), New Hampshire (Constitutional Law), Pennsylvania (Law En-forcement and Civil Rights), Illinois (Rights of the Accused), New Mexico (Constitutional Law for the Police), and so on. However, these were very short courses with time allotments

of one or two hours only. Within such brief, introductory
courses it would be next to impossible to inculcate in the
minds of trainees respect for the higher values of law identified as an important dimension of the historical model of police
human relations.

Some states laid more emphasis on police adherence to
the spirit of the Bill of Rights. Washington, for example,
offered courses on the U.S. Constitution and Supreme Court
as well as on the exclusionary rule. Included in these courses
was a discussion on current philosophy on the use of the exclusionary rule. In its law courses Iowa included a topic on
procedural due process in which trainees were taught to be
sensitive to the concept of due process as it applied to the
law enforcement functions. In Colorado the course entitled,
U.S. Constitution, was designed to impart knowledge to police
officers to the effect that theirs was a role to protect the
rule of law. In Florida the course on constitutional law was
utilized to drive home to trainees that the Constitution was
the basis for the criminal justice system. In North Carolina
the course on constitutional law was taught to familiarize them
with the applicable constitutional provisions relating to duties
and responsibilities of law enforcement officers. Philosophical
concepts like the Bill of Rights as the living body of law and
an embodiment of changing values of society were discussed.
In Wyoming the course entitled, Basic Law and the Constitution,
was taught to make police officers sensitive to continually
changing powers and constraints derived from the U.S. Constitution.

As against such topics with higher philosophical values,
there were also states which seem to be emphasizing rote mem-
orization of statutes by police trainees. It appears that in
Virginia various criminal law statutes were required to be
learned by heart while Mississippi seems to be teaching briefly
a segment called, Basic Law for Law Enforcement Officers.
West Virginia and Idaho seemed to be content offering only
a short introduction to the U.S. Constitution and its provisions
in their courses on constitutional law. In Louisiana there was
a course on constitutional law in which students were apparently required to be superficially familiar with the First, Fourth,
Fifth, Sixth, Tenth, and Fourteenth Amendments only.

Moral authority and democratic values had been given
sufficient importance through the state-mandated courses on

Ethical Ideals and Values, Understanding Human Behavior, Group Behavior, and Community Relations. The service aspect of policing had been adequately covered through the courses included in Dimensions of Variant Behavior, Crisis Management, Family and Domestic Disorders, Stress, Communication Skills, and Relations with Special Groups.

Looking at the consensus model it is noted that the contemporary definition of police human relations seems to include moral authority, democratic principles, willing spirit of service, and skills for service. There does not seem to be nationally adequate attention paid to include an appreciation of the higher values of law in human-relations training. This aspect of police human relations forms an important dimension in the historical model. It is reasonable to argue that probably teaching service attitude as well as moral and democratic principles were easier than the higher concepts of law. The latter called for a deeper understanding of the philosophy of law and an acceptance of the numerous constraints. Young police trainees with limited education did not seem to be amenable to imbibing such a spirit. This can be a reason for an apparently skeptical approach to the courses emphasizing the higher values of law. Presented in Table 1 are the elements of the topics included in the consensus model of police human-relations training.

TABLE 1:

Elements of the Courses in the Consensus Model

1. ETHICAL IDEALS AND VALUES

    a. Avoiding gifts, gratuities, bribes, and rewards.
    b. Knowledge regarding the exercise of caution in use of drugs, alcohol, and tobacco.
    c. Understanding of ethical values as the key to professionalism.
    d. Knowledge of the Code of Ethics adopted for law enforcement as a profession.
    e. Perception of the need to develop professional sensitivity toward unethical conduct in fellow officers.
    f. Knowledge of the need for ethical values for maintaining the quality of police work and an acceptable image.

TABLE 1 (cont.)

2. DIMENSION OF VARIANT BEHAVIOR

    a. Discussion of symptoms usually observable in the common types of mental illness, mental retardation, personality abnormalities, psychopathic personality, persons with physical handicaps (deafness, for example), alcoholics, drug addicts, and so on.

    b. Understanding of the psychologically tested techniques and safe handling of the mentally disturbed.

    c. Knowledge of the legal, moral, and social aspects of the issues in handling of abnormal personalities.

    d. Information regarding social agencies where services for abnormal personalities are available.

    e. Development of police professionalism as well as emotional detachment in dealing effectively with human aberrations.

    f. Awareness of the usually negative police responses toward abnormal personalities and the consequent effects.

3. CRISIS MANAGEMENT

    a. Knowledge of the major types of police crisis calls: understanding of the differnece between crisis and conflict.

    b. Explanation of the situations that are likely to cause stress, conflict, and crisis for citizens such as family disputes, landlord/tenant disputes, suicide attempts, criminal victimization, and emotional shocks.

    c. Understanding of the symptoms of persons in crisis, stress and conflict.

    d. Study of the verbal and nonverbal calmative, peace-restoring safety procedures for reduction of conflict, defusion of crisis, and safety of the persons, including the officer.

    e. Discussion of the operational steps in crisis management: initial contact, defusion of the situation, and restoration of calm, investigation of crisis, mediation, legal and remedial action (referral and counseling).

    f. Understanding of the psychological processes involved in mediation, reconciliation, advisement, as well as alternatives like civil remedies, prosecution, and arrests.

TABLE 1 (cont.)

g. Knowledge of the effectiveness of the police acting as the impartial third party in resolving conflicts, crisis, and stress.

h. Study of the ways to cope with crisis through exercise, diet, change of activities, and so on.

4. COMMUNITY RELATIONS

a. Projection of police work as a mission of professional community service.

b. Understanding of the impact of the factors like age, socio-economic conditions, school exposure, media, family, peers, and ethnicity in community attitudes towards the police.

c. Understanding of the negative impact of police apathy, unethical conduct, brutality, racial bias, and discrimination in community relations.

d. Police awareness of the coercive, violent role model of law enforcement, and the consequent psychological barriers between the police and citizens.

e. Study of officer's own conduct on community attitudes.

f. Perception of the importance of courtesy and positive attitudes towards the public and the media.

g. Understanding of the interlinking connection between community relations, ethical conduct, and professionalism.

h. Awareness of good relationship as a product of crime prevention through public support.

5. FAMILY AND DOMESTIC DISORDER

a. Knowledge of the characteristics of battering, battered mates, and battered children, and the causes associated with domestic disputes.

b. Knowledge of various steps in domestic dispute intervention: arrival at the scene, perceptive sizing up of the situation, assistance to victim, and coercive action like arrests.

c. Knowledge of handling shock, guiding victims regarding legal, financial, medical, child-care help, and helping sufferers make positive decisions.

d. Discussion of the risks and hazards in domestic disputes and violence.

TABLE 1 (cont.)

  e. Knowledge of the objectivity, restrained, and calming nonverbal and verbal expressions, resourcefulness of mind, and the statutory obligations of the police.

6. STRESS

  a. Knowledge of the positive and negative effects of occupational stress: the connection between stress and physical as well as mental disorders.
  b. Understanding of the causes of stress in the police because of the routine encounters with violence, danger, human suffering, emergency response, traumatic experience, and conflict situations.
  c. Discussion of the various types of adjustment mechanisms including alcoholism, drug abuse, and suicide.
  d. Study of psychological and physical techniques of stress management including professional assistance.

7. UNDERSTANDING OF HUMAN BEHAVIOR

  a. Understanding of sociological and psychological factors that shape human behavior: introduction to social psychology.
  b. Identification of the patterns of interaction between individual and society.
  c. Knowledge of the unique characteristics of human personality formed through experience, perceptions, and needs.
  d. Study of helping relationships with citizens, appreciation of helpee's perspectives, and regard for persons in need.
  e. Knowledge of self-perceptions and awareness of the impact of officer's own expectations on his behavior.
  f. Understanding of the public fear of police authority and police attitudes that confirm public stereotypes of the police.
  g. Discussion of the skills and abilities that police officers must acquire in order to deal with people, particularly those who are victimized, injured, or in trouble.
  h. Understanding of the nature of motivation, perception, self-image, behavior, attitudes, and power.

TABLE 1 (cont.)

8. COMMUNICATION SKILLS

    a. Understanding of the need for effective interpersonal communications in the professional career of a police officer.

    b. Discussion of the negative verbal and nonverbal communication techniques which are barriers to communication.

    c. Discussion of the effective means of communication as a learned art which calls for understanding of the basic communication skills.

    d. Knowledge of the effective communications as a tool for building relationships with citizens, dealing with abnormal behavior, and for carrying out law enforcement, order maintenance, and service functions.

    e. Discussion of the psychological and physical problems in communicating with the deaf, the mentally retarded, the sexual deviates, and the angry, hostile, and hysterical people.

9. GROUP BEHAVIOR

    a. Study of the legal, sociological, and psychological aspects of crowds, mobs, assemblies, and other forms of group behaviors.

    b. Explanation of arrest procedures, emergency first aid, use of chemical weapons, and psychological strategies.

    c. Discussion of squad formations, arrest chains, team work, immediate action, defusion of panic and mob hysteria, and differential application of force.

    d. Understanding of the importance of accurate assessment of crowd characteristics and the need for proper intelligence.

10. RELATIONS WITH SPECIAL GROUPS

    a. Knowledge of terminological usages in the area of juvenile delinquency, like delinquent child, dependent child, neglected child, and so on.

    b. Understanding of the ways to establish rapport with juveniles and the effect of formal police contact upon juveniles.

    c. Study of the reasons for police prejudice against

TABLE 1 (cont.)

certain types of juveniles and also common antagonism
of juveniles against police.
d. Understanding how, in spouse abuse situations, women
are normally the victims.
e. Knowledge of the history of race relations in the United
States of America.
f. Developing appreciation for the peculiar difficulties
and problems of ethnic minorities.
g. Discussion of racial prejudice of the police and its
effects on law enforcement.
h. Psychological understanding of the problems of the
deaf and the need to avoid misconceived actions.
i. Knowledge of the necessity and benefits of healthy relations between the police and the press.

Conclusion

In order to understand the contemporary nature of
police human relations in America, all POST commissions were
contacted and their curricula were obtained. On the basis
of the examination of the relevant courses taught nationally,
a consensus model of police human relations was noted. Included in this model were these topics: ethical ideals and
values, dimensions of variant behavior, crisis management,
community relations, family and domestic disorders, stress,
understanding human behavior, communication skills, group
behavior, and relations with special groups. Comparing the
two models of police human relations, it is observed that in
the contemporary model the emphasis is on moral authority,
democratic principles, willing spirit of service, and skills
for service. In the historical model the emphasis was also on
a deeper understanding of law.

References

Best, John W. (1981). Research in education. Englewood
Cliffs, NJ: Prentice-Hall.

Borg, W. R., & Gall, M. D. (1979). 2nd ed. New York:
David McKay.

Remington, F. J., Goldstein, H., & Krantz, S. (1973).
    Standards relating to urban police functions. New York:
    American Bar Association.

VanDalen, Deobold B. (1979). Understanding educational
    research. New York: McGraw-Hill.

Chapter 4

DIVERSITY IN UNDERSTANDING POLICE
HUMAN RELATIONS

Diversity in understanding police human relations can
be observed by examining state-mandated training in this
area. Certain issues in this regard deserve special attention.
First, states differed widely in their approach to human relations training and the content of the courses included there-
in. Secondly, in some states POST commissions provided adequate guidelines regarding how courses were to be developed
while others allowed their certified local academies full discretion in this regard. Thirdly, time allocations for human
relations training varied widely as diverse considerations de-
termined such allocations. Fourthly, course nomenclature
varied from state to state. Fifthly, qualifications of human
relations instructors as well as their views on this aspect
of police training present some important concerns. Finally,
there seemed to exist a wide diversity between concerns and
emphases found in the literature and those included in the
human relations courses.

Variation in Approach and Content

The differences in approach to human relations can be
seen from the way the courses were put in a particular block
of instruction. Generally, almost all states had their programs
divided into a few major blocks like law, patrol, investigation,
and so on. Many also had blocks like community relations and
human relations. But human relations courses were also included in different blocks of instruction. Ethics, for example,
was a course that claimed an important place in human relations training, but it was taught within diverse blocks of instruction including Introduction to Criminal Justice, Professional Orientation, Administration of Justice, Agency Politics

and Procedure, Patrol Tactics, Human Behavior, Community Relations, Social Psychology, Special Subjects, and Police Practice and Procedure. In one state ethics was a topic among the subjects offered during the First Week of Training.

As it is seen in Appendix A, the blocks of instruction under which human relations courses were included are rather varied. A few of the blocks were these:

- Human Relations
- Introduction to Law Enforcement
- Patrol Procedures
- Community and Police Relations
- Professional Orientation
- Administration of Justice
- Human Behavior
- Human Skills
- Proficiency Skills
- Police Function & Human Behavior
- Special Activities
- Police Role and Professional Development
- Providing Service and Rendering Assistance
- Sociological Development
- Police Problem
- General Police

Although a particular topic might be treated as a human relations subject, it could be included in any of the above-mentioned blocks of instruction, which indicated the uncertainty of states' approach to police human relations training. It could be guessed that a human relations topic included within a block of instruction like Introduction to Law Enforcement would probably be taught as an introductory course. Within Patrol Procedures the orientation of such a course would be different. Probably the important point to note here is that police human relations as it is taught in numerous police academies in the country is characterized by large diversity.

Human relations courses were similar in some states.
In New Mexico, the contents of various courses strikingly
matched those taught in California. In fact, historically some
of the POST commissions created first were widely copied
with regard to later structure and curricula. It was also
true that different states emphasized different elements in the
same topic. To illustrate this point, the elements of a few
courses in police ethics in several states could be taken into
consideration. In Alaska, the course Police Ethics and Standards of Conduct was taught highlighting ten elements that
include technical and general rules of conduct like compliance
with duty, avoiding gifts, bribes and gratuities, and desisting
from publicity. In Arizona, Ethics and Professionalism was
utilized for emphasizing the need for high moral and ethical
police performance standards. The stress was on the link
between ethics and professionalism. In Arkansas, Police Ethics
and Image had broadly two elements included in it: these
were familiarity with the Law Enforcement Code of Ethics and
public sensitivity to unethical police conduct. In this course
police image was stressed. In California, Ethics (including
unethical behavior) contained seven main concepts including
principles of morality, ethics as the key to professionalization,
acceptance of perennial norms of society, diagnosis of unethical
traits, and awareness of weak tendencies in one's character.
Thus, a wide diversity could be observed in the ways course
elements were understood and emphasized. While California
had a philosophical orientation, Alaska seemed to veer more
toward practical considerations. Arkansas emphasized the
image-building value of ethics, and Arizona concentrated on
the need of conforming to the professional standards of conduct.

Course Guidelines

Variation in understanding human relations can be observed by looking at the practices regarding publication of
descriptive course materials. In only 16 states did the POST
commissions provide complete course descriptions consisting
of course content, course goal, and performance objectives.
It was obvious that without adequate descriptive guidelines
an academy instructor was at liberty to teach a course according to his own understanding. This could cause a great
deal of variation in human relations courses.

Course content only was included in the curricula of
15 states and in almost all cases the content descriptions were
rather brief. Academy instructors were likely to get a somewhat limited idea of the content from such guidelines. To
appreciate this point, the following description found in the
curriculum of Wyoming could be considered:

> Police Role in Society (1 hour): A study of the
> policeman's concept of the police role and how it often
> contradicts the public's perception of his job. Dem-
> onstrates the absolute necessity for law enforcement
> to secure public assistance and acceptance in order
> to function effectively (Lynch, Personal Communication,
> May 10, 1983).

Nothing else was provided as course guidelines for the instructor. So far as academy instructors were concerned, such
brief content description provided little guidance on the subject.

In 18 states under review the published course materials
consisted primarily of course goal and performance objectives.
However, in the absence of a specific outline of course content,
it was difficult for instructors to visualize a complete blue-
print of a mandated topic on the basis of the information provided in that manner. In this respect a reference could be
made to Oregon for demonstrating how course goals and performance objectives served as the only source of guidelines
for instructors in some states. In a communication from the
Oregon Board on Police Standards and Training it was stated:

> We give our instructors some latitude in how they
> approach the classroom teaching, but require them to
> cover each performance objective contained in their
> particular unit of instruction (Bettiol, Personal
> Communication, March 2, 1983).

Although a content outline per se was omitted, the course
objectives were expected to provide a reasonable understanding of the content of the course.

Some commissions gave full scope to their academies to
develop the courses according to their understanding. In this
regard Arizona's practice was typical. In a letter from Arizona's Law Enforcement Officer Advisory Council, it was
mentioned that "each academy is responsible for covering
the required material in whatever manner they deem appropriate"

(Townsend, Personal Communication, March 30, 1983). Under these circumstances the POST commission's impact was likely to be minimal. New York followed the same policy in the matter of lesson plans. According to a letter received from the Division of Criminal Justice Services (McMahon, Personal Communication, March 15, 1983), academy instructors were to make their lesson plans from the short descriptions given by the POST commission under each course title. Missouri, too, had a similar approach since in that state, too, the academies had full freedom to design and plan the courses as they understood. In a letter from the POST Program, it was explained that they "do not hold course outlines per se at the Department of Public Safety--held at academies ..." (Baker, Personal Communication, May 20, 1983).

In Table 2 (pages 59-60) the availability of course content, course goals, and performance objectives is shown in each state. It will be noted that the full details provided by POST commissions are available in the curricula of some courses. As noted above there were many differnt practices in this regard. In Arizona the certified academies designed and planned the courses on human relations. While Arkansas POST commission published brief course details, Delaware did so only in a few courses. Wyoming, too, was somewhat like Delaware in this regard. Maryland did not publish course goals and performance objectives although course content was indicated in the curricula. Missouri left the human relations courses to be developed by the academies. Thus, the practices in regard to the degree of centralized direction by the POST commissions varied from state to state, and in some states the variation in control was noticeable from course to course.

Proportion of Human Relations to Basic Training

Tables 3 and 4 (pp. 61-64) contain a few details of basic and human relations training hours. The average proportion between the two segments of training is 8.4 percent. In basic training there is a little more agreement among the states in regard to the total hours since two groups of states numbering seven each offered the same number of hours (240 or 400 hours). In human relations training, however, the states are characterized by a much lesser degree of agreement. As it is seen the maximum number of states in agreement regarding specific time allocation is only five. Table 5 presents

TABLE 2:

Adequacy of Course Description

State	Number of Courses	Course Content	Course Goal	Performance Objectives
Alabama	6	X		
Alaska	5	X	X	X
Arizona	8	X		
Arkansas	6	X		
California	11	X	X	X
Colorado	8	X	X	X
Connecticut	11		X	X
Delaware	8	X		X
Florida	7	X		
Georgia	6		X	X
Hawaii	9	X		X
Idaho	7	X		
Illinois	13	X	X	X
Indiana	11	X		
Iowa	9	X	X	X
Kansas	6	X		
Kentucky	13	X		
Louisiana	9	X	X	X
Maine	13	X	X	X
Maryland	7	X		
Massachusetts	7	X	X	X
Michigan	4	X	X	X
Minnesota	8	X	X	X
Mississippi	5	X		X
Missouri	5	X		

TABLE 2 (cont.)

State	Number of Courses	Course Content	Course Goal	Performance Objectives
Montana	7	X	X	X
Nebraska	2	X		
Nevada	4	X	X	X
New Hampshire	5	X	X	X
New Jersey	21	X	X	X
New Mexico	9	X	X	X
New York	9	X		
North Carolina	7	X	X	X
North Dakota	5		X	X
Ohio	1	X		
Oklahoma	9		X	X
Oregon	5		X	X
Pennsylvania	6	X		X
Rhode Island	6	X	X	X
South Carolina	4	X	X	X
South Dakota	3	X	X	X
Tennessee	4	X		
Texas	4	X	X	X
Utah	8	X		
Vermont	10	X		
Virginia	8		X	X
Washington	6		X	X
West Virginia	6			X
Wisconsin	7	X		
Wyoming	2	X		

TABLE 3:

Basic Training Hours*

Value	Frequency	Percent	Valid Percent	Cumulative Percent
120	1	2.0	2.1	2.1
240	7	14.0	14.9	17.0
270	1	2.0	2.1	19.1
280	1	2.0	2.1	21.3
300	1	2.0	2.1	23.4
310	1	2.0	2.1	25.5
320	4	8.0	8.5	34.0
329	1	2.0	2.1	36.2
330	1	2.0	2.1	38.3
335	1	2.0	2.1	40.4
341	1	2.0	2.1	42.6
347	1	2.0	2.1	44.7
350	1	2.0	2.1	46.8
368	1	2.0	2.1	48.9
369	1	2.0	2.1	51.1
400	7	14.0	14.9	66.0
418	1	2.0	2.1	68.1
440	3	6.0	6.4	74.5
480	5	10.0	10.6	85.1
495	1	2.0	2.1	87.2
504	1	2.0	2.1	89.4
520	1	2.0	2.1	91.5

*Prepared by Dr. Michael H. Hazlett, Department of Law Enforcement Administration, Western Illinois University, Macomb, Illinois.

TABLE 3 (cont.)

Value	Frequency	Percent	Valid Percent	Cumulative Percent
525	1	2.0	2.1	93.6
560	1	2.0	2.1	95.7
618	1	2.0	2.1	97.9
954	1	2.0	2.1	100.0
999	3	6.0	Missing	
Total	50	100.0	100.0	

Mean	385.596	S E Kurt	1.965
Mode	240.000	Range	834.000
Kurtosis	6.134	Sum	18,123.000
S E Skew	.347	Median	369.000
Maximum	954.000	Variance	17,713.463
Standard Error	19.413	Skewness	1.622
Standard Dev.	133.092	Minimum	120.000

Valid Cases	47	Missing Cases	3

TABLE 4:

Human Relations Training Hours*

Value	Frequency	Percent	Valid Percent	Cumulative Percent
7	1	2.0	2.2	2.2
9	1	2.0	2.2	4.3
10	1	2.0	2.2	6.5
13	1	2.0	2.2	8.7
15	2	4.0	4.3	13.0
16	2	4.0	4.3	17.4
18	1	2.0	2.2	19.6
20	1	2.0	2.2	21.7
21	3	6.0	6.5	28.3
22	2	4.0	4.3	32.6
23	1	2.0	2.2	34.8
24	2	4.0	4.3	39.1
26	2	4.0	4.3	43.5
32	3	6.0	6.5	50.0
33	1	2.0	2.2	52.2
34	1	2.0	2.2	54.3
35	2	4.0	4.3	58.7
36	4	8.0	8.7	67.4
40	5	10.0	10.9	78.3
43	1	2.0	2.2	80.4
45	1	2.0	2.2	82.6
46	1	2.0	2.2	84.8

*Prepared by Dr. Michael H. Hazlett, Department of Law Enforcement Administration, Western Illinois University, Macomb, Illinois

TABLE 4 (cont.)

Value	Frequency	Percent	Valid Percent	Cumulative Percent
48	2	4.0	4.3	89.1
57	1	2.0	2.2	91.3
59	1	2.0	2,2	93.5
60	1	2.0	2.2	95.7
64	1	2.0	2.2	97.8
83	1	2.0	2.2	100.0
99	4	8.0	Missing	
Total	50	100.0	100.0	

Mean	32.587	S E Kurt	1.964
Mode	40.000	Range	76.000
Kurtosis	1.003	Sum	1,499.000
S E Skew	.350	Median	32.500
Maximum	83.000	Variance	253.892
Standard Error	2.349	Skewness	.827
Standard Dev.	15.934	Minimum	7.000

Valid Cases	46	Missing Cases	4

a consolidated statement of state-wide total basic hours, human
relations hours, proportion between the two, and various
ranks. The range of basic training is between 120 hours and
954 hours, while human relations training varies from seven
to 83 hours. Thus, the variation in range is wider in human
relations training.

The rank ordering presents some useful and interesting
information. Indiana ranks 12th among the states in basic
training, 34th in human relations, while its percentile ranking
(rank in proportion between human relations and basic training
hours) is 41. It shows that Indiana's rank is high in basic
training hours, but it is disproportionately low in human relations training. In that state the proportion between these
two aspects of training is very low, too. New York's rank in
basic training is 22nd, 8th in human relations, and 9th in the
proportion between the two segments of training. Thus, New
York has a higher amount of human relations emphasis in its
basic mandated program.

Using the data available from all states, it is observed
that there is a statistical relationship at the significant level
of .00032 between basic and human relations training. This
statistic, calculated using Pearson's Product-Moment Correlation
Coefficient, gives the R value of .485 with R^2 of .235. The
graphic representation is shown in Figure 1 (page 68).

Reasons for Variation in Human Relations Training Hours

One important reason for the variation from one state
to another in human relations hours seems to be the way the
states approach this training. In Pennsylvania human relations
was sought to be included within all the areas of basic training. According to a communication received from the Director
of Bureau of Training and Education in that state, it was
difficult for him to specify the human relations instruction
hours since it was included within many courses. Leiter
(Personal Communication, April 4, 1983) explains that he was
"attempting to manage the curriculum content by treating the
training program wholly. This approach is complicated, but ap-
appears to be possible." In Georgia, Ethics was taught in a
unit entitled, Introduction to Law Enforcement, while it was offered as an Administration and Justice course in Colorado.
Many states also included it specifically in their human relations
instruction.

TABLE 5:

State-wide Details of Training*

State	Basic Hours	Human Hours	Hum/Bas Hours	Basic Ranking	Human Ranking	Percentile Ranking
Alabama	240	15	6.2	41	41	34
Alaska	270	15	5.5	38	42	39
Arizona	440	36	8.1	13	19	26
Arkansas	280	23	8.2	37	31	24
California	520	32	6.1	5	24	36
Colorado	335	36	10.7	28	16	12
Connecticut	480	36	7.5	8	17	29
Delaware	368	35	9.5	24	21	16
Florida	320	32	10	32	25	14
Georgia	240	22	9.1	40	32	18
Hawaii	954	60	6.2	1	3	35
Idaho	347	24	6.9	26	29	31
Illinois	400	64	16	22	2	2
Indiana	480	21	4.3	12	34	41
Iowa	400	33	8.2	17	23	25
Kansas	320	40	12.5	31	14	4
Kentucky	400	32	8	21	26	27
Louisiana	240	9	3.7	42	45	43
Maine	504	57	11.3	6	5	10
Maryland	MIS	MIS	MIS	MIS	MIS	MIS
Massachusetts	480	45	9.3	11	9	17
Michigan	440	13	2.9	15	43	45

*Prepared by Dr. Michael H. Hazlett, Department of Law Enforcement
Administration, Western Illinois University, Macomb, Illinois

TABLE 5 (cont.)

State	Basic Hours	Human Hours	Hum/Bas Hours	Basic Ranking	Human Ranking	Percentile Ranking
Minnesota	MIS	MIS	MIS	MIS	MIS	MIS
Mississippi	320	43	13.4	32	10	3
Missouri	120	7	5.8	46	46	37
Montana	350	34	9.7	25	22	15
Nebraska	341	36	10.5	27	18	13
Nevada	240	16	6.6	39	40	33
New Hampshire	618	20	3.2	2	37	44
New Jersey	MIS	MIS	MIS	MIS	MIS	MIS
New Mexico	418	35	8.3	16	20	23
New York	400	46	11.5	20	8	9
North Carolina	369	40	10.8	23	11	11
North Dakota	310	18	5.8	35	38	38
Ohio	560	16	2.8	3	39	46
Oklahoma	300	26	8.6	36	28	21
Oregon	330	24	7.2	29	30	30
Pennsylvania	480	40	8.3	9	12	22
Rhode Island	480	59	12.2	10	4	6
South Carolina	329	22	6.6	30	33	32
South Dakota	240	21	8.7	43	36	20
Tennessee	240	10	4.1	45	44	42
Texas	400	48	12	18	7	7
Utah	400	48	12	19	6	8
Vermont	525	40	7.6	4	13	28
Virginia	MIS	MIS	MIS	MIS	MIS	MIS
Washington	440	83	18.8	14	1	1
West Virginia	495	26	5.2	7	27	40
Wisconsin	240	21	8.7	44	35	19
Wyoming	320	40	12.5	34	15	5

(MIS) = Values missing or unavailable.

GRAPHIC REPRESENTATION OF BASIC AND HUMAN RELATIONS HOURS

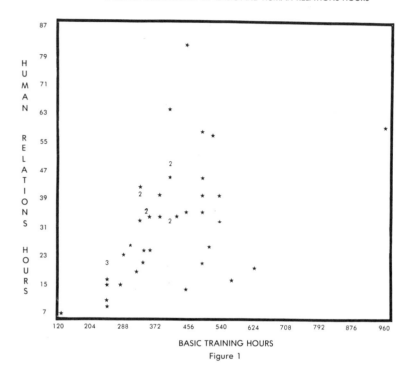

BASIC TRAINING HOURS

Figure 1

STATISTICS..

CORRELATION (R)-	.48595	R SQUARED	-	.23615	SIGNIFICANCE	-	.00031
STD ERR OF EST -	14.08343	INTERCEPT (A)	-	10.41360	SLOPE (B)	-	.05755
PLOTTED VALUES -	46	EXCLUDED VALUES-		0	MISSING VALUES -		4

★ = 1 STATE

2 = 2 STATES WITH SAME COORDINATES

3 = 3 STATES WITH SAME COORDINATES

Fig. 1

Training hours were naturally likely to vary according to the block of instruction in which a human relations course was included.

It could be learned from extensive discussion with POST commission officials that an additional reason for this low variation was that a number of considerations governed the duration of human relations training. Some of these were as follows:

1. Many states preferred to include even human relations courses within traditional police functions as it was believed that such a process would ensure a more familiar structure.

2. Some planners and administrators were apprehensive that the police courses taught as human relations might appear too impractical and unrelated to real police work. It could, it was feared, mean lesser attention from recruits. Accordingly, human relations courses were fitted into the traditional areas which shortened the hours actually devoted to this aspect of recruit training.

3. Many POST commissions took into account the views of instructors regarding the hours necessary to achieve the performance objectives. So different hours were allocated to various topics in preference to instructors' views.

4. Police academies also took note of the views and opinions of the chiefs in their areas which could alter the duration of human relations training from one area to another.

5. Apart from conforming to the needs and opinions of client departments, the POST commissions also generally followed the curricula from neighboring areas or well-known states. California had greatly influenced many states. It was further learned that because of the cost involved in conducting independent research in regard to performance objectives and course planning, many states followed what others had already done. This could affect time allocations for human relations training from region to region.

6. Some states like Maine conducted comprehensive surveys of the views of officers on the street regarding human relations training which were important in determining the duration. States also conduct public hearings, hold conferences

of trainers, and get the views of others connected with training for deciding the nature and hours for human relations
courses.

7.   Certain traditional subjects were to be given more
importance in minimum basic training, and the time for human
relations training was decided after earmarking the hours for
traditional courses.   Hence the time allotted for this aspect
of training was not always uniform.

8.   Views and understanding of POST commissions ex-
ecutives also played a significant part in the allocation of the
time and in deciding the content of human relations courses.
Many such officials had past police experience, and their
opinion was given considerable importance in the time allotment
for police training.

9.   In some states there were well-structured channels
of communication to the POST commissions.   In New York the
Municipal Training Council could make recommendations to
the Governor of the state regarding the courses to be included
in police training.   The training directors of the various academies in the state were also authorized to make their input
available.   These bodies played a role in shaping the various
aspects of the human relations training including its duration.

Thus, variation was normal in regard to the duration
of human relations training because of a number of administrative, political, and psychological reasons.

Terminological Diversity

Course nomenclature, too, was characterized by extensive
diversity and this could be observed by looking at one topical
area.   The course on ethics was taught with many different
titles which are presented in Table 6 (pages 71-73).   California and many other states referred to the course on ethics
as Police Ethics, Ethics, or Ethical Issues.   Illinois used the
term, Police Morality, for their ethics course.   In Kansas it
was Police Professionalism while Massachusetts included their
ethics course in Environment of Policing.   In South Dakota
ethics was taught within Police Community Relations, in Virginia
it was presented in Law Enforcement and the Community, and
in Connecticut it was included within Police Ethics, Moral

TABLE 6:

Terminological Diversity in Ethics Courses

Alaska	Police Ethics and Standards of Conduct
Arizona	Ethics and Professionalism
Arkansas	Police Ethics and Image
California	Ethics
Colorado	Law Enforcement Ethics
Connecticut	Police Ethics--Moral Development and Professionalism
Florida	Ethics and Professionalization
Georgia	Police Ethics and Professionalism
Idaho	Police Courtesy and Ethics
Illinois	Police Morality
Iowa	Ethics and Professionalism
Kansas	Police Professionalism
Kentucky	Police Ethics
Louisiana	Police Ethics
Maine	Police Ethics and Moral Issues
Maryland	Ethics
Massachusetts	Environment of Policing
Michigan	Police Courtesy and Ethics
Minnesota	Police Ethics

TABLE 6 (cont.)

Mississippi	Police Ethics
Missouri	Police Ethics and Professionalization
Montana	Police Ethics
Nebraska	Ethics
Nevada	Ethics and Professionalism
New Hampshire	Police Ethics and Unethical Behavior
New Jersey	Morals and Ethics
New Mexico	Ethics
New York	Ethical Awareness
North Carolina	Dealing with Victims and the Public
North Dakota	Law Enforcement Ethics
Oklahoma	Police Ethics
Oregon	Law Enforcement Profession
Pennsylvania	Police Community Relations, Police Public Relations, and Police Ethics
Rhode Island	Public Ethics
South Dakota	Police Community Relations
Tennessee	Police Ethics
Utah	Police Ethics and Professionalism
Virginia	Law Enforcement as a Profession
Washington	Ethics
West Virginia	Police Ethics

TABLE 6 (cont.)

Wisconsin   Police Ethics and Police Image

Wyoming   Professional Orientation

Development, and Professionalism. It is needless to say that such terminological diversity made communication between the states regarding these courses rather difficult. Consequently, the various POST commissions might fail to exchange meaningful ideas with each other. Terminological uniformity is an essential step in the development of a body of professional knowledge. Police human relations training has developed as a result of the need for police professionalization. But intense localism manifested by such phenomena as terminological diversity is a matter of concern for the ideals of police professionalism. One can easily discern the contradiction between localism and professionalism in this development.

On the basis of the discussion with the important officials of the POST commissions the following were found to be the reasons for terminological diversity:

1. Terminological variations were considered to be inevitable because the states acted in accordance with their understanding and unique circumstances including geographical and cultural distinctiveness.

2. This diversity could be explained by political necessities, too. A course entitled, Battered Women, was likely to find more favor with a particular lobby than the one with the title, Crisis Intervention. Hence, the title, Battered Women, might be preferred by some POST commissions.

3. Diversity in course titles existed not only between the states, but even academies within the same state came to notice for using different names for identical courses. This was due to variation in understanding, politics, and academic habits of local officials including instructors.

4. Some terminological variation was due to subtle attempts at subterfuge. A powerful, traditional chiefs' lobby might frown upon a course title such as Police Stress, because

such a nomenclature was not expected to conform to the so-
called tough, macho image of the police. But, at the same
time, it was realized that such courses were important in view
of the complexities of police responsibilities. So a course
on police stress might be authorized, but with a camouflaged
title like Police Professionalism. These considerations were
obstacles to developing truly descriptive titles.

5. POST commissions do not have research branches
and, hence, no systematic research on such topics as standardization of terminology was undertaken.

6. Many courses in human relations were devised as a
means of coping with sudden developments that confronted
trainers and managers. Hence, course titles became part of
the coping mechanism, and in such a process not much thought
or deliberation was given to course nomenclature.

7. Terminological diversity was also due to the different
intellectual disciplines, understanding, and training of the
people in POST commissions. Those with psychology backgrounds would use titles which might not be preferable to
persons with training in sociology.

Officials were queried as to whether standardization was
desirable and practical. Virtually all POST commissions felt
that standardization would help more in the dissemination and
exchange of ideas in the field. It was also maintained that
in view of the diversity of law enforcement practices and norms
in various parts of the country, such standardization would
be a herculean task. Nonetheless, certain suggestions in
regard to standardization of terminology could be made. In
the analysis of the curricula it was observed that ten topical
areas were more widely used in human relations training in the
state-mandated programs. These were (a) Variant Behavior,
(b) Crisis and Conflict Management, (c) Community Relations,
(d) Police Ethics, (e) Human Behavior, (f) Family Disputes,
(g) Stress-related Issues, (h) Communication Skills, (i) Group-
related Behavior, and (j) Treatment of Special Groups.

In the topical area of Variant Behavior courses such as
Handling Mentally Ill, Mentally Retarded, and Drug Addicts
were included. Since the officers were taught to be flexible
in their approach to such behavior patterns, the courses in
this area could be given the title, Dealing with Variant

Behavior, which was currently used in Illinois. Crisis Intervention and Conflict Management courses were taught in various states in a comprehensive manner. Crisis included stress,
domestic disturbances, and other kinds of disputes. The
courses in this area could be properly described by the terminology used in California, namely, Topics in Crisis Management. This is a more expressive title than the existing ones.
Since all the courses in police community relations dealt primarily with relationships, these courses were better described
as Police Community Relations.

Police Ethics was expected to generate value consciousness and concerned conduct, professionalism, idealism, and
so on. So, from an idealistic perspective, police ethics and
values could be given a descriptive course title conforming
to ethical orientation. Hence, Ethical Ideals and Values could
be a meaningful title. Understanding Human Behavior was a
course title that could cover all topics in psychology, sociology,
interpersonal relations, and other related areas. Family and
Domestic Events was a suggested title to encompass a variety
of courses offered in the areas of spouse abuse, domestic
violence, child molestation, domestic crisis intervention, and
so on.

Stress-related Issues was a title that could be used for
a variety of courses on police stress, causes of stress, and
management of stress. Communication Skills would be a fairly
adequate nomenclature to replace various titles like Human
Communication, Oral Communication, Interpersonal Communication, and other similar names. The title Group Behavior
Phenomena could be used for courses dealing with crowds,
mobs, unlawful assemblies, disputing labor groups, and many
other offerings on collective behavior. Relations with Special
Groups was a suggested title for the courses relating to all
unique groups including ethnic minorities, depressed socio-
economic groups, the physically impaired (deaf, blind, etc.),
juveniles, and others in need of special police considerations.

These suggested titles are really suitable for referring
to broad typologies. It is almost impossible to standardize
every possible course title and very detailed standardization
may not be worth pursuing. However, broad agreement and
understanding regarding the titles of the major topical areas
in the human relations area are expected to be useful. This
will generate better understanding not only between different

POST commissions, but also between the former and those engaged in research in the field. An account of the existing titles, topical areas, and suggested titles is given in Table 7 (pages 77-83).

Survey of Instructors

An exploratory study of the qualifications and views of the state-mandated human relations training instructors was undertaken on a limited scale. For the purpose, a survey instrument was designed to elicit data on the following four counts:

1. Qualification of human relations instructors
2. Methods of instruction
3. Effectiveness of police human relations training
4. Human Relations instructors' opinion regarding the degrees of involvement of police training authorities in this area of training.

On November 1, 1983, a letter was written to all POST commissions requesting them to forward the names of the instructors who taught human relations courses in basic mandated programs. The letter was followed by reminders on December 20, 1983, and February 3, 1984. A number of agencies were also contacted telephonically in order to expedite their replies. The names were solicited for the purpose of the administration of the instrument.

As a result of these communications, it transpired that there were 625 police academies in the country which offered state-mandated minimum basic recruit training for certification. But all did not offer human relations training. Among those offering such training, many did not employ instructors on a permanent basis. These academies depended on part-time, seasonal employees who were not readily available for the administration of the instrument. In view of this practice it was not possible to determine the exact number of people engaged in human relations instruction in the state-mandated programs. Nevertheless, on the basis of the inquiries, 175 instructors were identified and questionnaires were sent to them. Out of these, 85 were received back from 17 states, namely, Arizona, Arkansas, California, Delaware, Georgia, Kentucky, Michigan, Minnesota, Missouri, Montana, Nebraska,

TABLE 7:

Standardization of Terminology

Topical Area	Existing Nomenclature	Suggested Nomenclature
Police Confrontation with many patterns of abnormal behavior	1. Mental Illness 2. Handling Abnormal People 3. Mental Retardation 4. Dealing with Variant Behavior 5. Handling Abnormal Personalities 6. Alternatives to Incarceration 7. Handling the Mentally Disturbed 8. Handling the Emotionally Disturbed 9. Recognizing and Handling Abnormal Behavior 10. Handling the Mentally Ill 11. Abnormal Psychology 12. Dealing with People 13. Abnormal Behavior 14. Mental Illnesses and Retardation 15. Mentally and Physically Handicapped 16. Mentally Impaired 17. Mentally Ill 18. Recognizing and Handling the Mentally Ill 19. Recognizing and Handling Abnormal Persons 20. How to Recognize and Handle Emotionally Disturbed People	Dealing with Variant Behavior

TABLE 7 (cont.)

Standardization of Terminology

Topical Area	Existing Nomenclature	Suggested Nomenclature
	21. Handling Abnormal Persons	
Crisis/Conflict Disturbances/ Disputes	1. Crisis Management 2. Conflict Management 3. Crisis Intervention and Conflict Management 4. Crisis Intervention 5. Crisis Intervention/ Disturbance Calls 6. Family Disturbance and Crisis Intervention 7. Crisis Intervention and Conflict Resolution 8. Conflict-Crisis Intervention 9. Mental Health Procedures Act--Crisis Intervention 10. Intervention in Domestic Disturbances 11. Crisis Intervention Techniques	Topics in Crisis Management
Relationships with Community	1. Community Service Concept 2. Community Attitudes and Influences 3. Citizen Evaluation 4. Police Community Relations 5. Public Relations for the Peace Officer 6. Community Relations 7. Police and Public 8. Race Relations, An Extension of Police Community Relations 9. Police Citizen Relations 10. Building Respect for the Police	Police-Community Relations

TABLE 7 (cont.)

Standardization of Terminology

Topical Area	Existing Nomenclature	Suggested Nomenclature
	11. Police Image	
	12. Environment of Policing	
	13. Public Relations	
	14. Police Public Interrelations	
	15. Law Enforcement and the Community	
	16. Police Role in Society	
	17. Police Community Relations, Police Public Relations, and Police Ethics	
Ethical Issues	1. Police Ethics and Standards of Conduct	Ethical Ideals and Values
	2. Ethics and Professionalism	
	3. Ethics	
	4. Law Enforcement Ethics	
	5. Police Ethics and Image	
	6. Police Ethics-Moral Development and Professionalism	
	7. Police Ethics and Professionalism	
	8. Police Morality	
	9. Situational and Impartial Enforcement of the Law	
	10. Police Professionalism	
	11. Law Enforcement Profession	
	12. Code of Ethics	
	13. Environment of Policing	
	14. Police Courtesy and Ethics	
	15. Police Ethics and Professionalization	

TABLE 7 (cont.)

Standardization of Terminology

Topical Area	Existing Nomenclature	Suggested Nomenclature
	16. Police Ethics and Unethical Behavior	
	17. Ethical Awareness	
	18. Human Relations, Ethics, and Courtesy	
	19. Ethical Issues	
	20. Unethical Behavior	
Psychological and Sociological Topics	1. Human Relations	Understanding Human Behavior
	2. Human Behavior	
	3. Supervisor-Subordinate Relationships	
	4. Perception of Human Behavior	
	5. Police Psychology	
	6. Psychology of Suicide	
	7. Perception	
	8. Self-Perception	
	9. Police Authoritarianism and Discretion	
	10. Psychology of Human Relations	
	11. Human Relations: Cultural Awareness	
	12. Perception of Human Behavior	
	13. Emotional Stability	
	14. Human Relations and Social Values	
	15. Personality Theory	
	16. Perception Technique	
	17. Police Isolation and Alienation	
	18. Psychology for Law Enforcement, Self-Understanding and Handling Stress	
Disputes in Domestic Setting	1. Family Disputes	Family and Domestic Events
	2. Handling Family Disputes	

TABLE 7 (cont.)

Standardization of Terminology

Topical Area	Existing Nomenclature	Suggested Nomenclature
	3. Domestic Disputes and Crisis Intervention	
	4. Domestic Complaints	
	5. Battered Women	
	6. Child Abuse	
	7. Spouse Abuse	
	8. Conflict Resolution	
	9. Domestic Violence	
	10. Domestic Crisis Intervention	
	11. Domestic Disputes	
	12. Domestic Conflict Management	
	13. Handling Disturbances, Disputes, Domestic Violence and Child Abuse Complaints	
Stress, Its Effects and Management	1. Stress Management	Stress-Related Issues
	2. Police Stress	
	3. Stress Factors	
	4. Stress Behavior	
	5. Stress Management Training for Law Enforcement Professionals	
	6. Psychological Stress of Police	
	7. Job Related Stress	
	8. Stress/Crisis Intervention	
Communications of Various Types	1. Interpersonal Communications	Communication Skills
	2. Human Communications	
	3. Communications in the Police Environment	
	4. Personal Communications	
	5. Interpersonal Relations	

TABLE 7 (cont.)

Standardization of Terminology

Topical Area	Existing Nomenclature	Suggested Nomenclature
	6. Oral Communications	
	7. Communications	
	8. Effective Verbal Communications	
Control and Regulation of Groups	1. Crowd and Riot Control	Group Behavior Phenomena
	2. Crowd Control	
	3. Labor Disputes	
	4. Crowd Control/ Civil Disorders	
	5. Riot Control	
	6. Crowd Behavior	
	7. Response to Special Emergencies	
	8. Civil Disorders	
	9. Group Behavior	
	10. The Nature and Control of Civil Disorders	
	11. Crowd and Riot Control Operations	
	12. Crowds and Mobs	
	13. Mob and Crowd Control	
Handling Groups in Need of Special Attention	1. Police and Troubled Youth Relations	Relations with Special Groups
	2. Police Officer and the Female Citizen	
	3. Patrol Decision Making in Juvenile Matters	
	4. Police Minority Relations	
	5. Police Orientation to the Deaf	
	6. Handling Juveniles	
	7. Minority Relations	
	8. Police and Press Relations	
	9. Child Abuse and Battered Wives	
	10. Sociology	

TABLE 7 (cont.)

Standardization of Terminology

Topical Area	Existing Nomenclature	Suggested Nomenclature
	11. Social Services	
	12. Dealing with People	
	13. Police and Minority Groups	
	14. News Media	
	15. Minority Relations	
	16. Handling the Deaf	
	17. Officer/Violator Relationships	
	18. Racial and Ethnical Differences	
	19. Police and Juveniles	
	20. Tourist and Police Relations	
	21. Handling Individuals with Special Needs	
	22. Handling Sick, Injured, and Deceased Persons	

New Mexico, New York, Oregon, Pennsylvania, South Dakota, and Texas.

It is noted that 85 instructors from 17 states do not constitute a representative sample of those teaching in basic mandated police human relations training programs. However, given the constraints of resources, it can be regarded as the best available sample. Babbie (1973, p. 106) recognizes that there can arise "situations in which probability sampling could be prohibitively expensive." And, hence, "the researcher may wish to study a small subset of a larger population." Kerlinger (1973, p. 406), too, says that "exploratory studies" can be used to "lay the groundwork for later, more systematic and rigorous testing of hypotheses."

Instructors' Qualifications

Regarding educational qualifications, the information received was as follows:

Education	Number	Percent
Nondegree	5	6
Associate	9	11
Baccalaureate	27	32
Master's	32	38
Ph.D.	10	12

Work experience of the participants is indicated below:

Type of Experience	Number	Percent
Non-Law Enforcement	15	18
Law Enforcement (Street)	20	23
Law Enforcement (Street/ Supervisory)	50	59

The majority of the instructors (82%) had law enforcement experience. Most of them were experienced in both supervisory and street-level work.

On the basis of the utilization of a particular instructional method, instructors can be divided as follows:

Methods of Instruction	Number of Instructors	Percent
Lectures based on scholarly research	17	20
Lectures based on research and experience	29	35
Lectures based on anecdotes and experience	15	17
Seminar/group discussion based on research and experience	12	14
Seminar/group discussion based on anecdotes and experience	12	13

Teaching methods based on scholarly research and experience were used by the majority of the instructors. A style consisting of academic model (research) and "how-to" approach (experience) is used by the majority of those who teach human relations.

Instructors were also asked regarding the effectiveness of police human relations training. Their opinions are summarized below:

Levels of Effectiveness	Number of Instructors	Percent
Generally effective	41	48
Partially effective	43	51
Not effective at all	0	0
Not certain	1	1

It is noted that the levels of effectiveness perceived by the instructors are not based on any scientific method of measurement. This is a view based on their experience.

The instructors surveyed were asked two more questions in order to determine their views regarding the degrees of involvement on the part of those who were managing mandated training of police recruits. These were whether human relations training was merely used to lend a touch of sophistication to recruit training. They were further queried if such training was included in the certification curricula in order to meet

the criticism that traditionally police training was primarily
stereotyped. The responses were as follows:

Objectives	Number of Instructors	Percent
Lending a touch of sophisti- cation to police training	29	34
Meeting criticism against stereotyped recruit training	32	38

Summary of Issues

It is evident that there are a few important concerns
in regard to police human relations instructors and the related
issues.

First, almost one half of the instructors (49%) had only
baccalaureate degrees or no degrees (17%) at all. Also, 18%
of them had no law enforcement experience. Emphasizing the
need for experience and education, the Task Force Report:
the Police (The President's Commission on Law Enforcement
and Administration of Justice, 1967, pp. 177, 139) suggests
the utilization of "experienced officers," "talented instructors,"
and "civilian specialists" for police training. The National
Advisory Commission on Criminal Justice Standards and Goals
(1973, pp. 376, 382-383, 409-410) recommends "quality instructors" who are "academically qualified." Its emphasis is
on instructors' "work experience and educational and professional credentials." According to the commission, academy
instructors must "retain close contact with the field performance of the subject they teach." Further, the commission
recommends "rotation of police training instructors through
operational assignments or periodic assignments to field observation tours of duty." Recognizing the need for "expertise
... beneficial to the training objective," it advocates "use of
outside instructors." Bittner (1980, pp. 81-82) recommends
that for police training there should be professional schools
staffed by educated teachers to be "drawn from within the
occupation." Conrad (1979, p. 17) maintains that a well-
educated instructor should be able to save the teaching process from becoming "anecdotal, unsystematic, and worst of all,
unrelated to the objective." Stratton (1984, pp. 69,74) comments that "the trainers have to be exceptional people." He
adds that "they have to be streetwise, willing to share their

practical experiences," and "academically oriented." They
need to "spend time on the street; attend classes, seminars,
or talk with other teaching professionals." Frost and Seng
(1983, p. 299) observed that "law enforcement experience
and education" were considered essential for police instructors.
Obviously, there is a need for human relations instructors
with more adequate qualifications based on formal education
and experience.

Second, 34 percent of instructors were of the opinion
that human relations courses were included in mandated police
training in order to lend a touch of sophistication to it. Also,
38 percent of them stated that human relations training was
a means of appeasing the critics who criticized police training
as purely mechanical. This cynical attitude needs careful
probing as such an attitude on the part of more than one-
third of the instructors may have an adverse effect on this
aspect of police training.

Third, about 51 percent of the sample felt that the effectiveness of this aspect of police training was only partial.
The perception needs to be explored further to determine
whether it is true. Such an investigation may also provide
insights into some problems in police human relations training.
It may, for example, enable POST commissions to understand
better the challenges in teaching human relations to police
recruits.

Fourth, 30 percent of the instructors teach police human
relations courses through anecdotal methods. It is true that
the methods of instruction in police academies have been found
generally conventional and archaic. Brown (1981, pp. 88-89)
notes that recruit training is marked by "emphasis on obedience, the concern for obedience to trivial rules" and, hence,
the methods of instruction tend to be authoritarian. Klockars
(1983, p. 384) says that police academies think that they can
inflate the ego of police recruits "by making the initiation experience extremely severe--seeing how much you can take."
Chapman (1982, p. 248) points out that instructors are beginning to shift their emphasis to "hands-on" methods and "student participation." Nevertheless, McCreedy (1983, p. 37)
comments that methods of instruction are generally conventional.
Police academies (Goldstein, 1977, p. 273) place heavy emphasis on "committing to memory large tracts of irrelevant facts,"
and conveying "only one point of view on controversial matters

in a manner intended to avoid open discussion." According to
Harris (1978, p. 287), most instructors tend to use "gimmicks,"
"sexual jokes," and also "pictures of nudes" to make their
lectures more interesting. However, anecdotal methods cannot
be the ideal vehicle for imparting human relations skills and
values to police recruits.

Recognizing the need for "effective," "experiential
methods" in police academies, Roberg (1976, p. 102) explains
that military-vocational "instruction is along how-to lines,"
while the academic model is geared toward "contemplative and
precise scholarship." He says that police academy instruction
style should be a balanced mixture of the two with a view to
teaching officers to "make very rapid decisions in highly
variable situations involving complex human interactions."
Gaines and Forester (1983, p. 210) maintain that police instructors should have experience and knowledge to ensure that
"important skills and abilities have been internalized by trainees." It is evident that a balanced, hands-on method is likely
to be more effective for imparting police human relations
training. In this rather abstract area of training, the need
is for a technique capable of strengthening values, awareness,
and attitudes.

It may be worthwhile to examine some of the recommendations of the National Advisory Commission (1973, pp. 383, 409)
in this regard. The commission advocates that police trainers
should make use of "the most communicative" teaching procedure with "the greatest emphasis on student-oriented instruction methods." Suggestions have been made for the
consideration of instructional techniques such as "role playing,
situation simulation, group discussion, and reading and research projects." In order to add "realism and impact," use
of audio-visual aids, "preconditioning materials," "self-paced
individualized instruction methods," and "computer assistance"
have been enthusiastically endorsed. Another measure suggested is this:

> Periodic monitoring of the presentation of every police
> training instructor to assist him in evaluating the ef-
> fectiveness of his methods, and the value of his
> materials.

These clear guidelines should make classroom instruction on
human relations lively and active.

It may be beneficial for POST commissions also to have a look at competency-based assessment technique developed at Alverno College (Milwaukee, Wisconsin). In that college, students enrolled in liberal arts courses are required to internalize certain skills and values which help them in life and work. This technique which has proven very effective is implemented as follows:

> At the beginning of each course, the instructor spells out the course goals in the syllabus, including the competence levels a student may be ready to demonstrate as a result of the course experience. In the syllabus, the instructor relates the particular materials and assignments to course goals. The syllabus also specifies the assessment techniques that will be used, and enumerates the criteria upon which the students' work will be judged. (The Alverno College Faculty, 1979, p. 8)

Competency-based assessment technique may prove useful for state-mandated police human relations instruction.

On the basis of this exploratory study, it can be argued that further improvement in police human relations training was possible through more adequately qualified instructors, who shared a wider agreement in regard to its objectives and utilized more suitable instructional methods.

Conclusion

In the country today, police human relations training is marked by wide diversity in approach and course content, adequacy of guidelines from POST commissions to the academies where such courses are taught, proportion of human relations to basic training from state to state, and utilization of terminology for course nomenclature. A survey of human relations instructors shows that they were educationally generally qualified, even though some lacked police experience. Many were not convinced about the real need of police human relations and somewhat skeptical about its effectiveness. Methods of instruction in this sophisticated area of police training were not very suitable in many states.

References

The Alverno College Faculty. (1979). Assessment at Alverno College. Milwaukee, WI: Alverno Productions.

Babbie, E. R. (1973). Survey research methods. Belmont, CA: Wadsworth Publishing.

Best, J. W. (1981). Research in education. Englewood Cliffs, NJ: Prentice-Hall.

Bittner, E. (1980). The functions of the police in modern society. Cambridge, MA: Oelgeschlager, Gunn & Hain.

Brown, M. K. (1981). Working the street. New York: Russell Sage Foundation.

Chapman, S. G. (1982). Personnel management. In B. L. Garmire (ed.), Local government in police management. Washington, DC: International City Management Association.

Conrad, J. P., & Myren, R. A. (1979). Two views of criminology and criminal justice. Chicago: Joint Commission on Criminology and Criminal Justice Standards and Education.

Cox, S. M., & Fitzgerald, J. (1982). Police in the community. Dubuque, IA: Wm. C. Brown.

Das, D. K. (1985). A review of progress toward state-mandated police human relations training. The Police Journal, 58(2), 147-162.

_____. (1984). Some issues in state-mandated police human relations training. Journal of Police Science and Administration, 12(4), 412-424.

Frost, T. M., & Seng, M. J. (1983). Police recruit training in urban departments: a look at instructors. Journal of Police Science and Administration, 2(3), 296-302.

Gaines, L. K., & Forester, W. (1983). Recruit training processes and issues. In C. J. Swank, & J. A. Conser (eds.), The police personnel system. New York: Wiley.

Goldstein, H. (1977). Policing a free society. Cambridge, MA: Ballinger.

Harris, R. N. (1978). The police academy and professional
    self-image. In P. K. Manning & J. Van Maanen (eds.),
    Policing: a view from the street. Santa Monica, CA:
    Goodyear.

Kerlinger, F. N. (1973). Foundations of behavioral research.
    New York: Holt, Rinehart and Winston.

Klockars, C. B. (1983). Thinking about police: contempor-
    ary readings. New York: McGraw-Hill.

McCreedy, K. (1983). Entry-level police training in the
    1980s. The Police Chief, 50 (10), 32-37.

National Advisory Commission on Criminal Justice Standards
    and Goals. Police. Washington, DC: U.S. Government
    Printing Office.

The President's Commission on Law Enforcement and Adminis-
    tration of Justice. (1967). Task force report: the police.
    Washington, DC: U.S. Government Printing Office.

Roberg, R. R. (1976). The changing police role. San Jose,
    CA: Justice Systems Development.

Stratton, J. G. (1984). Police passage. Manhattan Beach,
    CA: Glennon.

Wilson, J. Q. (1972). The police in the ghetto. In R. F.
    Steadman (ed.), The police and the community. Baltimore:
    Johns Hopkins University Press.

Chapter 5

VARIATION IN UNDERSTANDING HUMAN RELATIONS
BETWEEN THE LITERATURE AND THE COURSES

Views in the Literature

Examined here is whether ideas and concepts taught
through the courses in mandated human relations programs and
those found in the relevant literature are identical. Three frequently utilized courses have been selected for detailed review:
police community relations, ethics, and urban disorders. In
the literature review of the first two courses principal thoughts
of noted scholars have been highlighted and compared with the
primary contents of the courses. In the analysis of the mandated instructions on urban disorder the literature review high-
lights the lessons that the police can learn from past experiences.

The views in the police community relations literature
can be discussed under three major assumptions, namely, historical, psychological, and pragmatic. Historically, Peel's
Metropolitan Police constables are the prototype of American
police (Radelet, 1980; Manning, 1977; Reppetto, 1978; & Rubinstein, 1973). The British police officers recruited by Peel's
commissioners were exhorted to internalize the historical
common-law tradition that the police were the public and the
public the police (Brogden, 1982, p. 218; Critchley, 1967, p.
52; & Reith, 1956, p. 140). In today's changed English context,
too, the assumption that the police are a part of the community
continues to be reiterated. According to Osborn (1980, pp.
30-33), the British police public relations, rooted historically
in the tradition that the police are "a part of society--not
apart from it," are "the envy of the world." It is argued by
McNee (1983, p. 232) that Metropolitan Police needed "to be
well informed of the needs and demands of its local communities." He implies that this was expected because they were
part of the people they policed.

Never was the historical concern for police rapport with

the people so strongly advocated in this country as in the period following the traumatic 60s. The President's Commission (1967, pp. 98-100), for example, advocated that "police-citizen relationships on the street" should be meaningful "person-to-person encounters." It, therefore, recommended a reexamination of "fundamental attitudes" of the police toward the people. Its position was that community relations should not be viewed as "public-relations programs to sell the police image." On the contrary, the commission called upon the police to become "more active and valued members of the community." They were asked to value the ideals of mutual "respect" and the "sense of identity" with the public as partners in the same mission.

An important dimension of police community relations, Radelet (1980, p. 22) maintains, "is providing some beneficial service to the community" which can be psychologically gratifying to the police. Regarding the psychological benefits from service functions, the President's Commission (1967, p. 98) said that "opportunities to be friendly and useful are psychologically valuable." Various psychopathological consequences including coercion, suspicion, alienation, cynicism, authoritarianism, and the like are inevitable characteristics of a policeman's occupation (Niederhoffer, 1967; Westley, 1970; Skolnick, 1975; and Bittner, 1980). Service functions (Rubinstein 1973, p. 348) are, therefore, healthy for police officers because if he did nothing but remain on crime control he would be a strange human being. Banton (1978, p. 3) recommends a "variety of services" for the police because without them the police are likely "to narrow their role."

Further, trainees can be made to appreciate that positive community relations achieved through service functions can be particularly psychologically rewarding because of a number of reasons. First, those whom the police serve in this capacity are generally from the uneducated, economically depressed, and vulnerable segment of community. Specifically, they are blacks in the urban ghettos of America (Cumming et al., 1965; Wilson, 1974; Radelet, 1980). Second, they are also the principal targets of aggressive law enforcement strategy (Chevigny, 1969; Muir, 1977; and Bittner, 1980). Third, they are "more likely to give negative ratings to the police" (Decker, 1981, p. 81). For such reasons welfare activities to this special group of clients could be satisfying to police officers seeking to achieve "internalization of the traditional humanistic values of the ancient professions" (Niederhoffer & Blumberg, 1976, p. 19).

The community-oriented police experiment in San Diego showed that involvement with the community could provide police officers "with a greatly enriched sense of accomplishment" (Boydstun & Sherry, 1975, p. 76). According to Brown and Locke (1985, pp. 95-96), some of the benefits of good public relations are "greater feelings of job satisfaction," "sensitivity," and judgment." Muir (1983, pp. 4-9) notes that "a vigorous part in community affairs, including politics," can alleviate cynicism and the other negative consequences of police "preoccupations with the morbid side of life." Toch et al. (1975, pp. 8-9) recommend "positive, meaningful contacts between police and public" as "these contacts integrate the officer in the community, and give him a sense of participation and vested interest in a larger social order." According to them, the "alienated" police officer regards himself as "misunderstood," "unappreciated," and "disrespected." Mottaz (1983, p. 29) argues that positive community relations can reduce police alienation. Brown (1981, p. 58) comments that sharing values with the community, officers can mitigate the undesirable impact of "the separation between the police and the community."

According to the Peelian principles which dwelt upon many pragmatic advantages of public approval and respect, police effectiveness, in fact, depended upon community good will. As noted elsewhere, it was stressed that public cooperation, their voluntary compliance with the law, and execution of police work with the minimal use of physical force could be achieved through sound working relationships with people. Nurtured on public approval, the Metropolitan Police (Tobias, 1972, p. 117) were successful in reduction of crime and elimination of "prejudices that greeted the introduction of the force in 1829." Tobias (1972, p. 9) adds that public support toward the police shielded the government from the charges of "the tyranny of a police state." Stead (1977, p. 83) enumerates that "stability and security" of the social order, alleviation of "the wildness and brutality of so much of English life," "the public decorum of 19th-century London," and "the amelioration of urban life" were the practical contributions of the popular Metropolitan Police.

Many benefits of public goodwill and cooperation are mentioned in the literature. According to McDowell (1977, p. 375), crime prevention responsibilities ought to be shared between the "official sector" and the public for the sake of effectiveness and results. Latessa and Allen (1980, p. 69) observed that assistance and participation of citizens could "significantly reduce crime." Citizen "information and expertise" are for the police their "principal resource" (Formby & Smykla, 1981, p. 403). Lavrakas and Herz (1982, p. 48) conclude that "citizens may play the major role in the control and prevention of crime." Sherman (1983, p. 29) refers to "information" patrol officers could obtain through "personal relationships with storekeepers, members of the clergy, and others."

It has been argued that the disorders of the 60s could have been prevented, and, also, controlled far better with good police public rapport (The President's Commission, 1967; The National Advisory Commission on Civil Disorders, 1968). Wilson (1972, p. 85) maintains that the most useful method for "easing of tension" is "an active partnership between citizens and the police."

The foregoing conclusions point out that there are historical, psychological, and pragmatic reasons for police community relations. It is expected that these considerations should be brought to the attention of police trainees during their courses on community relations.

State-mandated Training in Community Relations

All community-relations courses were carefully analyzed and reduced to their basic elements (Appendix B). Further, the recurring elements were identified using the criterion of the frequency-of-use across the nation. Elements discussed variously in these courses were (a) minority relations including race relations as well as relations with special groups like juveniles, women, and the elderly; (b) projecting a desirable police image to the community; and (c) an awareness of the negative police characteristics like subculture that affected police relations with the public. However, the similarity in police community relations courses was limited. Approximately 27 percent of the courses dealt with minority relations, police image was stressed in 36 percent of the courses, police subculture figured in 18 percent of them, and the focus in the rest of the courses (about 20 percent of them) was rather diverse. Both in the literature and the courses there were references to police subculture, alienation, cynicism, and other

negative occupational consequences. While therapeutic, cura-
tive aspects of community relations were stressed in the
literature, the courses were not emphatic in this regard. Public relations including image-building efforts were emphasized
in the courses which the literature did not encourage.

Diversity in the courses was readily noticeable (Appendix
B) and 100 different elements were found in the courses under
review. Probably the diversity in the courses was indicative
of the following:

1. Lack of understanding regarding what police recruits
    should learn in their basic police community-relations
    courses.

2. Absence of exchange of ideas on the subject among
    various states.

3. Nonavailability of sophisticated coordination in regard
    to these courses.

It was also examined if the views in the literature were
reflected in any particular community-relations course. As a
result, it is noted that in the California course, Community
Service concept, community service as a historical mission
of police work was emphasized. Courtesy, openness, and
positive attitudes in dealing with the public were stressed
in the course, Public and the Police, taught in Georgia.
Creating an environment of cooperation (New York, The Police
and the Public); cultivating honor, faith, and trust in relations with the people (South Carolina, Police Community Relations); and developing an area of common interests with the
community (Utah, Police Community Relations) were another
set of elements. Such sentiments were echoed in a few other
courses in some other states too. In them, officers were
charged with the responsibility of building rapport with the
"man on the street" to carry out their historical community-
relations role (California, Community Evaluation; Colorado,
Police Community Relations; and Kentucky, Police Community
Respect).

Concepts identical to psychosocial assumptions were
noted in a number of separate courses. Goodwill toward the
public as a means of self-control was focused in Public Relations taught in Missouri. Satisfaction derived from cooperation

with citizenry was discussed in Human Relations, a course in
Michigan. Insights into the nature of police prejudice were
projected through a course in New York, namely, Police and
Minority Groups. Psychologically cultivated attitudes on the
part of the police were emphasized in South Carolina's course
on community relations.

Specific elements endorsing pragmatic assumptions
were found in individual courses. In New Hampshire the relationships between crime prevention and public support were
stressed in the course, Police/Community Relations. Public
support as a motivator of police excellence was emphasized in
The Police and the Public, a course offered in New York.
Connection between crime prevention and community participation was taught in Utah in the course, Police Community Relations.

Recommendations

Incorporation of the important views found in the literature is expected to result in better conformity between the
views of the researchers and those stressed in the courses.
Presently, historical, psychological, and pragmatic assumptions
are not nationally adequately reflected in the community-
relations courses. This phenomenon can be attributed to the
variation in the concept of police community relations between
the scholars in the area and the designers of the community-
relations courses.

State-mandated Police Training in Ethics

An evaluation of state-mandated courses in ethics is
attempted below with a view to exploring whether the courses
reflect the major recommendations found in the literature.
Certain thoughts would also be offered for the consideration
of those responsible for police training in this area.

Views in the Literature

A review of the literature in regard to important ethical
concerns in policing reveals the following:

1. The need for police appreciation of the sacred obligations toward law, i.e., legal professionalism.

2. Cultivation of conduct based on principles and values.

3. Avoidance of corruption.

According to Skolnick (1975, pp. xvi-xviii), the "rule
of law" implies that the police are not merely bureaucracies
engaged in administration of law. They have a more sacred
obligation, and he describes it "as strengthening the rule of
law." In the enforcement of law, says Skolnick, the police
must develop "a deeper and more thoughtful set of values"
including the acceptance of the paradox that a purpose of
law "is to make their tasks more difficult." As "front-line
workers" (Punch, 1979, p. 45) they should not take upon
themselves the responsibilities of judges and prosecutors.
One of the principles of Sir Robert Peel, (Davis, 1973, p.
113), was that the police should "never appear to usurp the
powers of the judiciary."

Sherman (1982, pp. 14-15, 19, 44) points out that
police culture and environment tend to encourage "lying and
deception" as well as scant regard toward procedural law.
Police officers learn to scoff at due process as it appears to
be "only a means of protecting criminals at the expense of the
law abiding." Sherman (1982, p. 10), therefore, maintains
that there is an urgent need for "examining police problems
in the light of basic moral principles and from the moral point
of view." According to him (1982, p. 44), many "ethical
questions" arise in police practices regarding use of informers,
surveillance, keeping of dossiers, and so on, requiring each
officer to make a moral decision. Heffernan (1982, pp. 31-32)
also recommends ethical awareness on the part of police officers in regard to "perjury," "government participation in
deceit," "individual privacy versus the public security," and
other violations of similar nature.

The exemplary conduct of the British police has been
enthusiastically praised as the single most important source
of their unwritten authority. Banton (1964, p. 232) equates
the police with "the monarchy and the church," one of the
"central institutions" in British life. The cultivation of un-
blemished, moral conduct is considered more challenging than
mere conformity to legal norms. While the former calls for

ethical and humane values, the latter may be satisfied through mechanical compliance. Callahan (1982, p. 64) argues that "the requirements of morality go beyond those of the law," and adds that kindness, empathy, altruism, and the like, without which a profession will be "dangerous," are "traits" that law does not require. Potts (1981, p. 132) recommends "personal rectitude among individual police officers" to eliminate the evils of "abuse of authority, insulting language, ethnic slurs, and other forms of social impropriety." The President's Commission (1967, p. 181) recommended that all police departments should have well-defined policies regarding "need for courtesy," "conduct," and for prohibiting "racial epithets." Black and Reiss (1972, p. 196) mention that civility does not mean "humor and joviality toward citizens." It must be "based" on the appreciation of "the rights and dignity of individuals and recognition of them as persons."

Goldstein (1977, p. 173) suggests that sensitivity to "citizen complaints" can provide the police with useful means for improvement. According to him, "special interest" in studying public accusations of "verbal abuse," "appearing callous," as well as other "situations that prompt a citizen to complain" can help the police to polish their conduct. The Standards and Goals Commission (1973, p. 402) notes that police discrimination could "destroy the trust essential for public support." Brown (1978, p. 64) maintains that "stereotyped concepts of minorities" and, also, the "tendency to place value judgments on cultural differences" generally resulted in police discrimination toward these people.

While discussing police conduct based on principles and values, the question of deadly force cannot be avoided. In regard to the use of deadly force, Elliston (1981, p. 97) observes that justice could not be "achieved by the use of deadly force." Moreover, the police task was not to "dispense justice," and, as pointed out earlier, the police are only responsible for "bringing the offender to justice." Muir (1977, p. 45) says that a police officer's authority, status, sense of civility and reasonableness should "impose terrible limits on his freedom to react successfully to the extortionate practices of others." Fyfe (1982, p. 311) indicates that training should enable the police to develop "skills" in avoiding "the escalation of violence," and "encourage the use of less drastic alternatives."

The police are expected to honor the code of conduct
adopted by the International Association of Chiefs of Police.
Potts (1981, p. 132) mentions that the "code is not the same
thing as inculcation of ethical values" since a code could
merely be a "wishful expression of principles." It was, nevertheless, useful as a "careful articulation of the values" attending the police mission.

The most common form of corruption is "the misuse of
authority by a police officer in a manner designed to produce
personal gain for the officer or for others" (Goldstein, 1977,
p. 188). In many other forms of abuse of authority "there
is no indication that the abuse was motivated by a desire for
personal gain." Goldstein adds that "corruption is considered
morally wrong by the community" (1977, p. 205), while officers
accused of excesses may often receive "widespread community
approval." Sherman (1974, p. 5), too, defines "corruption as
bribery." Manning and Redlinger (1978, p. 157) describe
corruption as "departures from correct procedure in exchange
for some goods, services or money," and they consider "bribe-
taking is the most common form of corruption." Walker (1983,
p. 182) says that "the most serious form of corruption" is
regular "pay-offs" for vice protection.

Murphy (1982, p. 53) states that police corruption "un-
dermines public confidence," "destroys respect for law,"
and harms departmental discipline and police morale. Enumer-
ating the sources of corruption, Murphy (1983, pp. 50-60)
presents a long list of sources: "ignoring vice," "fixing
traffic tickets," "bargaining with the criminal," "accepting
small gratuities," "taking kickbacks," "stealing," and "internal
payoffs." His list generally illustrates Sherman's (1974, pp.
191-199) observation that the moral career of a police officer
involves "a painful process of choices." In this complex process a key role is played by peer pressure which resolves for
the individual officer the "conflict between police group values
and those of the larger society." Minor "perks" which initiate
the recruit to corruption are not rejected by him since the
"peer pressure to accept them is great." Stoddard (1983,
p. 347), too, identifies "the sanction of group acceptance"
as of "paramount" importance in developing insensitivity to
corrupt practices.

State-mandated Training in Ethics

Most of the states (78 percent of those participating) include ethics in their state-mandated minimum basic programs.

On the basis of the examination of the curricula, it was found that there are diverse elements in the courses under review (Appendix B). The following were identified as frequent elements:

1. Avoiding gifts, gratuities, bribes, and rewards.

2. Knowledge regarding the exercise of caution in use of drugs, alcohol, and tobacco.

3. Adoption of a law enforcement code of ethics to demonstrate commitment to professionalism.

4. Practice of ethical values for a public image.

5. Perception of the need to develop professional sensitivity toward unethical conduct in fellow officers.

Police commitment to strengthening the rule of law, did not appear to have been generally incorporated in the ethics courses included in the state-mandated programs. A handful of states, however, included some legal concerns in their instruction in ethics. In California, the course entitled, Ethics, was utilized for a discussion of "false or colored testimony." It also focused attention on "violations of civil rights through false arrest," "illegal serach," "denial of right to counsel, and right to bail," as well as other acts of impropriety in law enforcement. In the course, Police Morality offered in Illinois, there were references to "abuse of authority" and "perjury." Included in the New Hampshire course in Police Ethics and Unethical Behavior, was a discussion of "false arrest," and "civil liability." "Respect for civil rights," "acceptance of limitations of authority," and "concern for honest prosecutions" were elements of the course, Police Ethics, taught in South Dakota. In the rest of the states, legal professionalism was not a part of the ethics courses.

In the literature, personal rectitude, civility of manners, sensitivity to public complaints, abjuring of discrimination, and avoidance of brutality were some of the principles recommended for police ethics. These principles were considered as the endurable foundation of police conduct. All these

concerns, however, were not really reflected in the ethics
courses mandated by the various POST commissions. In the
review of the literature, the mere adoption of a code of ethics
did not emerge as an important area of concern. But in the
courses taught, knowledge of the code of ethics had been
given importance. Open espousal of ethical norms was recommended in the courses for the sake of maintaining a good public image. The concern for public image, however, could be
indirectly interpreted as a desire for cultivating "sensitivity
to public complaints" which has been recommended in the
literature. Moderation in the use of intoxicating substances
was a vital element in the courses, although it did not emerge
as a major concern in the review of the literature.

Conformity to some other values and perspective recommended in the literature was partially seen in a few states.
"Brutality," "racial prejudice," and "discourteous conduct"
were discussed as unethical in a course taught in California.
In Connecticut, "the role of courtesy" was one of the elements
in Police Ethics--Moral Development and Professionalism. In
South Dakota "respect for all interests" and "demonstration of
trust and fairness" were taught in Police Ethics. Ethical Issues, a course taught in Wyoming, contained references to
"coercive force" and "courtesy."

Only one recommendation noted in the literature, namely,
"sensitivity to public complaints," was generally included in
ethics courses. However, even this concept was found only
indirectly emphasized in discussion of the relationship between
ethical norms and public image. Trainees were taught to be
sensitive to the ways the public developed perceptions about
the police in an Arkansas course entitled, Police Ethics and
Image. In Maryland, the course titled, Code of Ethics, is
utilized to emphasize that police officers were fully exposed
to public view and, hence, there was a need for exemplary
morality. The relationship between ethical conduct and community relations was discussed in ethics courses in Louisiana,
Michigan, Missouri, Kentucky, Massachusetts, Nebraska, and
Nevada.

In brief, an opinion expressed in the literature regarding
principled conduct and found in ethics courses, namely, sensitivity to public complaints, was indirectly covered through
discussion of the relationship between ethical behavior and
public image of the police. Other recommendations like

personal rectitude, civility, renunciation of discrimination, and abjuring of violence are only partially emphasized in a few states. Avoidance of excess in drugs and alcohol as well as knowledge of the code of conduct were two additional perspectives observed in course elements although not emphasized in the literature.

An analysis of the course elements showed that mandated programs highlighted the importance of avoidance of all illegal gratifications including bribery. The types of police corruption as well as opportunities for corruption were important elements in Environment of Policing, a course on ethics mandated in Massachusetts. Perception of integrity was a part of the Nevada course entitled, Ethics and Professionalism. In New Hampshire, corrupt practices that destroyed professionalism were discussed in the course, Police Ethics and Unethical Behavior. Ethics, a course in New Jersey, was designed to make trainees aware of the opportunities and avenues of dishonesty in police. Similarly, lack of dignity in corruption as well as opportunities for immoral practices in policing were emphasized in Ethical Awareness, a course taught in New York's state-mandated program. The nature of corruption was discussed in Law Enforcement Profession, a course in Oregon.

In regard to avoidance of corruption, there arose a number of important concerns in the relevant literature. But only two such concerns, namely, desisting from all forms of illegal gratifications including bribery and the diverse impact of peer pressure were incorporated in the mandated courses. A few states paid attention to matters such as avenues of corruption and its impact upon the police. All the other concerns discussed in the literature in connection with corruption were missing in the courses under review.

Recommendations

A review of the literature showed that three most important concerns in the area of police ethics were legal professionalism, principled conduct, and avoidance of corruption. It is observed that the ethics courses under review did not seem to have been planned taking into account the main considerations highlighted in the literature. Hard philosophical concerns were missing from the courses in numerous programs. There was no common focus on the recognition of the higher

values of law. Concerns with brutality, discrimination, personal rectitude, and so on, were not emphasized in connection
with police conduct. The connection between bribery and
debasement of the social order represented by the police was
not highlighted in the discussion of corruption. More simplis-
tic ideas like avoidance of excessive use of drugs and alcohol,
formal obeisance to the code of ethics and nonacceptance of
gifts were common elements in the state-mandated ethics courses.

It is true that the above-mentioned ideas provided easy
and pragmatic guidelines for a newly recruited police officer.
Moreover, the time allocated to this aspect of training was
minimal. It was not possible to focus attention on philosophical discourses within such a limited time frame. It was probably also true that many police recruits did not enter the
service with the academic background needed for sophisticated
discussion of the matters of ethical subtleties. Nevertheless,
these constraints probably needed to be carefully discussed
in view of the police claim to professional status. As professionals, police officers make important decisions affecting individuals and society without direct supervision and guidance.
They use discretion and judgment constantly. Without a deep
and abiding sense of legal professionalism, principled conduct,
and integrity of highest standards, a police officer cannot be
morally competent to adequately shoulder sensitive responsibilities. The need for well-designed, properly planned, and
fully comprehensive courses based on research findings in
ethics cannot be neglected to narrow the gap between the
literature and the mandated courses.

Handling Urban Disorders

This is an attempt to analyze whether state-mandated
courses in riot control take into account the lessons learned
from past practices which may help the police to avoid similar
mistakes in the future.

In the area of urban disorders critical comments on
police practices are as follows: (a) overreaction to protests
and demonstrations, (2) misconceived notions about the people
who participate in disturbances, and (3) racial discrimination
in the treatment of agitators. Commenting on police behavior
in the urban disorders of the 1960s, Gary T. Marx (1970, p.

21) maintained that the police could exacerbate the aggressiveness of agitators. Police methods were responsible for giving
rise to "strong feelings of generational loyalty" (The President's Commission on Campus Unrest, 1970, p. 26) that es-
calated the tempo of youth violence. According to Rainwater
(1970, p. 214) "a riot seems almost always to begin with an
incident in which the police make an effort at enforcing one
or another law." Boskin (1976, p. 135) mentions that the
riots in Harlem (1964), Newark (1967), Detroit (1967), and the
Los Angeles Chicano protests (1970) were sparked by police
overreaction. According to him, the "spark was the classic
one: a trivial police accident." He (1976, p. 108) says that
1964 Harlem riots started as follows:

> The crowd marched off to 123rd street police station....
> The police tried to seal off the block. "that's it!" a
> police inspector cried, "Lock 'em up!" Officers hustled
> 16 demonstrators inside and started bullying others
> down the streets. Almost in a matter of minutes
> Central Harlem was aflame with hatred.

Marx (1970, p. 20) mentions that the police have justified aggressive reaction to urban disorders. In 1968 the New Jersey
State Patrolmen's Benevolent Association vehemently protested
against charges of undue force leveled by their own superiors.
They objected to charges of overreaction as follows:

> Were any of the commissioners who accuse police of
> using undue force on the firing line? Do they really
> know what they are talking about? Use of the term
> "undue force" is an exercise in tortured semantics
> that police refuse to accept. Not only is the charge
> without merit, it is an insult of the brave men who
> risked their lives for the public and equally unaccept-
> able to reasonable people.

Miron and Wasserman (1980, p. 51) caution the police
regarding "the basic role conflict" inherent in militaristic
handling of civil disorders. According to them, the police
should bear in mind that they are not "military personnel."
Basically, they are "citizens of a community who have chosen
to serve that community." The Report of the National Advisory
Commission on Civil Disorders (1968, pp. 174-177) advocates
"sufficiently strong" discipline for the police to be able to
avoid being "provoked into unilateral tactics." The Commission

argues that deadly force applied against agitators may kill or
injure innocent bystanders or passersby. It is likely that in
use of armed force against looting or vandalism, somebody
may be killed for "stealing a six-pack of beer." The Commission adds that "the inappropriate display of weapons" may be
"inflammatory" and it violates the police principle of "minimum
use of force." Moreover, weapons used in civil disorders can
be "brutalizing and demeaning."

A suggested alternative to the use of force is cultivation
of methods that do not aim at "suppression but the avoidance
of conflict" (Deane-Drummond, 1975, p. 25). Suppression can
lead to abuse of power while the practice of conflict avoidance
demands psychological skills. Deane-Drummond elaborates
this suggestion as follows:

> What is required is knowledge of the roots of our own
> behavior, as individuals or in a crowd, as spectators,
> as demonstrators taking part in political action, and
> as members of the agencies whose duty it is to maintain
> law and order ... crowd psychology and behavior of
> people en masse are subjects that deserve serious
> study.

The Task Force on Disorders and Terrorism (1976, p. 185) al-
luded to the risk of police "responding too visibly or too
strongly" to acts of civil disorders and added that life in a
society that had to witness such behavior could be uncertain
and distasteful.

In the 1960s, according to Skolnick (1969, p. 262), the
police viewed agitations and protests as conspiratorial acts
of a few disgruntled, antisocial and mischievous elements.
Platt (1971, p. 34) identified that attitude as a "riffraff"
theory which labeled "participants in popular disturbances as
mob or rabble." In accordance with this seventeenth-century
perspective, demonstrators were branded as "demagogues or
professional agitators." For example, it was observed that
(Skolnick, 1969, p. 263) the then F.B.I. Chief Hoover attributed the unique student revolts at Berkeley to the Com-
munists who were reportedly "in the forefront of civil rights,
antiwar, and student demonstrations."

Explaining the reasons for this attitude of the police,
Niederhoffer and Blumberg (1976, p. 12) say that the police

are made to act like "a social lightning rod" in protests and
disturbances. Their function is to act as a "buffer in insul-
ating and protecting existing political and social structures."
This could drive the police toward self-righteous obstinacy
and a supercilious feeling of being the defenders of the
society. They add:

> They perform a further, more subtle role in acting as
> a controlling radar calculated to keep a society within
> structural confines that tend to be somewhat narrower
> than its stated ideological commitments. Thus, the
> police are the vehicle by which the limits, boundaries,
> and permissibility of social tolerance are tested.

Learned opinions and research findings do not substan-
tiate the police labeling of demonstrators as "riffraff" elements.
The Fact-Finding Commission (1968, p. 4) was convinced that
the violent student protestors at Columbia University were the
"best informed, most intelligent, and the most idealistic, this
country has ever known." The President's Commission on
Campus Unrest (1970, p. 52) referred admiringly to the idealism of the youthful protestors. Lipset and Wolin (1965, p.
xii) observed that the protesting students at Berkeley demonstrated "sensitivity to social issues" and signs of a "new gen-
eration." According to the National Commission on the Causes
and Prevention of Violence (1970, p. 188) many of the protesting young people were "highly motivated by the ideals."
They were frustrated because of "the gap between the ideals
we preach and the many injustices."

In the 1960s the police apprehensions about the nature
of the protesting student led them to respond to the campus
agitations with an undue show of force. Dynes et al. (1974,
p. 53) attributed the destruction and damage at Ohio State
University to misconceived notions about the protestors. They
observed that scenes like the following were the consequences
of police nervousness:

> In about a 10-hour period, three major confrontations
> occurred between the police and rioters that resulted
> in more than 240 police officers being injured, 900
> persons being eventually arrested, and several thous-
> and persons being treated for effects of tear gas. At
> least 150 persons received treatment at hospitals, in-
> cluding at least seven for gunshot wounds.

Similar police apprehensions and misgivings were responsible for the tragedy at Southern University in Baton Rouge, Louisiana. The Commission of Inquiry (1973, pp. 26-27), which investigated the facts surrounding the death of two student protestors at the campus, expressed amazement that the police built up a massive stockpile of arms to deal with a body of unarmed students. Some of the weapons found with the police on the campus were these:

12 gauge shotguns	44
.30 caliber carbines	11
.37mm tear gas guns	3
.30-.30 caliber rifles	1
M-1 carbines	1
7.62mm caliber rifles	1
AR 15 rifles	1
Thompson submachine guns	2

These arms were in addition to "Big Bertha," an armored vehicle.

It has been suggested that one way of avoiding the waste of human lives and scarce resources is for the police to develop an insight into the nature of protestors. As explained above, the national commissions and scholars found that the protesting students of the 1960s were idealistic and sensitive. A survey (Katzenbach, 1980, pp. 6-15) conducted after the Miami riots of 1980 revealed that, out of the approximately 1,000 people arrested mainly for looting, the vast majority were working people without arrest records. Typically, a rioter was about 28 years old, single, and male. Probably, he dropped out of school and was working in a blue-collar job with an annual income below $10,000. Allen (1970, p. 8) observed that rioters did not differ from non-rioters in absolute income. They were not hard-core unemployed and, also, they were better integrated into the community than nonrioters. Allen adds:

> Characteristics of rioters, as compared with nonrioters, clearly refute the "riffraff" theory, which holds that rioters are the irresponsible deviants, the emotionally disturbed, or the criminals of the community.

It can be argued, however, that notwithstanding the idealism of the protestors, demonstrations are fraught with the

possibility of violence. Campus disorders bore ample evidence
of that danger. All protests (Etzioni, 1970, p. 2) have an
inherent "danger which is uniquely theirs: a tendency to
escalate from peaceful to obstructionist and from obstructionist
to violent action." The police, therefore, have to intervene
forcefully in order to protect life and property. Violent
strikes are also illegal (Fortas, 1968, p. 66):

> The words of the First Amendment mean what they
> say. But they mean what they say and not something
> else。 They guarantee freedom to speak and freedom
> of the press--not freedom to club people or destroy
> property. The First Amendment protects the right to
> assemble and to petition, but it requires, in plain
> words--that right be peaceably exercised.

But the possibility of violence should not provoke the
police to irrational response to protests. Their action is
likely to be tempered with moderation if it is based on proper
diagnosis of the reasons for such violence. It is pointed out
by Conant (1970, p. 36) that violent movements became "the
weapon of last resort available to labor" in the early part of
the century. The rationale for labor violence was their experience that no effective nonviolent alternative was available
to them. According to Conant the "ghetto riots of the 1960s"
were violent because blacks realized that "nonviolent protests
would not result in effective application of national laws and
policies." Piven and Cloward, too (1979, pp. 18-19) explain
that the poor invariably look upon mass defiance and spectacu-
lar disruption as more potent weapons than conventional elect-
oral politics. On the basis of the survey data from Watts,
Newark, and Detroit, Platt (1971, p. 35) observed that blacks
looked upon riots as "useful and legitimate forms of protests."
According to the blacks interviewed in Los Angeles, "riot was
a purposeful event which had a positive effect on their lives."

The police were also accused of being unduly aggressive
against blacks and other minority rioters. According to Supreme Court Justice Thurgood Marshall (1943, pp. 50, 232-234),
in the 1943 Detroit riots, the police enforced the law with
"unequal hand." They used "persuasion" against white rioters,
but blacks received "the ultimate in force: night sticks, re-
volvers, riot guns, submachine guns, and deer guns." According to Boskin (1976, pp. 14-15), in all the major riots
of the past the white groups "sparked the incident by attacking

members of the minority group." But the police, so argued
this analyst, "sided with the attackers." Another view (Becker & Murray, 1971, p. XV) is that the use of undue force
against black rioters is a part of everyday "police brutality
... in slums, ghettos, and inner cities." Feagin and Hahn
(1973, p. 153) maintained that the ghetto riots of the 1960s
turned into ugly, hostile confrontations between police and
blacks because of police discriminations.

An exhaustive study of the issue concerning the race
riots led the National Advisory Commission on Civil Disorders
(1968, p. 157) to conclude that "abrasive relationships between
police and Negroes and other minority groups have been a
major source of grievance, tension, and ultimately, disorder."
It was further observed (1968, pp. 3-5) that "Negro civilians"
suffered the highest casualties in all urban disorders. Iron-
ically, "police actions in almost half the cases" were the most
immediate cause of all such disorders. A typical rioter was
"better educated" than his nonrioting black neighbors, and
he was "seeking fuller participation in the social order"
rather than rejecting it. The Commission said:

> The police were not merely a "spark" factor. To
> some Negroes police have come to symbolize white
> power, white racism, and white repression. And, the
> fact is many police do reflect and express these white
> attitudes. The atmosphere of hostility and cynicism
> is reinforced by a widespread belief among Negroes
> in the existence of police brutality and in a "double
> standard" of justice and protection--one for Negroes
> and one for Whites.

It is also pointed out by the same commission that the causes
of disorders were "embedded in a tangle of issues and circum-
stances--social, economic, political, and psychological."

The National Commission on the Causes and Prevention
of Violence (1970, p. 125) observed that police abuse of the
rights of ghetto citizens could "contribute substantially to
disaffection with government." The President's Commission
on Law Enforcement and Administration of Justice (1967, p.
100) felt that "too many policemen do misunderstand, and are
indifferent to minority group aspirations, attitudes, and customs." The National Advisory Commission on Criminal Justice
Standards and Goals noted with alarm (1973, p. 30) that "some

segments of society have ... no confidence in their police."
It warned the police that "this lack of confidence could develop
into a chasm of total misunderstanding."

It has been argued that discrimination, mistrust, and
bitterness between the police and the minorities continue in
the 1980s. According to Miron and Wasserman (1980, pp. 64-
65), the Miami riots were "the result of narrowly defined but
widely shared grievances against the police or criminal justice
system." They maintain that the police could hardly do anything to remove the causes of poverty, stress, congestion,
and other negative consequences of life in the urban ghettos.
However, they could help the situation by developing understanding and appreciation of these problems. Such an attitude
would enable them to shed their prejudice and discrimination.
They added:

> The lessons learned from Dade County have been ac-
> quired at great cost and they will, no doubt, have
> to be learned again and again. In applying these
> lessons, police departments will need to assume a dif-
> ferent type of leadership in the 1980s. They will
> need to be less reticent in sharing with others their
> knowledge of neighborhood conditions which contribute
> to violence and disorder. When tensions are due to
> police failures, publicly acknowledged corrective action
> must be taken in order to maintain the credibility of
> the department.

Review of the Course Elements

The lessons from the past mistakes discussed above do
not appear to be incorporated in the courses which were designed to familiarize the recruits with riot drill, use of weapons, safety precautions, and other mechanical details.

A few courses were, however, fairly broad-based and
included a variety of socio-psychological and constitutional
discussions. In the course, Crowd Control, California had
laid stress on the constitutional responsibility of the police
in protecting the rights of demonstrators. In Illinois, the
course entitled, Crowd Behavior contained references to the
need for understanding types of crowds and psychological
methods of handling them. A similar emphasis on the

psychological aspects of crowd control was observed in the
course, Group Behavior which is taught in New Jersey. Prevention and defusion of mob hysteria were elements in Crowd
and Riot Control Operation in New York. In Crowds and
Mobs, a course offered in South Carolina, psychological factors
like anonymity, force of numbers, destructiveness of mobs,
and so on, had been highlighted.

Sociological aspects of protests and consequences of
police overreaction had been rarely included in the courses
under review. However, in Michigan, Civil Disorders was
a course taught with a view to enabling the trainees to understand sociological causes of public unrest. In that state,
emphasis was also laid on the application of strictly lawful
methods in riot control. In New York the course on the Nature
and Control of Civil Disorders was taught with a discussion
regarding use of force and danger of overreaction. Civil Disorders, a course taught in North Carolina, focused upon sociological, psychological, and constitutional aspects of riots,
riotous behavior, and riot control. In Texas, too, the impact
of open confrontations and provocative gestures on the part
of the police was discussed in the course entitled Crowd Control.

Recommendations

In the past the police have come to adverse notice in
handling urban disorders primarily on three counts: (a) overreaction to protests, (b) misconceived concept of demonstrations, and (c) racial discrimination. Many of the riots and
disturbances of the 1960s as well as the 1970s were reported
to have been aggravated by the unduly severe police response.
It has been suggested that physical force can be counterpro-
ductive in that it may cause uncalled-for injury and damage.
Misconceived notions about participants in protests can be
interpreted as one of the reasons for harsh police measures.
The police need to be familiar with the research findings that
demonstrators are idealistically alive and sensitive. Racial
discrimination has played a significant role in police response
to minority demonstrators. It is necessary that the police
try to develop a proper understanding of minority culture,
aspirations, and problems. Such understanding is likely to
help them avoid discriminatory treatment of demonstrators.

Most of the mandated courses do not seem to be taking into account the lessons that could be derived from the past police practices. While some states had highlighted the socio-logical and psychological aspects of dealing with crowds, the majority were offering instruction on the mechanical prepara-tions for handling mass agitations. This was not a happy development since the police needed to avoid the past mistakes and learn from the research findings regarding such practices.

The courses on police and protests needed to incorporate the lessons learned from past mistakes as it is believed that the incorporation of these lessons will make the courses con-form better to the views expressed by scholars, researchers, and various national commissions.

Conclusion

In this chapter three mandated police human-relations topics, namely, police community relations, police ethics, and police handling of urban disorders, have been discussed. The main purpose of this discussion is whether there is a variation between the views expressed in the literature regarding these topics and the contents of the courses. It is noted that the variation in this regard is wide.

Generally, the courses are not entirely based on the recommendations found in the relevant literature. It is true that certain elements stressed in the literature are also found in individual courses. However, this is the exception rather than the rule. In view of this, it has been suggested that an attempt should be made to conform the courses to the literature. It is expected such a conformity should make those courses more comprehensive, useful, and contemporary.

References

Allen, V. L. Toward understanding riots: some perspectives. Journal of Social Issues, 26(1), 1-17.

Attorney General's Special Commission on Inquiry on the South-ern University Tragedy of November 16, 1972. (1973). The report. Baton Rouge, LA: Department of Justice.

Banton, M. (1978). Crime prevention in the context of criminal policy. Police Studies, 1(2), 3-9.

_____. (1964). The policeman in the community. New York: Basic Books.

Becker, T. L., & Murray, V. G. (1972). Government lawlessness in America. New York: Oxford University Press.

Bittner, E. (1974). Florence Nightingale in pursuit of Willie Sutton: a theory of police. In The potential for reform of criminal justice. Beverly Hills, CA: Sage Publications.

_____. (1980). The functions of the police in modern society. Cambridge, MA: Oelgeschlager, Gunn, & Hain.

Black, D. J., & Reiss, A. J. (1972). Pattern of behavior in police and citizen transactions. In C. E. Reasons & J. L. Kuykendall (Eds.), Race, crime, and justice. Pacific Palisades, CA: Good Year Publishing.

Boskin, J. (1976). Urban racial violence. Beverly Hills, CA: Glencoe Press.

Boydstun, J. E., & Sherry, M. E. (1975). San Diego community profile: final report. Washington, DC: Police Foundation.

Brogden, M. (1982). The police: autonomy and consent. Padstow, Cornwall (England): T. J. Press.

Brown, L. P. (1978). The Multnomah County, Oregon Experience. In D. Hoel and J. Ziegenhagen (eds.), Police-minority community relations: the control and structuring of police discretion. Wayzata, MN: Spring Hill Center.

_____, & Locke, H. (1980). The police and the community. In R. A. Staufenberger (Ed.), Progress in policing: essays on change. Cambridge, MA: Balinger.

Brown, M. (1981). Working the street. New York: Russell Sage Foundation.

Callahan, D. (1982). Applied ethics and criminal justice. Criminal Justice Ethics, 1(1), 2, 64.

Chevigny, P. (1969). Police power: police abuses in New York City. New York: Vantage Books.

Conant, R. W. (1970). The prospects for revolution. New York: Harper & Row.

Cord, R. L. (1971). Protest, dissent and the Supreme Court. MA: Winthrop.

Cox, S. M., & Fitzgerald, J. D. (1983). Police in community relations. Dubuque, IA: Wm. C. Brown.

Critchley, T. A. (1967). A history of police in England and Wales, 900-1966. London: Constable.

Cumming, E., Cumming, I., & Edell, L. (1965). The police-man as a philosopher, guide and friend. Social Problems, 12(2), 276-286.

Dahlke, O. H. (1952). Race and minority riots. Social Forces, 30(4), 419-425.

Davis, E. M. (1973). Professional police principles. In E. Eldefonso (Ed.), Readings in criminal justice. Beverly Hills, CA: Glencoe Press.

Deane-Drummond, A. (1975). Riot Control. London: Royal United Services Institute.

Decker, S. H. (1981). Citizen attitudes toward the police: a review of past findings and suggestions for future policy. Journal of Police Science and Administration, 9(1), 80-87.

Dynes, R. R., Quarantelli, E. L., & Ross, J. L. (1974). Police perspectives and behavior in a campus disturbance. In H. Hahn (ed.), Police: perspectives, problems, and prospects. New York: Praeger.

Elliston, F. A. (1981). Police use of deadly force: an ethical analysis. In S. Lagoy (Ed.), New perspectives on urban crime. Jonesborough, TN: The Pilgrimage.

Etzioni, A. (1970). Demonstration democracy. New York: Gordon and Breach.

The Fact-Finding Commission Appointed to Investigate the Disturbances at Columbia University in April and May, 1968. (1968). Crisis at Columbia. New York: Vintage.

Feagin, J. R., & Hahn, H. (1973). Ghetto revolts. New York: Macmillan.

Formby, W. A., & Smykla, J. O. (1981). Citizen awareness in crime prevention: do they really get involved? Journal of Police Science and Administration, 9(4), 398-403.

Fortas, A. (1968). Concerning dissent and civil disobedience. New York: New American Library.

Fyfe, J. J. (1982). Observations on police deadly force. In J. J. Fyfe (Ed.), Readings on police use of deadly force. Washington, DC: Police Foundation.

Goldstein, H. (1977). Policing a free society. Cambridge: Balinger.

Heffernan, W. C. (1982). Two approaches to police ethics. Criminal Justice Review, 7(1), 28-35.

Katzenbach, J. (1980). Overwhelmed in Miami. Police Magazine, 3(5), 6-15

_____. (1981). World police leaders hash out human rights issues. Law Enforcement News, November, 7.

Latessa, E. J., & Allen, H. E. (1980). Using citizens to prevent crime: an example of deference and community involvement. Journal of Police Science and Administration, 8(1), 69-74.

Lavrakas, P. J., & Herz, E. J. (1982). Citizen participation in neighborhood crime prevention. Criminology, 20(3-4), 479-498.

Lipset, S. M., & Wolin, S. S. (1965). The Berkeley student revolt. New York: Doubleday.

Manning P. K., & Redlinger, L. J. (1978). Invitational edges of corruption: some consequences of narcotic law enforcement. In P. K. Manning & J. Van Manen (eds.),

Policing: a view from the street. Santa Monica, CA: Good Year.

_____. (1977). Police work: the social organization of policing. Cambridge, MA: MIT Press.

Marshall, T. (1976). The Gestapo in Detroit. In J. Boskin (ed.), Urban racial violence in the 20th century. Beverly Hills, CA: Glencoe Press.

Marx, G. T. (1970). Civil disorders and agents of social control. Journal of Social Sciences, 26(1), 19-57.

McDowell, C. P. (1977). Police in the community. Cincinnati, OH: Anderson.

McNee, Sir D. (1983). McNee's Law. London: Collins.

Miron, J. H., & Wasserman, R. (1980). Prevention and control of urban disorders: issues for the 1980s. Washington, DC: University Research Corporation.

Mottaz, C. (1983). Alienation among police officers. Journal of Police Science and Administration, 11(1), 23-30.

Muir, W. K., Jr. (1977). Police: street corner politicians. Chicago: University of Chicago Press.

_____. (1983). Police and politics. Criminal Justice Ethics, 2(2), 3-9.

Murphy, P. V. (1982). Corruptive influence. In B. L. Garmire (ed.), Local government police management. Washington, DC: International City Management Association.

National Advisory Commission on Civil Disorders. (1970). The report. Washington, DC: Government Printing Office.

National Advisory Commission on Criminal Justice Standards and Goals. (1973). Police. Washington, DC: Government Printing Office.

The National Commission on the Causes and Prevention of
    Violence. (1970). To establish justice, to insure domestic
    tranquility. New York: Bantam.

Niederhoffer, A. (1969). Behind the shield: the police in
    urban society. Garden City, New York: Doubleday.

_____, & Blumberg, A. S. (1976). The police in social and
    historical perspective. In A. Niederhoffer & A. S. Blum-
    berg (eds.), The ambivalent force. Ma: Xerox College
    Publishing.

Osborn, R. B. (1980). Policing in tune with society. Police
    Studies, 3(2), 30-37.

Piven, F. F., & Cloward, R. A. (1977). Poor people's move-
    ments. New York: Vintage.

Platt, A. M. (1971). The politics of riot commissions. New
    York: Collier.

Potts, L. W. (1981). Higher education, ethics and the police.
    Journal of Police Science and Administration, 9(2), 131-134.

The President's Commission on Campus Unrest. (1970). The
    report. Washington, DC: U.S. Government Printing Of-
    fice.

President's Commission on Law Enforcement and Administration
    of Justice. (1967). The challenge of crime in a free
    society. Washington, DC: U.S. Government Printing Of-
    fice.

_____. (1967). Task force report: the police. Washing-
    ton, DC: Government Printing Office.

Punch, M. (1979). Policing the inner city. Hamden, CT:
    Archon Books.

Radelet, L. A. (1980). The police and the community. New
    York: Macmillan.

Rainwater, L. (1970). Open letter on white justice and the
    riots. In J. R. Gusfield (Ed.), Protests, reform and re-
    volt. New York: Wiley.

Reith, C. (1956). A new study of police history. Edinburgh: Oliver and Boyd.

Reppetto, T. A. (1978). The blue parade. New York: Free
Press.

Rubinstein, J. (1973). City Police. New York: Farrar,
Straus, and Giroux.

Sherman, L. W. (1982). Ethics in criminal justice education.
New York: Hastings Center.

_____. (1982). Learning police ethics. Criminal Justice
Ethics, 1(1), 10-20.

_____. (1983). Police in the laboratory of criminal justice.
In K. R. Feinberg (ed.), Violent crime in America. Washington, DC: National Policy Exchange.

Skolnick, J. H. (1969). The politics of protest. New York:
Simon and Schuster.

_____. (1975). Introduciton: Professional police in a free
society. In J. H. Skolnick and T. C. Gray (eds.), Police
in America. Boston: Educational Associates.

_____, & Gray, T. C. (1975). Origins and development
of the police. In J. H. Skolnick & T. C. Gray (eds.),
Police in America. Boston: Educational Associates.

Stead, P. J. (1977). The new police. In D. H. Bayley
(Ed.), Police and society. Beverly Hills, CA: Sage Publications.

Stoddard, E. R. (1983). Blue coat crime. In C. B. Klockars
(ed.), Thinking about police: contemporary readings.
New York: McGraw-Hill.

Task Force on Disorders and Terrorism. (1976). The report.
Washington, DC: U.S. Government Printing Office.

Tobias, J. J. (1972). Nineteenth-century crime in England.
New York: Barnes & Noble.

Toch, H., Grant, D. J., & Salvin, R. T. (1975). Agents

of change: a study in police reform. Cambridge, MA:
Schenkman.

Walker, S. (1983). The police in America. New York:
McGraw Hill.

Westley, W. A. (1970). Violence and the police: a sociological study of law, customs and morality. Cambridge, MA:
MIT Press.

Wilson, J. Q. (1980). Police research and experiment. In
R. A. Staufenberger (ed.), Progress in policing: essays
in change. Cambridge, MA: Balinger.

Wilson, J. Q. (1972). The police in the ghetto. In R. F.
Steadman (ed.), The police and the community. Baltimore:
Johns Hopkins University Press.

Chapter 6

CONCLUSIONS

In order to understand police human relations, we
started with an exploration of the historical roots of American
police. It was noted that policing in this country was envisioned to be permeated with humane values and concerns. The
sources for the historical model of police human relations are
the Bill of Rights, Peel's Metropolitan model, and service
tradition of American police. Embodied in the Bill of Rights
is police responsibility for upholding the higher values of law
which calls for a humane attitude. These values demand
police respect for the spirit of law to ensure preservation of
individual dignity and inviolability. Peel's model upon which
American police were indeed founded underscored the importance of democratic principles and moral values. These are
the roots that give vitality and nourishment to police human
relations. Traditionally the police have been asked to respond
to various service functions because of their unique nature.
Demands for service continue making it necessary for the police to achieve the appropriate attitude and professional skills
for performing their multifarious helping role effectively.

Human relations emerging from the mandated training is
marked by wide diversity in understanding. Numerous courses
are regarded by the POST commissions as appropriate topics
of human relations. Their content, nomenclature, and duration
vary from state to state. They are taught within different
blocks of instruction. Notwithstanding the diversity, certain
topics emerged as the most commonly used courses in human-
relations training. These are ethics, variant behavior, crisis
management, community relations, understanding human behavior, family and domestic disorders, stress, communication
skills, group behavior, and police relationship with special
groups. Since these topics have been nationally extensively
utilized in human-relations training, they can be said to

constitute the contemporary American definition of police human relations. This is the consensus model of human relations that has been discussed in this book in order to facilitate an understanding of police human relations. Evaluated against the historical model, the courses in the consensus model are found to contain little in regard to the police need for appreciation of the higher values of law.

Extreme diversity in police human-relations training indicates that it is not generally clearly understood as to what should be taught in this area. Such diversity, however, seems to be also saying that human relations for the police cannot be really confined to a distinct segment of training. Human relations is needed in every aspect of police work. Police have to be guided by humane concerns in their investigative tasks. They cannot abandon the need of unbiased attitude in their patrol functions. Neither can they afford to be insensitive to humane ideals and values in handling an aggressive and angry mob (Das, 1985, p. 160). A human-relations orientation seems to be needed as an underlying foundation of all aspects of preparation for police work. Radelet (1980, p. 512) says:

> Human relations training for police, as with school teachers and others, is not simply a matter of what is taught in a given curriculum, no matter how imaginative it may be in content or method. Ideally, it is an emphasis, an orientation in all aspects of the given organization or type of activity. A good teacher of astronomy can teach the subject with a human-relations slant. Good teachers of police management courses can teach the subject similarly, espousing management theory that is human-relations oriented.

It is, therefore, felt that human-relations orientation should permeate the entire fabric of police training which includes law, patrol practices, administration and management, investigation, and so on. Probably, a comprehensive approach of that nature will be more useful and effective than specific courses in police human relations per se.

In fact, diverse practices observed in human-relations training indirectly underscore the need that police work must demonstrate a total commitment to human relations. In this connection the following extract from the New York curriculum is relevant:

> Every aspect of police training and education should
> conspicuously and repetitively reflect the necessity
> for an effective relationship with the public [Bureau
> for Municipal Police, New York: Basic Course Syl-
> labus].

In Pennsylvania the efforts are continuing to treat the "training program wholly" (Leiter, April 4, 1983).   In Minnesota
the Board of POST has started depending on "colleges and
vocational-technical schools to present the basic course to
individuals entering law enforcement" (Dysinger, March, 1983).
This is the result of their concern for producing a wholly
integrated police personality to be shaped through a process
of trained sensitivity, intellectual pursuit, and academic discipline.   Hence, the POST commission in Minnesota says that
the "learning objectives" imparted through college education
are expected to add a refreshing, dimension to the recruit's
personality.   They believe that "requiring a minimum of two
years of college training may assist our program for exposing
these students to different attitudes and values than people
who were law enforcement candidates before" (Dysinger, March
8, 1983).   To treat the program "wholly" also has been the
concern of Oregon.   Their policy is to "inform all our instructors of our wishes to have 'human relations' discussions included in all units of instruction.   We feel we have been successful in this effort" (Bettiol, March 2, 1983).

As a matter of fact, more states have started following
an integrated, comprehensive approach to police training including the human-relations aspect of it.   A year ago New
Jersey taught the following topics as human-relations courses:

Community Relations	6 hrs.
Ethics	4 hrs.
Group Behavior	2 hrs.
Mentally and Physically Handicapped	4 hrs.
Personal Communications	3 hrs.
Youth Relations	6 hrs.

Now the state has taken an integrated approach by specifying
performance objectives in different "functional areas."   In
this state the areas within which human-relations concerns
are taught cover Professional Development, Police Community
Relations, Law, Communications, Emergency Medical Care,
Patrol Concepts, and Traffic Enforcement.   According to the

New Jersey Police Training Commission (Schaeffer, Personal Communication, February 27, 1985), they are "implementing a performance objective system of training," through an "open-ended" program without mandating specific hours. Maryland, too, has changed to a holistic approach by including human relations within major blocks of instruction. In response to our query regarding how much time was spent in human relations, Police and Correctional Training Commission (Schuyler, Personal Communication, February 8, 1985) said:

> It, therefore, is impossible to answer you query in your terms of measurement. The certified entrance-level academies (14 active) have the latitude to design their own program devoting the time they deem necessary to accomplish the minimum performance objectives.

It was also mentioned that all academies in the state exceeded the minimum of 400 hours mandated by the commission, some by a considerable margin. Virginia has recently adopted a curriculum consisting of performance objectives which each trainee must successfully complete. This has been done without specifying the minimum time requirement for the achievement of those objectives. Included in the objectives are human-relations concerns.

A question that may be considered is whether a holistic approach can be used to train rookies in the consensus model, and acquaint them also with the dimensions of the historical model. As noted elsewhere, the difference between the two models is that in the consensus model the courses highlighting higher values of law are not found. The courses dealing primarily with ethical values, democratic principles, as well as attitudes and skills for service are incorporated in that model. It should be borne in mind that the acquisition of a proper orientation toward law and internalization of ethical and democratic values are concerned primarily with the change in the trainee's attitudes. But courses in regard to dealing with variant behavior, handling domestic disputes, crisis management, and so on, also demand practical skills in addition to an attitude of willing service. A holistic approach seems to be more valuable for change of attitudes. Human orientation adopted in teaching of law, investigation, patrol procedures, and so on, may be useful in attitudinally orienting the trainee to imbibe the proper spirit of law as the guiding principle in all police work. This approach is advocated by Siegel et al. (1970, p. 6):

> We are not interested in giving police officers human
> relations per se, but are interested in modifying their
> behavior from professional human-relations point of view.
> We are interested in training police officers in the "hu-
> man" relations aspect of their work.

According to Coffee et al. (1982, p. 151), such an approach
to human-relations training will be useful in order to enable
the trainee to avoid brutality, develop healthy attitudes, and
ensure enforcement of law with understanding and sensitivity.

It may be more pragmatic to teach the skills-oriented
courses within a separate block of instruction. However, such
skills, too (Toch, 1973, p. 92), need to be strengthened with
sensitivity training and therapeutic appreciation. Even in
the area of skills, the police trainee has to be made sensitive
to values. As Toch suggests, a proper response to service
tasks calls for acquiring familiarity with contemporary social
issues like urbanization, poverty, unemployment, and discrimination. He adds:

> Police candidates can thus come to view themselves
> as playing a crucial role in producing the type of
> social order in which crime and other symptoms of
> interpersonal conflicts are reduced. Such a view can
> be fully justified. Unlike many of us, law enforcement
> officers are not encumbered with archaic quasi-medical
> or quasi-educational model of social change. The
> police may thus be in a unique position to lead the
> way toward the redefinition of professional roles which
> the pressures of our day demand.

Compartmentalization of human-relations training may
give trainees a wrong notion of police work and, hence, from
that point of view, too, a holistic approach has much to recommend. In this connection it is interesting to note the following remark of Washington State Criminal Justice Training
Commission:

> A program's responsiveness to reality, and its value
> to the trainees who must subsequently work with
> realities, depend upon its integration of subjects, and
> to the extent possible, presentation of information
> along a continuum of simple to complex, theoretical
> to the practical, and response to solution. An example

is "use of force." Although "use of force" is set
forth as a separate four-hour block of instruction with
specific learning goals and student performance objectives, the subject additionally is addressed in criminal law, criminal procedures, patrol procedures, crisis
intervention, "shoot-don't-shoot" simulation, and certain mock scenes involving field interviews, building
searches, traffic stops, felony stops, and domestic
disturbances.

In the process of a holistic approach, "an emphasis," and "an
orientation" (Radelet, 1980, p. 512) are most important. Without the emphasis a course which can be taught from the angle
of human relations may be presented as a purely technical
matter. This observation can be illustrated by an examination
of the descriptive materials published in regard to a course,
namely, Use of Force, in a few states.

In New Jersey this course is taught within the legal
block of instruction. A glance at the goal and performance
objectives of the course is enough to convince one that there
seems to be no human-relations orientation. As the "unit
goal," it is stated that a police officer is "justified under
N.J.S.A. 2C in using force, including deadly force." But the
officer is warned against "the consequences that might result
from the use of unlawful force." It is stated as performance
objectives that the trainee should be able to define various
terms like "force," "deadly force," "unlawful force," and so
on. Performance objectives also included knowledge of the
"agency's policy concerning the use of warning shots," the
crimes for which a police officer might use deadly force, and
some such mechanical details.

In Virginia, Use of Force is taught within a block of instruction called Protection of Life which looks capable of being
treated with human-relations orientation. An examination of
the performance objectives of the course, however, does not
show any such concern. In this course the learning goal is
that "the officer shall know the laws pertaining to the use of
weapons and deadly force by law enforcement officers." Included among the performance objectives are definitions of the
elements of justifiable use of deadly force, "the legal relationship between fear and the use of deadly force," and so on.
No humane concerns with use of deadly force are observed
in the treatment of the subject.

However, the course, Use of Force, taught in Washington in an independent block of instruction, seems to have an unmistakable human relation orientation. As a learning goal the trainee is asked to learn to "identify the use of force and when it may be used by a police officer." Among the performance objectives, there is a reference to the need for a police officer to "become familiar with other factors which affect use of force." Considerable emphasis is placed on personal changes which may take place in "an officer who uses fatal force." (A detailed description of these courses is in Appendix C.)

In the field of human-relations training, it is necessary that practices in each state are standardized so that they can learn from each other. In founding human-relations training on the historical model, NASDLET can play a useful role. It should be possible for NASDLET to seek the views of the states in each of the major problems discussed in this book, and through such discussion, as well as exchange of ideas, police training in this country can benefit a great deal. In the areas other than human relations, training practices seem to be more standardized. Investigation or patrol practices are considerably more uniform throughout the country. But, as it has been seen, extreme diversity is the hallmark of human-relations training. It is, therefore, more important for NASDLET to play a more synthesizing role in regard to this segment of police training. Such a role will result in better understanding of police human relations in this country.

References

Bureau for Municipal Police. (1985) Basic course syllabus. New York.

Coffey, A., Eldefonso, E., & Walter, H. (1982). Human Relations: law enforcement in a changing community. Englewood Cliffs, NJ: Prentice-Hall.

Das, D. K. (1985). A review of progress toward state-mandated human relations training. Police Journal, 58(2), 147-162.

Radelet, L. A. (1980). The police and the community. New York: Macmillan.

Siegel, A. I., Federman, P. J., & Schultz, D. G. (1973). Professional police-human relations. Springfield, IL: Charles C. Thomas.

Toch, H. H. (1973). Psychological consequences of the police role. In Edward Eldefonso (ed.), Readings in criminal justice. Beverly Hills, CA: Glencoe Press.

Appendix A:

IMPORTANT COURSE DETAILS

State	Total Mandated Hours	Human Relations Hours	Subjects	Hours Per Subjects	Block of Instruction	Remarks
Alabama	240	15	History of Law Enforcement and Law Enforcement as a Profession	1	Introduction to Law Enforcement	
			Handling the Emotionally Disturbed	6	General Topics	
			Public Relations	1	Community/Public Relations	
			News Media/Law Enforcement	1	"	
			Community Relations	4	"	
			Extremist Groups & Targets	2	"	
Alaska	270	15	Community Service Concept	1	Role of Police	
			Community Attitudes and Influences	1	Role of Police/ Community Relations	
			Citizen Evaluation	5	Interview & Interrogation, Officer Violator Contact, Etc.	
			Police Ethics and Standards of Conduct	1	Ethics & Code of Conduct	
			Police Stress	7	Stress	
Arizona	400	Variable	Ethics and Professionalism	Variable	Introduction to Law Enforcement	According to Sergeant William F. Taylor, Research Analyst (January, 1985), the State requires that each topic mandated be taught
			Domestic Disputes and Crisis Intervention	"	Patrol Procedures	
			Mental Illness	"	"	

State	Total	No.	Topic	Hours	Category
Arizona (cont.)			Crowd and Riot Control	"	"
			Public Relations for Peace Officers	"	Community & Police Relations
			Social Psychology for Peace Officers	"	"
			Human Communications	"	"
			Crime Prevention Theory and Practice	"	"
Arkansas	280	25	Police Ethics and Image	2	First Week
			Occupational Stress	3	"
			Crisis Intervention and Conflict Management	7	
			Human Relations	2	Fifth Week
			Community Relations	2	"
			Interpersonal Violence	7	"
California	520	31	Ethics (also Unethical Conduct)	2	Professional Orientation
			Community Service Concept	2	Police Community Relations
			Community Attitudes and Influences	5	"
			Citizen Evaluation	2	"
			Crime Prevention	3	"
			Stress Factors	5	"
			Interpersonal Communications	3	Communications
			Family Disputes	4	Patrol Procedures
			Agency Referral	1	"
			Crowd Control	4	"

Arizona (cont.)

in a given block of instruction required to have a minimum number of hours of instruction. He adds that this procedure provides suitable flexibility for the various basic academies throughout the state to address the needs of their specific client agencies.

California

In his letter, Dr. James Norborg, Ph.D., Test Validation and Developmental Specialists (January, 1985), mentioned that "our academies have considerable autonomy in presenting the basic peace officer training course. For example, the time allocated to a particular topic varies considerably from one academy to next.... The values I entered are means for all academies."

State	Total Mandated Hours	Human Relations Hours	Subjects	Hours Per Subjects	Block of Instruction	Remarks
Colorado	335	36	Law Enforcement Ethics	4	Administration of Justice	
			Police-Community Relations	4	Human Relations	
			Crime Prevention	4	"	A course is taught on Crime Prevention but it is purely technical in concept
			Stress Management	6	"	
			Conflict Management	8	"	
			Handling Family Disputes	4	Patrol Procedures	
			Crowd Control	4	"	
			Handling Mentally Ill	2	"	
Connecticut	480	36	Human Behavior (incl. spouse train.)	5	Community Relations	
			Police Ethics and Professionalism	2	"	
			Police and the Public	3	"	
			Police and Youth	5	"	
			Supervisor/Subordinate Relationships	2	"	
			Crisis Intervention	6	Patrol Procedures & Traffic Services	
			Crowd Control/Civil Disorders	3	"	
			Domestic (Including Spouse) Violence	3	"	
			Recognition & Handling Abnormal Behavior	2	"	
			Special Communications - Deaf & Hearing Impaired	3	"	
			Mental Retardation	2	"	
Delaware	368	35	Race Relations: An Extension of Police-Comm. Relations	4	Community Relations	

State			Course	Hours	Category
Delaware (cont.)			Community Relations - Project	1	"
			Police Officer and the Female Citizen	3	"
			Crime Prevention	7	"
			Crisis Intervention	6	Crisis Intervention
			Handling Abnormal People	4	Handling Abnormal People
			Police Discipline and Courtesy	2	Police Discipline & Courtesy
			Riot Control	8	Civil Disorder & Riot Control
Florida	320	32	Human Behavior	12	Human Skills
			Officer Stress	4	"
			Human Problems and Services	6	"
			Juvenile Delinquency and Dependency	2	"
			Civil Disorders	2	Proficiency Skills
			Ethics and Professionalization	2	Introduction to Criminal Justice System
			Communication	4	Patrol Procedures
Georgia	240	20	Police Ethics and Professionalism	2	Introduction to Law Enforcement
			Interpersonal Communications	4	Community Relations
			Police and the Public	2	"
			Mental Retardation	4	"
			Police Stress	2	"
			Crisis Intervention	6	Police Procedures
Hawaii	954	60	Coping with Stress	6	Functional Police Skills
			Professional Ethics Development	6	"

Course details in Hawaii are left to the discretion of individual instructors.

State	Total Mandated Hours	Human Relations Hours	Subjects	Hours Per Subjects	Block of Instruction	Remarks
Hawaii (cont.)			Civil Disturbance Exercise (Field Training)	16	"	
			Telephone Courtesy	2	Communications	
			Visual Communications (Sign & Body Language)	1	"	
			Deaf Awareness	1	"	
			Police-Public Interrelations	1	"	
			Tourist and Police Relations	1	"	
			Emotional Crisis Intervention	26	"	
Idaho	347	24	Police Courtesy and Ethics	2	Police Human Relations	
			Stress Awareness	4	"	
			Juvenile Procedures	7	"	
			Interpersonal Communications	6	"	
			Death Notification	1	"	
			Domestic Disputes	2	Patrol Procedures	
			Crime Prevention	2	"	
Illinois	400	64	Battered Women	4	The Police Function & Human Behavior	
			Child Abuse	2	"	
			Communication in the Police Environment	20	"	
			Crisis Intervention/Disturbance Calls	6	"	
			Crowd Behavior	4	"	
			Dealing with Variant Behavior	4	"	
			Modern Police Role & Organization Structure	4	The Police Function & Human Behavior	

State			Hours	Topic	Category
Illinois (cont.)			2	Patrol Decisions in Juvenile Matters	"
			4	Perception of Human Behavior	"
			6	Police Citizen Relations	"
			4	Police Morality	"
			4	Stress Behavior	"
Indiana	480	22	2	Police-Minority Relations	Human Relations
			2	Handling Abnormal Personalities	"
			3	Conflict Management	"
			4	Police Stress	"
			2	Orientation to the Deaf	"
			1	Introduction to Human Behavior	"
			1	Death Notification	"
			2	Suicide Management	"
			1	Alternatives to Incarceration	"
			1	Police-Victim/Witness Relations	"
			2	Personal Communications	Criminal Investigation/ Forensic Sciences
Iowa	400	33	1	Ethics and Professionalism	Professional Orientation
			6	Community Services	Community Services
			2	Law Enforcement and Minority Groups	Human Relations & Communication
			1	Communication Skills	"
			4	Crisis Intervention	"
			4	Mentally Impaired	"
				News Media	"
			1	Death Notification	"
			14	Psychology for Law Enforcement, Self Understanding and Handling Stress	"

State	Total Mandated Hours	Human Relations Hours	Subjects	Hours Per Subjects	Block of Instruction	Remarks
Kansas	320	42	Police-Community Relations	5	Human Relations	
			Police Professionalism	3	"	
			Crime Prevention	6	"	
			Internalization/Externalization of Stress	3	"	
			Interpersonal Communications - General	7	"	
			Interpersonal Communications - Family	16	"	
Kentucky	400	24.5	Police Image	1	Introduction to Law Enforcement	
			Police Ethics	3	"	
			Police and Community Relations	1	The Police & Community Service	
			Police, Community, & Minority Relations	1	"	
			Police and Press Relations	1	"	
			Psychological Stress of Police	2	"	
			Self-Perception	1	Self-Perception	
			Handling the Mentally Ill	2	The Police Patrol Function	
			Agency Referral	1	"	
			Crowd Control	2	"	
			Family Disputes	4	"	
			Patrol Call: Dealing with Intoxicated Persons	1	"	
			Crime Prevention	4	"	

State	Hours	Topic	Hours/Topic	Special Activities
Louisiana	240	Variable		
		Crisis Intervention	1-3	Special Activities
		Handling Juveniles	"	"
		Handling the Mentally Disturbed	"	"
		Police Ethics	"	Police Community Relations
		Situational and Impartial Enforcement of the Law	1-3	Police Community Relations
		The Police Role	"	"
		Minority Relations	"	"
		Building Respect for the Police	"	"
		Crime Prevention	"	"
Maine	504	57		
		Interpersonal Communication	4	Human Behavior/Interpersonal Skills
		Stress Management	3	"
		Dealing with Variant Behavior	4	"
		Perception of Human Behavior	3	"
		Police Ethics and Moral Issues	7	Police Role & Professional Development
		Police Citizen Relations (Minority Relations)	2	"
		Police and the Public	4	"
		News Media Relations	2	"
		Crisis Conflict Management	16	Police Patrol Procedures
		Juvenile Behavior and Control	3	"
		Child Abuse	3	Patrol Investigation Functions
		Spouse Abuse	3	"
		Crowd Control and Civil Disorder	3	Practical Police Skills

According to Mr. Ben Garris (March 1, 1985), Acting Director, Louisiana Commission on Law Enforcement, a set number of hours is not mandated. Normally 1-3 hours are devoted to each topic.

State	Total Mandated Hours	Human Relations Hours	Subjects	Hours Per Subjects	Block of Instruction	Remarks
Maryland	400		Ethics	Variable	Administration	According to John A. Schuyler, Exec. Director, Dept. of Public Safety and Correctional Serv., (Feb. 8, 1985), the state mandates performance objectives within blocks of instruction, and the certified entrance-level academies (14 active) have the latitude to design their own program devoting the time they deem necessary to accomplish the minimum performance objectives. He also adds that all academies currently exceed the minimum number of 400 hours mandated by the Commission, some by a considerable margin.
			Media Relations	"	"	
			Family Disputes	"	"	
			Handling Victims	"	"	
			Conflict Management	"	"	
			Crime Prevention	"	"	
			Communication Skills	"	"	
			Handling Mentally Disturbed Persons	"	"	
Massachusetts	480	45	Police Role in Modern Society	2	Patrolling	
			Environment of Policing	3	"	
			Interpersonal Relations	7	Providing Service & Rendering Assistance	
			Conflict Resolution	10	"	
			Crisis Intervention	10	"	

State					
Massachusetts (cont.)			Oral Communication	5	Documenting & Recording
			Police Stress	8	Stress
Michigan	440	13	Interpersonal Relations	4	Interpersonal Relations/ Conflict Mediation
			Family Disputes Mediation	4	"
			Handling Abnormal Persons	3	Patrol Procedures
			Dealing with Families of Juveniles	2	"
Minnesota		Not Specified	Police Ethics		Human Behavior
			Career Influences		"
			Stress and Crisis Intervention		"
			Conflict-Crisis Intervention		"
			Emotional Stability		"
			Dealing with People		Law Enforcement Operations and Procedure
			Crime Prevention		"
			Community Relations		

According to Dr. Dake W. Dysinger, Ph.D., Evaluator (March 15, 1985), Minnesota Board of Peace Officers Standards and Training, the state does not use an academy training for the basic course, but delivers this training through certified colleges and vocational schools in the state. The content of the training is specified through learning objectives rather than "hours of training." Therefore, at some schools there is a three-credit-hour course in crisis intervention, while at another school, this segment of the learning objectives is only a part of a course.

State	Total Mandated Hours	Human Relations Hours	Subjects	Hours Per Subjects	Block of Instruction	Remarks
Mississippi	320	42	Police Ethics	1	Police Knowledges	
			Human Relations	8	"	
			Police Image	1	"	
			Crime Prevention	2	"	
			Officer Survival and Crisis Intervention	30	Police Skills	
Missouri	120	7	Human Relations	1	Community Relations	
			Police and Minority Groups	1	"	
			Public Relations	1	"	
			Police Ethics and Professionalization	1	Introduction to Law Enforcement	
			Domestic Complaints	3	Patrol Procedures	
Montana	350	34	Abnormal Behavior	6	Abnormal Behavior	There is no grouping of the curriculum into basic divisions. Every subject is treated as a block of instruction. According to Ted Huber (December 4, 1985), Criminal Justice Programs Manager, "the segments are presented according to the availability of the instructor."
			Crisis Intervention	4	Crisis Intervention	
			Effective Communication	8	Effective Communication	
			Officer Perception	2	Officer Perception	
			Police Ethics	2	Police Ethics	
			Police Stress	8	Police Stress	
			Crime Prevention	4	Crime Prevention	
Nebraska	341	36	Understanding Human Behavior	24	Understanding Human Behavior	

State			Topic		Course Area
Nevada	240	16	Ethics and Professionalism	4	Police Ethics
			Mental Illness	4	Handling the Mentally Ill
			Domestic Violence	4	Domestic Violence
			Crisis Intervention	4	Crisis Intervention
New Hampshire	618	20	Police Ethics and Unethical Behavior	4	Intro. to Criminal Justice System
			Police-Community Relations	4	Community Relations
			Mental Illness and Retardation	2	"
			Domestic Complaints	4	Criminal Investigation
			Stress	6	Police Officer Stress
New Jersey	Variable	Variable	Morals and Ethics	Variable	Professional Development
			Career Influences	"	"
			Identification of Techniques Dealing with Stress	"	"
			Police Responsibility to Provide Community Service	"	Police Community Relations
			Community Relations-Crime Prevention	"	"
			Community Relations-Referral	"	"
			Community Relations-Minority Subcultures	"	"
			Community Relations-Youth	"	"
			Community Relations-Crisis Intervention	"	"
			Handling Individuals with Special Needs	"	"
			Awareness of Emotional Reactions	"	"

According to Geri Schaeffer, Deputy Executive Secretary, New Jersey Police Training Commission, (June 26, 1985), their training is open-ended. No hours are mandated by them and a trainee must pass the program within 18 months of appointment in the time the school allows for the training. It has been found that academies generally require more than 700 hours to cover the mandated performance objectives.

State	Total Mandated Hours	Human Relations Hours	Subjects	Hours Per Subjects	Block of Instruction	Remarks
New Jersey (cont.)			Use of Force	"	Law	
			Telephone Communication	"	Communications	
			Oral Communications	"	"	
			Alcoholism as a Disease	"	Emergency Medical Care	
			Dealing with Intoxicated Persons	"	"	
			Observation and Perception	"	Patrol Concepts	
			Handling Disturbances, Disputes, Domestic Violence and Child Abuse Complaints		"	
			Handling Sick, Injured, and Deceased Persons	"	"	
			Riot and Crowd Control	"	"	
			News Media Relations	"	"	
New Mexico	418	34	Ethics (also Unethical Behavior)	3	Professional Orientation	
			Community Service Concept	3	Police-Community Relations	
			Community Attitudes and Influences	1	"	
			Citizen Evaluation	1	"	
			Crime Prevention	2	"	
			Stress Factors	1	"	
			Crime and Elderly	2	"	
			Crisis Intervention/Interpersonal Relations	19	Patrol Procedures	
			Mental Illness	2	"	

State			Topic	Hours	Category
New York	400	65.5	Ethical Awareness	14	Community Relations
			Police and Minority Groups	4	"
			The Police and the Public	3	"
			News Media Relationship	2	"
			Domestic Violence	14.5	Police Procedures/Patrol Functions
			The Nature and Control of Civil Disorder	2	"
			Intoxication	2	Police Functions
			Mental Illness	3	"
			Social Agency Services	1	The Administration of Justice
North Carolina	369	44	Civil Disorders	12	Civil Disorders
			Crisis Management	10	Crisis Management
			Deviant Behavior	10	Deviant Behavior
			Dealing with Victim and the Public	8	Dealing with Victim and the Public
			Observations and Perceptions		Patrol Techniques
			High Incidents Calls for Service		"
			Crime Prevention Techniques	4	Crime Prevention Techniques
North Dakota	310	34	Law Enforcement Ethics, & Moral Issues	2	Sociological Development
			Human Relations and Social Values	4	"
			Minority Relations	2	"
			Dealing with Variant Behavior	2	Patrol Procedures
			Crisis Intervention	8	"

State	Total Mandated Hours	Human Relations Hours	Subjects	Hours Per Subjects	Block of Instruction	Remarks
Ohio	292	16	Human Relations	16	Human Relations	According to Wilfred Goodwin, Executive Director, Ohio Peace Officer Training Council (December 30, 1985), they have "written a new curriculum and it was test taught at our central academy in the summer months at approximately 551 hours ... Sometime in 1987 it should be put in place across the state."
Oklahoma	300	29	Police Community Relations	2	Police-Community Relations	
			Crime Prevention	2	"	
			Police Ethics	2	"	
			Unethical Behavior	2	"	
			Psychology of Human Relations	4	"	
			Minority Relations	3	"	
			Interpersonal Communications	4	Communications	
			Crisis Intervention	8	"	
			Mentally Ill	2	Patrol	
Oregon	330	24	Domestic Conflict Management	4	Human Behavior	
			Law Enforcement Profession	4	"	
			Contemporary Society Awareness	4	"	
			Police Discretion	4	"	
			Sexual Abuse and Child Neglect	8	"	

State			Topic	Hours	Category
Pennsylvania	480	56	Police-Community Relations, Police-Public Relations, and Police Ethics	16	Human Values and Problems
			Human Relations: Cultural Awareness	8	"
			Mental Health Procedures Act - Crisis Intervention	20	"
			Service Calls	12	"
Rhode Island	480	58.5	Police Community Relations	40	Social Services
			Domestic Violence	2	"
			Crime Prevention	2	"
			Police and the Media	1.5	"
			Police Ethics	10	"
			Police Stress Management	3	"
South Carolina	329	22	Handling the Deaf	1	Police Problems
			Police-Community Relations	5	Police Community Relations
			Crowds and Mobs	2	Patrol Procedures
			Crisis Intervention	6	Crisis Intervention
			Child Abuse	4	Not Available
			Domestic Violence	4	"
South Dakota	240	21	Police-Community Relations	3	Police Community Relations
			Human Behavior	10	Human Behavior
			Family Stress	4	Family Stress
			Crime Prevention	4	Crime Prevention
Tennessee	240	10	Police Ethics	2	Patrol
			Domestic Disturbance	2	"
			Recognizing and Handling Mentally Disturbed People	4	Investigative Topics

State	Total Mandated Hours	Human Relations Hours	Subjects	Hours Per Subjects	Block of Instruction	Remarks
Tennessee (cont.)			Stress Management	2	General Police	
Texas	400	54	Crime Prevention and Public Service	32	Patrol	
			The Peace Officer's Role in Society			
			Crowd Control	8	Investigative Patrol	
			Recognizing and Handling Abnormal Persons	8	Miscellaneous	
				6	Miscellaneous/Investigative Patrol	
Utah	400	38	Police Ethics and Professionalism	2	Human Relations	
			Police-Community Relations	4	"	
			Personality Theory	4	"	
			Abnormal Behavior	4	"	
			Crisis Intervention	12	"	
			Officer-Violator Relationship	4	"	
			Decision Making (Police Discretion)	2	"	
			Interpersonal Communications	6	"	
Vermont	525	40	Dealing with Death	2	Communication	
			Handling the Emotionally Disturbed	2	"	
			Interpersonal Communication	12	"	
			Police Discretion	3	"	
			Police and the Press	2	"	
			Public Relations	3	"	

State		Courses	Hours	Core / Curriculum	Hours
Vermont (cont.)		Domestic Crisis Intervention		Police Patrol Procedures	8
		Crowd Management		Defensive Tactics	4
		Spouse Abuse		Investigative Procedures	2
		Stress Management		Others	2
Virginia	315	Law Enforcement as a Profession		Core Curriculum	Flexible
		Communication		Communication	"
		Persuasion Techniques		Interview and Interrogation Techniques	"
		Perception Techniques		Patrol Techniques	"
		Family Disputes		"	"
		Mentally Ill		"	"
		Agency Referral		"	"
		Crime Prevention		Crime Prevention	"
Washington	440	Ethics	86.5	Criminal Investigation	4
		Crime Prevention		"	8
		Crisis Intervention		Crisis Intervention	40
		Miscellaneous Service Calls		Patrol Procedures	6.5
		Communications Skills		Communication Skills	24
		Use of Force		Use of Force	4
West Virginia	495	Police Ethics	26	Introduction to Law Enforcement	2
		Police Minority Relations		"	2
		Communication Skills		"	2

According to Mr. L. T. Eckenrode, Executive Director, Department of Criminal Justice Services (March, 1985), his department mandates a total number of hours required as a minimum for completion of entry level law enforcement training. The time required for each subject is dependent upon classroom time, practice time, test time, and the number of students attending the session.

These courses have been included in human relations on the basis of the course titles only. Neither

State	Total Mandated Hours	Human Relations Hours	Subjects	Hours Per Subjects	Block of Instruction	Remarks
West Virginia (cont.)			Crisis Intervention	8	"	outlines nor any other descriptive material were received.
			Public Speaking	10	"	
			Handling Abnormal Persons	2	Patrol Operations & Procedures	
Wisconsin	240	19	Human Relations	4	Fundamentals of Human Behavior	
			Racial and Ethical Differences	2	"	
			Effective Verbal Communications	4	"	
			How to Recognize and Handle Emot. Disturbed People	2	"	
			Crisis Intervention Techniques	3	"	
			Police and Juveniles	2	Juvenile Procedures	
			Professional Ethics and Police Image	2	Introduction to Police Work	
Wyoming	320	40	Professional Orientation	24	Professional Orientation	
			Professional Skills	16	Professional Skills	

Appendix B:

ELEMENTS OF HUMAN RELATIONS COURSES

ALABAMA

- History of Law Enforcement and Law Enforcement as a Profession

  (1) Presentation of a historical account of law enforcement.
  (2) Discussion of law enforcement as a profession.
  (3) Consideration of advantages, disadvantages, and implications of policing as a profession.

- Handling the Emotionally Disturbed

  (1) Recognition of characteristics of the emotionally disturbed.
  (2) Instruction on methods of handling such individuals.
  (3) Knowledge of agencies for referrals and assistance.

- Public Relations

  (1) Explanation of the need for effective public relations in all phases of law enforcement.
  (2) Appreciation of the impact of individual officers' official and unofficial activities on public relations.

- News Media/Law Enforcement

  (1) Acknowledgment of the importance of good relations with the media.
  (2) Familiarization with methods of preparing, editing, and sub-mitting news releases.

- Community Relations

  (1) Discussion of the functions of a viable community relations program.
  (2) Consideration of good relations with the public for bridging the gap between the community and the police.

- Extremist Groups and Targets

  (1) Knowledge of extremist groups in the U.S., specifically in Alabama.
  (2) Study of leaders, known followers, goals, objectives, and methods of operation of such groups.

ALASKA[1]

- Police Ethics and Standards of Conduct

  (1) Knowledge of the rules of official conduct.
  (2) Study of relevant departmental rules for practical application.
  (3) Awareness of unbecoming conduct.
  (4) Understanding of the need for compliance with duty.
  (5) Learning to be cautious concerning use of drug, alcohol, and tobacco.
  (6) Knowledge of the ways to avoid gifts, gratuities, bribes, and rewards.
  (7) Discussion of the ways to avoid advertisement, endorsement, public statements, and so on.

- Police Stress

  (1) Definition of physical and mental stress.
  (2) Discussion of specific sources of police stress, conflict of values, racial situations, job ambiguity, and job overload.
  (3) Study of reaction to stress according to physical and psychological characteristics of individuals.
  (4) Knowledge of the ways to deal with stress.

ARIZONA

- Ethics and Professionalism

  (1) Appreciation of the highest moral and ethical standards of performance by the police.
  (2) Discussion of peace officers' rights and responsibilities.

- Domestic Disputes and Crisis Intervention

  (1) Description of techniques and procedures used in handling husband-wife and parent-child disputes.
  (2) Explanation of the difference between domestic disputes and civil problems.
  (3) Knowledge of crisis intervention including suicide prevention, handling family crises, and delivery of death notifications.

- Mental Illness

  (1) Discussion of the common types of mental illnesses and their symptoms.
  (2) Description of the proper techniques for handling the mentally disturbed.
  (3) Explanation of legal procedures used in emergency as well as routine cases.

- Crowd and Riot Control

  (1) Study of unruly crowds, riots as well as prevention and

control techniques.

(2) Discussion of Arizona law in regard to handling public disorder.

(3) Demonstration of lethal and nonlethal weapons used in riot control.

- Public Relations for Peace Officers

  (1) Enumeration of the elements conducive to building and maintaining the right climate for citizen-police relations.

  (2) Discussion of police responsibilities in regard to relationship with the press.

- Social Psychology for Peace Officers

  (1) Understanding of the impact of sociological and psychological factors in human behavior.

  (2) Discussion of cultural backgrounds of various ethnic groups.

  (3) Identification of the patterns emerging in the course of interaction between society and the individual.

- Human Communications

  (1) Analysis of interpersonal communication dynamics.

  (2) Discussion of the means of effective communication with minority groups.

  (3) Prescription of the dos and don'ts in interpersonal communications.

- Crime Prevention Theory and Practice

  (1) Discussion of methods, theories, and practices regarding safety procedure applicable to residential and business establishments.

  (2) Study of neighborhood watch programs.

  (3) Consideration of assistance to the elderly through crime prevention programs.

ARKANSAS

- Police Ethics and Image

  (1) Discussion of the Code of Ethics.

  (2) Understanding of the perception about the police on the part of community, fellow citizens, and general public.

- Occupational Stress

  (1) Awareness of the characteristics and effects of the social role of the police.

  (2) Knowledge of various kinds of psychological pressures on officers.

(3) Knowledge of occupational factors influencing behavior, attitude, and response.

- Crisis Intervention and Conflict Management

    (1) Provision of information and practice for effective handling of crisis calls.
    (2) Knowledge of the major types of police crisis calls.

- Human Relations

    (1) Discussion of the problems likely due to policeman's cynical attitude, intolerance, and prejudice.
    (2) Awareness of stereotyping, discourtesy, nonverbal communication, anger, and provocation.
    (3) Understanding of the public view of the police.

- Community Relations

    (1) Knowledge of the factors useful for building up proper climate for citizen-police relations.

CALIFORNIA

- Ethics (Including Unethical Conduct)

    (1) Appreciation of honor and morality as the basis for police conduct.
    (2) Appreciation of ethics as the key to professionalization of the police.
    (3) Recognition of the links between ethics and honest law enforcement.
    (4) Understanding of the social norms for ethically sound values.
    (5) Knowledge of the Code of Ethics.
    (6) Recognition of unethical conduct resulting from (a) dishonesty, (b) brutality, (c) racial prejudice, (d) gratuities, (e) misappropriation of prisoner's property, (f) false or colored testimony, (g) violation of laws, (h) infringement of civil rights, (1) discourteous conduct, (j) deliberate inefficiency, (k) divulging of confidential information, and (1) violation of privileged communications.
    (7) Discussion of the lack of ethics associated with excessive drinking, undesirable sexual activities, gambling, and so on.
    (8) Development of sensitivity toward unethical conduct in fellow officers.
    (9) Understanding of the harmful consequences of carrying tales against fellow officers.

- Community Service COncept

    (1) Understanding of police work as a mission involving five community services, namely (a) order maintenance, (b) crime

prevention, (c) law enforcement, (d) helping service, and (e) public education.

- Community Attitudes and Influences

  (1) Study of community attitude toward the police as a product of individual sentiments, socio-economic conditions, and psychological factors.
  (2) Knowledge of the elements that can influence community attitudes like: (a) school exposure, (b) the media (TV, radio, newspaper), (c) family, (d) peers, and (e) minority status.

- Citizen Evaluation

  (1) Discussion of response time and police methods of handling public requests.
  (2) Impact of police/citizen contacts, crime rate, and other police practices on citizen evaluation of the police.
  (3) Appreciation of society's expectations from the police as problem solvers responsive to community needs.
  (4) Study of the consequences of: (a) police apathy, (b) unethical conduct, (c) brutality, (d) racial bias, and (e) discrimination.

- Crime Prevention

  (1) Understanding and knowledge of the role of crime prevention for the police.
  (2) Ability to encourage citizens' cooperation in police crime prevention programs.
  (3) Familiarity with the techniques of opportunity reduction, crime problems, and crime prevention programs.
  (4) Instruction on how to conduct security surveys of residential and commercial establishments.

- Interpersonal Communications

  (1) Knowledge of interpersonal communication methods and problems.
  (2) Study of physical gestures, facial expressions, and body language.
  (3) Discussion of negative nonverbal communications like offensive and abusive manner, disrespectful attitude, and discourteous body movement.
  (4) Knowledge of negative verbal communications like profanity, derogatory language, ethnically offensive terminology, and occupational jargons.

- Family Disputes

  (1) Knowledge of the dangers inherent in family dispute situations with awareness of safety precaution.
  (2) Definition of family disputes as disputes between spouses,

parent and child, siblings, boyfriends or girlfriends, as well as between relatives.

(3) Discussion of the causes of disputes which may include property, custody of children, alcohol consumption, and so on.

(4) Knowledge of operational techniques such as calming down, mediation, separation, restraining, and referral.

- Agency Referral

  (1) Knowledge of agencies available for help in drug problems, alcoholism, juvenile problems, and so on.

- Crowd Control

  (1) Study of legal and constitutional aspects of crowd control
  (2) Understanding of the need to protect the rights of demonstrators and members of the public.
  (3) Discussion of the ways for the police to gain immediate control of a situation involving crowd control.
  (4) Explanation of chemical agents, arrest procedures, emergency first aid, etc.

COLORADO

- Law Enforcement Ethics

  (1) Discussion of the Law Enforcement Code of Ethics and the Canons of Police Ethics.
  (2) Importance of ethics as a guide to an officer's on-duty and off-duty conduct.
  (3) Cultivation of responsibilities for proper response to unethical behavior in fellow officers.

- Police Community Relations

  (1) Discussion of the effects of police officer's conduct on community attitude.
  (2) Knowledge of characteristics of law enforcement and the consequent problems in community relations.
  (3) Knowledge regarding responsibilities of every officer for promoting positive police community relations.

- Crime Prevention

  (1) Knowledge of the concepts and purpose of crime prevention.

- Stress Management

  (1) Discussion of occupational factors responsible for police stress.
  (2) Explanation of methods useful for reducing stress.
  (3) Knowledge of the effects of stress on a police officer's behavior.

- Conflict Management

  (1) Knowledge of crisis and conflict.
  (2) Explanation of situations causing stress or crisis for citizens.
  (3) Description of the symptoms of a person in crisis.
  (4) Discussion of verbal and nonverbal methods alleviating conflict and crisis.
  (5) Awareness of psychological reactions to victimization.
  (6) Discussion of family dynamics responsible for promoting conflict and crisis.

- Handling Family Disputes

  (1) Learning to mediate in family disputes.
  (2) Recognition of child abuse and neglect situations.

- Crowd Control

  (1) Discussion of crowd control tactics.

- Handling Mentally Ill

  (1) Knowledge of the legal aspects of handling mental illness.
  (2) Learning to handle the mentally ill with consideration and patience.
  (3) Safe and proper methods of handling madness.

CONNECTICUT[2]

- Human Behavior

  (1) Knowledge of interpersonal dynamics affecting behavior.
  (2) Understanding of the process of socialization.
  (3) Awareness of police behavior capable of causing public resentment.
  (4) Discussion of the separate perceptions of the police by different ethnic groups.
  (5) Appreciation of the impact of bias and prejudice on an individual's attitude and behavior.
  (6) Knowledge of community social agencies available for referrals.

- Police Ethics—Moral Development & Professionalism

  (1) Knowledge of the Law Enforcement Code of Ethics and the nature of public trust in the police.
  (2) Importance of maintaining calm attitude in all situations.
  (3) Elaboration of the role of courtesy in everday police conduct.
  (4) Explanation of the association between police professionalism and ethical conduct.
  (5) Knowledge of the relationship between a police officer's everyday actions and the public image of the department.
  (6) Explanation of unethical implications inherent in gratuities, drinking, sex, larceny, nonenforcement, and vindictiveness.
  (7) Insights into public stereotypes of the police.

- Police and the Public

  (1) Discussion of various ways citizens tend to evaluate the police.
  (2) Explanation of the reasons that may lead to withdrawal of public support to the police.
  (3) Study of the effects of age, status, and levels of development in public attitude toward the police.
  (4) Discussion of the methods and programs that can promote better police-public relations.
  (5) Comprehension of the relationship between crime prevention and public relations.

- Police and Youth

  (1) Knowledge of the technical terms like delinquent child, juveniles in need of custody, nonjudicial and protective supervision, neglected child, dependent child, and uncared-for child.

  (2) Understanding of various techniques of establishing rapport with juveniles, correct and incorrect ways of interviewing, and the effects of juvenile contacts with the police.

  (3) Knowledge of social agencies for referral.

- Supervisor/Subordinate Relationships

  (1) Awareness of the need and importance of supervision.
  (2) Knowledge of supervisor's responsibilities toward management and subordinates.
  (3) Discussion of the impact of prejudice, personality conflicts, and favoritism in supervisor/subordinate relationships.

- Crisis Intervention

  (1) Awareness of foreseen and unforeseen crises.
  (2) Recognition of the need for crisis intervention techniques useful for preventive purposes.
  (3) Knowledge of personality types and emotional characteristics responsible for differences in social interactions.
  (4) Understanding of the need for personal safety and flexibility.
  (5) Knowledge of the importance of initial contact, defusion of situation, restoration of calm, investigation of crisis, mediation, referral, arrest, and so on.

- Crowd Control/Civil Disorders

  (1) Knowledge of the provisions of Connecticut State Statutes relating to riots.
  (2) Understanding of the type, nature, and character of demonstrations.
  (3) Knowledge of crowd control with force or show of force.
  (4) Instruction on chemical agents and dispersal formations.
  (5) Discussion regarding agencies which can help in civil disorders.

- Domestic Complaints

  (1) Knowledge of intervention techniques including contact, restoration of calm and fact-finding in domestic complaints.
  (2) Cultivation of professional attitude for avoiding emotional involvement.
  (3) Discussion of short- and long-range uses of crisis intervention
  techniques and referrals to nonpolice agencies.
  (4) Insights into the psychological factors likely to operate in
  domestic complaints.
  (5) Knowledge of the importance of officer's attitude in handling
  domestic complaints.
  (6) Understanding of the common types of domestic complaints
  and the unique risks involved in each type.

- Recognizing and Handling Abnormal Behavior

  (1) Recognition of the signs of a mentally disturbed person.
  (2) Knowledge of the methods of handling persons with mental
  problems.
  (3) Ability to identify clues connected with mental disorders.
  (4) Insights into internal defense techniques and mechanism involved in coping.

- Mental Retardation

  (1) Recognition of a mentally retarded person.
  (2) Learning to handle an encounter with a mentally retarded
  person.
  (3) Appreciation of the distinction between mental retardation
  and mental illness.
  (4) Knowledge of community resources available to law enforcement
  personnel.

DELAWARE

- Community Relations Projects

  (1) Definition of police community relations.
  (2) Appreciation of good relationship between the police and the
  community.

- Mob and Riot Control

  (1) Explanation of the need for police neutrality, objectivity, discipline, and resoluteness in riot situations.
  (2) Discussion of the causes and nature of riots and police problems created by such events.
  (3) Instruction on operational strategy suitable for riots.
  (4) Knowledge of tactical formations and uses of various weapons.

- Crime Prevention

  (1) Understanding of preventive philosophy of the British police.

(2) Comparison of reactive and proactive forms of policing.
(3) Knowledge of various strategies of crime prevention including target hardening, security lighting, and positive interactions between the police and the citizens.

- Police Officer and the Female Citizen

  (1) Understanding of the complex nature of sexual victimization of women and children.
  (2) Discussion of the nature, consequences, and circumstances of various sexual assaults.
  (3) Elaboration of the need for sensitivity, courtesy, and common sense in police handling of sexual victims.

- Race Relations: An Extension of Police Community Relations

  (1) Knowledge of the history of race relations training for police officers.
  (2) Understanding of minority groups, police community relations, prejudice, and minority membership traits.
  (3) Explanation of various sources of prejudice.

- Handling Abnormal People

  (1) Identification of the behavioral factors involved in handling abnormal persons.
  (2) Discussion of the influence of group norms on individual behavior.
  (3) Understanding of unusual behavior with a view to mastering effective ways of dealing with such behavior.
  (4) Knowledge of commitment procedures of abnormal people.

- Police Discipline and Courtesy

  (1) Appreciation of the need for police discipline and courtesy.
  (2) Cultivation of proper behavior, discipline and courtesy.

- Crisis Intervention

  (1) Study of confusion, helplessness, dependency, disorder, and depression associated with crisis.
  (2) Awareness of predictable (divorce) and unpredictable crisis (sudden event).
  (3) Importance of immediate response in crisis.
  (4) Familiarity with safety procedures for officers and others.
  (5) Knowledge of applicable methods like authoritative and calm manner, separation of disputants, sense of humor, mediation and referral.

FLORIDA

- Human Behavior

(1) Understanding of the principles of human behavior including psychological factors affecting behavior.
(2) An overview of human motivation, attitudes, and situations responsible for criminal or antisocial behavior.
(3) Instruction on how to improve interpersonal skills.
(4) Improving the trainee's capacity to recognize and deal effectively with prejudice and bias.

- Officer Stress

(1) Recognition of psychological and physiological stress agents.
(2) Ability to identify emotional, cultural, and job-related stressors.
(3) Learning to use techniques and resources for avoidance of internalization of stress as well as for resolution of personal crisis.

- Human Problems and Services

(1) Awareness of noncriminal and nonarresting situations required to be handled frequently by the police.
(2) Knowledge of social service agencies for referrals.
(3) Understanding of problems and services involving mental illness, mental retardation, and alcoholism.

- Juvenile Delinquency and Dependency

(1) A brief overview of the causes of juvenile delinquency.
(2) Recognition of the symptoms of dysfunctional, disruptive, delinquent and dependent children.
(3) Study of the preventive role an officer may play.

- Civil Disorders

(1) Understanding of the patterns of disorder, levels of violence, extent of damage, characteristics of riot participants, and initial incidents.
(2) Knowledge of psychological influences on individuals involved in mob situations.
(3) Explanation of crowd and mob control techniques.
(4) Understanding of various types of crowds and gatherings.

- Ethics and Professionalization

(1) Discussion of the Law Enforcement Code of Ethics and the Canon of Police Ethics.
(2) Discussion of law enforcement as a professional endeavor.
(3) Understanding of the need for ethical behavior and attitude on the part of law enforcement officials.

- Communication

(1) Knowledge of various communication equipments.
(2) Importance of telephone courtesy.

- Crisis Intervention

  (1) Recognition of stress in criminal and noncriminal situations.
  (2) Knowledge of the techniques for reducing, diverting, and resolving crisis situations.
  (3) Information on agencies available for referrals.
  (4) Learning how to avoid additional stress.

GEORGIA

- Police Ethics and Professionalism

  (1) Recognition of ethical and unethical police behavior.
  (2) Knowledge of the characteristics of a profession.

- Interpersonal Communications

  (1) Knowledge of the psychological and sociological factors affecting human behavior.
  (2) Understanding of the relationship between citizen cooperation and police communication skills.

- Police and the Public

  (1) Importance of police courtesy and positive attitude toward the public and the media.
  (2) Discussion of public access to police files and records.

- Mental Retardation

  (1) Recognition of the characteristics of mental retardation.
  (2) Knowledge of the techniques used in handling mentally retarded offenders and nonoffenders.
  (3) Understanding of the legal obligations to retarded persons in police custody.
  (4) Understanding of the distinction between mental retardation and mental illness.

- Police Stress

  (1) Appreciation of the positive and negative effects of occupational stress.
  (2) Insights into frustrations causing stress in police work.
  (3) Identificaiton of adjustment mechanisms including alcoholism, drug abuse, and suicide.

- Crisis Intervention

  (1) Understanding of the ways for handling crisis situations arising from family fights, landlord/tenant disputes, suicide attempts, criminal victimization, and emotional trauma.
  (2) Knowledge of the disposal methods including arrest, counsel, and referral.

(3) Awareness of the soothing and restorative effects of certain intervention techniques.

(4) Recognition of safety procedures to be followed by intervening officers.

HAWAII[3]

IDAHO

- Police Courtesy and Ethics

  (1) Appreciation of the need for ethical and moral conduct for a professional officer.

  (2) Recognition of the link between an officer's conduct and public attitude toward the police.

  (3) Awareness of ethical dilemmas involved in gratuities, drinking, sex, larceny, nonenforcement, and vindictiveness.

  (4) Identification of the unfavorable public stereotypes of the police.

  (5) Insights into the race relations.

- Stress Awareness

  (1) Explanation of the nature and characteristics of police.

  (2) Identification of stress factors like rotating shifts, anger and frustration on the job, role conflict, disagreements with other components of the criminal justice system, and fear.

  (3) Recognition of physical and psychological manifestations of stress.

  (4) Knowledge of stress-reducing techniques such as exercise, diet, change in activity, and recreation.

- Juvenile Procedures

  (1) Identification of delinquent child and juveniles not in need of custody.

  (2) Knowledge of the differences between effective and ineffective techniques of establishing rapport with juveniles.

  (3) Proper understanding of moral and legal obligations in handling delinquent children.

- Interpersonal Communication

  (1) Importance of interpersonal relations in individual conduct.

  (2) Understanding of the process of socialization to develop insights into the courses of disputes and arguments.

  (3) Appreciation of the reasons for differences in perception about the police by various ethnic groups.

  (4) Insights into the forms of police behavior which are resented by the public.

- Death Notification

    (1) Understanding of general attitude toward death.
    (2) Appreciation of the dynamics of grief.
    (3) Recognition of the special needs of families following death notification.

- Domestic Disputes

    (1) Explanation of domestic complaints with special emphasis on the aspects of personality causing abrasive relationship.
    (2) Importance of officer's attitude while handling domestic complaints.
    (3) Understanding of precautionary measures useful in handling hostile domestic situations.
    (4) Knowledge of the various steps of intervention like initial contact, restoration of calm, fact-finding, and so on.

- Crime Prevention

    (1) Appreciation of the concept of crime prevention.
    (2) Knowledge of the measures which can help prevent crime.
    (3) Need for different crime prevention techniques according to geographical variation.

ILLINOIS

- Battered Women

    (1) Knowledge of the relevant sections of the Illinois Domestic Violence Act, orders of protection, and authorized use of arrest in domestic situations.
    (2) Awareness of police responsibilities including writing reports, arranging transportation, protecting victims, and legal action.

- Child Abuse

    (1) Understanding of neglect, physical abuse, and sexual exploitation of children.
    (2) Discussion of interactions between family and criminal justice system in the process of enquiry.

- Communication in the Police Environment

    (1) Knowledge of basic skills for conducting successful interviews.
    (2) Recognition of gestures and other nonverbal movements which normally precede violent action.
    (3) Identification of the responses associated with assertiveness.
    (4) Discussion of police handling of emotionally upset persons, emergency messages, and inquiries regarding progress of a case.

- Crisis Intervention /Disturbance Calls

  (1) Knowledge of different types of crisis situations.
  (2) Discussion of the techniques used for assessing gravity and appropriate intervention.
  (3) Knowledge of safety procedures used in handling violent or potentially violent situations.
  (4) Familiarization with the processes of mediation, reconciliation, advisement, and other courses of actions including civil remedies, prosecution, arrest, and so on.

- Crowd Behavior

  (1) Knowledge of the types and characteristics of crowds including those engaged in demonstrations and strike activities.
  (2) Study of the psychological and physical methods of handling crowds and the relevant legal provisions.

- Dealing with Variant Behavior

  (1) Working knowledge of psychosis, neurosis, personality disorders, substance abuse, and other psychological disorders.
  (2) Knowledge of the Illinois State Mental Health Code and the legal provisions regarding handling of mentally ill persons.
  (3) Psychological handling of mentally ill individuals and provision of assistance to them.

- Modern Police Role & Organizational Structure

  (1) Discussion of the historical roots of policing, contemporary police functions, organizational policies, political leadership, and sociological factors and their impact on police role.
  (2) Appreciation of the impact of cynicism, role dilemmas, and anxieties in police morale and performance.

- Patrol Decisions in Juvenile Matters

  (1) Knowledge of peer conformity and rebellion against authority as unique juvenile characteristics.
  (2) Development of interaction skills with juveniles.

- Perception of Human Behavior

  (1) Insight and sensitivity to the problem of human behavior.
  (2) Understanding of the role of experience, characteristics of misperception, human needs, and self-others encounters.
  (3) Perception of behavioral clues involving any situation handled by the police.
  (4) Understanding of police behavioral failures in their daily activities.

- Police Citizen Relations

  (1) Discussion of the forms of police behavior creating barriers

between the police and the community.
(2) Awareness of the factors like television and the press that tend to generate stereotypes about the police.
(3) Recognition of racist, crime-fighting, and discriminating "cops."
(4) Understanding of the need for special behavior toward minority groups (ethnic), older persons, and other weaker sections.

• Police Morality

(1) Knowledge of professional standards and principles, canons of police ethics, abuse of authority, corruption, and perjury.
(2) Discussion of the Blue Curtain phenomenon.

• Stress Behavior

(1) Awareness of police stress because of routine encounters with violence, dangers, human suffering, emergency situations, and traumas and conflicts.
(2) Knowledge of behavioral, psychological and physical reactions to stress.
(3) Understanding of psychological and physical techniques of stress management, and other forms of professional assistance.

• Crime Prevention

(1) Discussion of the patrol officer's role in crime prevention.
(2) Encouragement of citizens' participation in crime prevention measures.
(3) Knowledge of crime prevention as it relates to public information, personal safety precautions of citizens, and security precautions against property crime.

INDIANA

• Police Minority Relations

(1) Awareness of traditional suspicion and distrust of the police by minorities.
(2) Recognition of police attitude of mistrust toward people.
(3) Development of insights into police prejudice and misconceptions.

• Handling Abnormal Personalities

(1) Study of the objective criteria applicable to assessment of

personality abnormalities.

(2) Knowledge of cautious and safe methods of handling such personalities.

(3) Understanding of suicide management process including sensitivity to warning signs, depression, disoriented motive, defiant orientation, dependency, etc.

(4) Appreciation of legal issues involved in voluntary and involuntary commitment of mental patients.

- Domestic Complaints

  (1) Knowledge of police responsibilities in domestic disputes like maintaining order, protecting the innocent, and safeguarding property.

  (2) Discussion of various types of domestic complaints made to the police.

  (3) Knowledge of procedures for ensuring safety of officers.

  (4) Comprehension of the importance of calm, impartial and objective behavior.

  (5) Understanding of the need for flexible techniques including referral.

- Conflict Management

  (1) Knowledge of the psychological factors in conflict management.

  (2) Understanding of good listening as an effective tool in conflict management.

  (3) Knowledge of helpful steps like neutrality toward the parties involved, comprehension of the causes of conflict, separation of the parties, allowing the parties to give vent to their feelings in words, and safety procedures for the officer.

- Police Stress

  (1) Knowledge of occupational stresses in policing.

  (2) Explanation of physical, mental, and social consequences of police stress in the officer's on-duty and off-duty life.

  (3) Discussion of coping and reduction techniques.

- Orientation to the Deaf

  (1) Understanding of the problems of the deaf.

  (2) Knowledge of patient means of communicating with the deaf.

  (3) Discussion of what to do and what not to do while confronting a deaf person.

  (4) Knowledge of agencies which can help in understanding the deaf.

- Introduction to Human Behavior

  (1) Understanding of the need for continual adjustments between desires and restraints in everyday life.

  (2) Understanding of the unique differences in persons, the state

of flux characterizing individuals and environment, and distinctive reaction of each individual to life's experience.

(3) Knowledge of the importance of recognition by others for every person.
(4) Police encouragement of an attitude of self-policing in violators.
(5) Appreciation of the barriers an individual can face in satisfying basic drives and motives.
(6) Awareness of the connection between frustrations in satisfying needs and wants, and illegal acts.
(7) Insights into four general areas of reaction--direct action, positive substitute, negative substitute, and retreat from society.

- Death Notification

    (1) Understanding of the nature of grief and despair on hearing about death of a beloved one.
    (2) Recognition of the police role in such situations as service and protection.
    (3) Discussion of the need for calm and patient ways of divulging such sad news.
    (4) Arrangement for the protection of the aggrieved people.

- Alternatives to Incarceration

    (1) Knowledge of tact, caution, and consideration in handling the mentally impaired persons.

- Suicide Management

    (1) Understanding of Freud's concept of "death wish" and Durkheim's views on suicide.
    (2) Knowledge of direct versus indirect self-destructive behavior and symptoms indicating suicide threats.
    (3) Understanding of various intervention techniques.

- Police Victim/Witness Relations

    (1) Appreciation of victim's rights.
    (2) Knowledge of many possible forms of police assistance to victims including referrals, transportation, evaluation of physical and emotional trauma, sympathetic treatment, and provision of information regarding prosecution.
    (3) Knowledge of the State codes protecting the rights of victims and witnesses of crime.

- Personal Communications

    (1) Knowledge of effective verbal, nonverbal, and written communications.
    (2) Understanding of harmful effects resulting from breakdown of communications.
    (3) Explanation of the importance of communications for police work.

IOWA

- Communication Skill

    (1) Effective and professional use of written, oral, and mechanical media.
    (2) Skills to evaluate situations and circumstances with discretion, control, and safety.

- Ethics and Professionalism

    (1) Discussion of positive and negative aspects of policing as a profession.
    (2) Knowledge of professional principles and their application to law enforcement.
    (3) Awareness of the need for the highest ethical and moral standards for the police.
    (4) Knowledge of the Law Enforcement Code of Ethics.

- Community Services

    (1) Crime prevention, public education, service delivery, and law enforcement as contributions of the police to the community.
    (2) Working knowledge of crime prevention concepts.
    (3) Impact of officer's conduct on community attitudes and influences.
    (4) Knowledge of the special needs of racial and ethnic minorities, women, certain economic groups, the elderly, and the physically handicapped for police assistance.
    (5) Appreciation of citizens' evaluation of the police, their expectations from the police, and negative stereotypes of the police.
    (6) Knowledge of crime prevention programs.
    (7) Discussion of opportunity reduction strategy in crime prevention.
    (8) Understanding of police citizen cooperation in prevention of crime.

- Law Enforcement and Minority Groups

    (1) Discussion of problems, attitude and motives of minority groups.
    (2) Recognition of the role of the police officer toward minorities.
    (3) Recognition of the possibility of the police behaving as a minority group.
    (4) Insights into police prejudice, discrimination, segregation, and racism.

- Crisis Intervention

    (1) Identification of the officer's responsibilities at crisis situations as keeping the peace and finding solution to the problem.

(2) Appreciation of the need for the officer's tact and reason in crisis situations.
(3) Knowledge of various methods of handling crisis.

- Mentally Impaired

  (1) Understanding and acceptance of the handicapped in every-day life.
  (2) Recognition of the handicapped on encounters.
  (3) Effective communication and use of discretion with the handicapped.
  (4) Knowledge of social agencies for referrals.

- Death Notification

  (1) Knowledge of techniques and procedures for delivering a death message.

- Psychology for Law Enforcement Self-Understanding and Handling Stress

  (1) Recognition of psychological problems involved in law enforcement.
  (2) Discussion of psychological theories of behavior.
  (3) Knowledge of police stress and techniques utilized in controlling it.
  (4) Recognition and handling of inappropriate behavior.

- News Media

  (1) Appreciation of the need for good relationships between the police and the media for the sake of police image, public relations, and dissemination of information.
  (2) Appreciation of the rights of the media as guaranteed by law.

KANSAS

- Police Community Relations

  (1) Study of the history and development of police and community relations programs in America.
  (2) Appreciation of the police officer's role as community service.
  (3) Importance of police conduct for fostering harmonious police community relations.
  (4) Knowledge of the role of the media in police community relations.

- Police Professionalism

  (1) Discussion of the attributes of professionalism such as ethics, service ideal, and knowledge.
  (2) Knowledge of anti-professional aspects of policing including political interference, low standards for employment, and failure to regulate conduct.

(3) Understanding of the Law Enforcement Code of Ethics and the need for ethical values for the police.
(4) Role of individual officers and unions in ensuring ethical values and standards.

- Crime Prevention

(1) Understanding of the police role in crime prevention.
(2) Knowledge of programs and hardware effective in prevention and reduction of crime.

- Internalization/Externalization of Stress

(1) Knowledge of the causes of stress in police officers.
(2) Study of the effects of stress upon a police officer's life and career.
(3) Recognition of various coping mechanisms.
(4) Understanding of the connection between stress and physical as well as mental disorders.
(5) Physical exercise for stress reduction.

- Interpersonal Communications--General

(1) Knowledge of defusion of tension and arbitration while handling civil disturbances.
(2) Study of verbal and nonverbal communication processes and sensitivity training.
(3) Discussion of disputes and abnormal behavior.
(4) Skills for handling civil disturbances without resorting to enforcement.
(5) Knowledge of various ways of handling abnormal persons.

- Interpersonal Communications--Family

(1) Knowledge and skills to assist families to deal with personal problems.
(2) Familiarity with various types of referral agencies for battered wives, children, and victims of family crisis.
(3) Mental and physical preparedness for handling crisis and family disturbance calls.
(4) Knowledge of caution and tact in police intervention in family disputes.
(5) Understanding of legal and service aspects in crisis intervention.

KENTUCKY[4]

- Police Image

(1) Knowledge of public attitude and prejudice toward the police.
(2) Discussion of the need for a presentable image.

- Police Ethics

  (1) Understanding of the relationship between ethics and law enforcement.
  (2) Appreciation of ethical practices for public respect.

- Police and Community Relations

  (1) Knowledge of a cadet's possible contribution to good police community relations

- Police, Community, and Minority Relations

  (1) Perceptions of the need for special concerns toward minorities.

- Police and Press Relations

  (1) Awareness of the need for healthy relationship between the police and the media.
  (2) Understanding of constitutional limitations, and public service obligations on the part of the media.

- Psychological Stress of Police

  (1) Understanding of psychological stress in general.
  (2) Knowledge of the impact of stress on occupational performance.

- Self-Perception

  (1) Knowledge of self-conception and expectations, and their impact on policemen's behavior.

- Handling the Mentally Ill

  (1) Knowledge of proper ways to handle the mentally ill.

- Agency Referral

  (1) Knowledge of all agencies to which the police can refer citizens in need.

- Crowd Control

  (1) Familiarity with the basic concepts of crowd control.

- Family Disputes

  (1) Knowledge of the methods capable of producing positive effects in family disputes.

- Patrol Calls: Dealing With the Intoxicated Person

  (1) Recognition and effective handling of persons under the influence of alcohol.

- Crime Prevention

  (1) Understanding of the concepts of crime prevention.

- Juvenile Delinquency and Child Abuse

  (1) Knowledge of laws, investigative methods, and techniques applicable to each specific stage of delinquency and child abuse.

LOUISIANA

- Crisis Intervention

  (1) Discussion of the psychological factors causing dominance of emotions over reason.
  (2) Knowledge of the special characteristics of domestic disputes.
  (3) Study of "psychiatric first aid" including professional advice to disputants.
  (4) Knowledge of disputes arising from repossession, landlord-tenant disputes, and so on.

- Handling Juveniles

  (1) Study of the relevant provisions of juvenile code.
  (2) Knowledge of interrogation of juveniles.

- Handling the Mentally Disturbed

  (1) Knowledge of types, degrees, symptoms, etc., of mental disturbances.
  (2) Study of special techniques for handling mentally ill persons.
  (3) Knowledge of agencies for mentally disturbed or retarded persons.

- Police Ethics

  (1) Knowledge of the principles and scope of professional ethics.
  (2) Application of ethics to law enforcement.
  (3) Study of ethics for maintaining the quality in police work and satisfaction of the community.

- Situational and Impartial Enforcement of the Law

  (1) Study of discretion as a useful tool in police work.
  (2) Insights into the factors affecting police decisions for enforcement or nonenforcement.

- The Police Role

  (1) Discussion of the police role involving order maintenance, crime prevention, public education, service delivery, law enforcement.

(2) Understanding of the expectations of various segments of society from the police.

- Minority Relations

    (1) Understanding of psychological factors for developing insight into minority problems.
    (2) Inclusion of women, sexually distinct groups, the elderly, and the physically handicapped in the study of ethnic and racial minorities.

- Building Respect for the Police

    (1) Knowledge of the importance of appearance, courtesy, action, and communication in public evaluation of the police.
    (2) Recognition of prompt response, willing service, sympathetic behavior, and fair treatment as factors conducive to good public relations.

- Crime Prevention

    (1) Effective policing, public education, and public awareness essential for crime prevention.
    (2) Building of crime prevention programs through proper communication, group interaction, and public acceptance.

MAINE

- Interpersonal Communication

    (1) Discussion of qualities desirable in an interviewer.
    (2) Understanding of the need for rapport on the part of an interviewer.
    (3) Study of effective interview techniques and benefits of controlling the interview techniques.

- Stress Management

    (1) Knowledge of the symptoms of physical, mental, and occupational stress.
    (2) Discussion of coping mechanisms.

- Dealing With Variant Behavior

    (1) Recognition of the symptoms of psychosis, neurosis, personality disorders, substance abuse, and suicide.
    (2) Comprehension of the legal and psychological aspects of handling a mentally ill person.

- Perception of Human Behavior

    (1) Knowledge of role awareness, reference groups, motivation and human needs, and so on, for proper understanding of perception.

(2) Study of "erroneous perception" and "selective perception."

(3) Knowledge of the causes limiting human perception.

(4) Awareness of the means for improving perception.

- Police Ethics and Moral Issues

  (1) Recognition of the need of high standards of ethical and moral behavior for the police.

  (2) Discussion of the consequences of unethical or immoral conduct by an officer or the department.

  (3) Identification of certain forms of immoral behavior involving gratuities, favoritism, criminal temptation, confidential information, and misuse of authority.

  (4) Knowledge of the Law Enforcement Code of Ethics and its relations to daily law enforcement activity.

- Police Citizen Relations

  (1) Understanding of racial, religious, cultural, and ethnic backgrounds of minority or special groups.

  (2) Role of ideas, values, attitudes, habits, and social situations in cultural development.

  (3) Recognition of police prejudice.

  (4) Discussion of effective police conduct and practices for strengthening police relations with subculture groups and ethnic minorities.

- Police and the Public

  (1) Study of the methods for creating a suitable climate for healthy police-citizen interaction.

  (2) Awareness of the role of individual officers in fostering positive community attitude toward the police.

  (3) Discussion of crime prevention as a primary basis of community relations efforts.

  (4) Identification of the most important forms of crime prevention undertaken by the police.

- News Media Relations

  (1) Understanding of the role of the news media in a democratic society.

  (2) Recognition of the conflict inherent in police need for confidentiality and constitutional freedom of the press.

  (3) Appreciation of the role of the media in prevention of crime and location of criminals.

- Crisis Conflict Management

  (1) Knowledge of the causes of crisis situations needing police intervention.

  (2) Recognition of the impact of personality and emotional maturity in crisis intervention situations.

- Juvenile Behavior and Control

  (1) Study of problem youths, and the need for proper attitude, methods, and techniques for dealing with them.
  (2) Enumeration of common juvenile offenses.
  (3) Appreciation of relationships of the juvenile officers' responsiveness to the needs of youths.
  (4) Discussion of young people's problems and encouragement of strong community relations with juveniles.
  (5) Overview of community agencies engaged in work with youths.

- Child Abuse

  (1) Recognition of negligence, physical abuse, and sexual abuse.
  (2) Awareness of proper reporting and referral procedures in child abuse cases.

- Spouse Abuse

  (1) Promotion of self-awareness and empathy of officers in spouse abuse cases.
  (2) Knowledge of various ways of handling spouse abuse cases.
  (3) Understanding of the complex causes of these cases, the dynamics of violence, and the ways of prevention.

- Crowd Control and Civil Disorder

  (1) Discussion of the different aspects of civil disorder, various levels of violence, and types of damages.
  (2) Knowledge of the patterns of disorder and traditional methods of disorder control.
  (3) Identification of prevention techniques and alternatives to the use of force in crowd control.

MARYLAND

- Ethics

  (1) Recognition of ethics as key to professionalism.
  (2) Awareness of the visibility of police officers and the consequent need for exemplary morality.
  (3) Identification of the importance of discipline in an efficient quasi-military organization such as a police department.

- Media Relations

  (1) Understanding of the importance of good public and press relations for police morale.
  (2) Knowledge of the need for achieving a healthy state of communication.
  (3) Discussion of policy and procedures to be followed by an individual officer for releasing information to the media.

(4) Demonstration of ability by a police officer to respond to questions from the public, maintain confidentiality, and refer problems to appropriate agencies.

- Family Disputes

  (1) Discussion of various types of service calls including calls for intervention in family disputes.
  (2) Understanding of the need for an officer's patience and safety.
  (3) Knowledge of the magnitude of child abuse and battered wives problems.
  (4) Information about supporting agency resources available to a disputant.

- Handling Victims

  (1) Explanation of many patterns of sexual development, various classes of rapes, and their psychological characteristics.
  (2) Understanding of the rape trauma syndrome.
  (3) Appreciation of the psychological responses of a crime victim like feelings of helplessness, lack of control, self-blame, blaming of others, and fear of attack.
  (4) Knowledge of the techniques for defusing crisis or stress of victims.

- Conflict Management

  (1) Identification of the duties of a police officer while intervening in interpersonal conflicts.
  (2) Management of intervention following rape or other kinds of sexual offenses, racial incidences, crime against the elderly, burglary, armed robbery, domestic violence, missing persons, homicide, kidnapping, arson, theft, poisoning, and suicide.
  (3) Knowledge of various steps in resolving a conflict situation including arrest, separation, mediation, and referrals.

- Communication Skills

  (1) Acknowledgment of the need for caution and courtesy in telephone conversation.
  (2) Awareness of the importance of prompt answering, appropriate greeting, courteous listening, accurate recording of information, demonstrated interest and sincerity, quick and accurate routing of calls, provision of service and information, and courteous termination of calls.
  (3) Understanding of the relationship between police image and effective communication.
  (4) Identification of profanity, derogatory language, ethnically offensive terminology, and inappropriate use of police jargons as detrimental to public relation.
  (5) Understanding of the impact of past experiences, maturity, mental and physical conditions, environment, and emotional

involvement in the process of perception.

(6) Instruction on effective communication with hostile, angry, hysterical, drunk, very old, very young, and racist persons.

(7) Awareness of special problems in interviewing young children, the elderly, the mentally retarded, and the emotionally impaired.

- Crime Prevention

(1) Discussion of an effective crime prevention strategy including devices, public awareness, and other details.

(2) Recognition of police officers' duty to speak to citizens about poorly protected areas and unsafe practices.

(3) Demonstrations of security hazards in residential structures, commercial establishments, and security locking devices.

- Handling Mentally Disturbed Persons

(1) Knowledge of destructive abnormal behavior.

(2) Understanding of the need for protecting the public while ensuring the welfare and humane treatment of the mentally ill.

(3) Ability to ignore verbal abuse, avoid excitement, and minimize the use of force.

MASSACHUSETTS

- Police Role in Modern Society

(1) Study of the historical development of the police and the criminal justice system.

(2) Enumeration of the duties of the police.

(3) Recognition of the impact of community expectations, officer's preferences, political influences, and discretion in police role.

(4) Appreciation of police discretion and its abuse.

- Environment of Policing

(1) Understanding of the Law Enforcement Code of Ethics.

(2) Discussion of professionalism as a goal of law enforcement, changing police role, and the qualities required for professional officers.

(3) Explanation of the need for positive police-community relations, its purposes and objectives.

(4) Enumeration of various forms of corruption including pervasive unorganized corruption, persuasive organized corruption, grass eaters, meat eaters, police theft from burglarized premises, sale of information, peddling, and so on.

(5) Discussion of departmental sanctions like oral reprimand, written reprimand, suspension, demotion, and dismissal.

- Interpersonal Relations

    (1) Study of human behavior for developing professional attitude and building respect.
    (2) Knowledge of verbal and nonverbal techniques of communications.
    (3) Discussion of barriers to communication such as stereotyping and language.
    (4) Knowledge of the art of persuasion.
    (5) Importance of interpersonal skills in dealing with ordinary citizens, handling abnormal people, responding to group challenges, and controlling disorderly or unruly people.

- Conflict Resolution

    (1) Knowledge of the nature of conflicts including interpersonal and intrapersonal conflicts.
    (2) Understanding of the police role including legal responsibilities in conflicts.
    (3) Awareness of effective communication skills and information-gathering techniques in interviewing complainants and victims.
    (4) Knowledge of intervention and conflict resolution techniques which may include problem solving, mediation, counseling, referral, and arbitration.

- Crisis Intervention

    (1) Identification of different types of abnormal behavior resulting from being emotionally charged, mentally ill, deranged, anti-social, self-destructive, retarded, suicidal, or intoxicated.
    (2) Instruction on handling and controlling different types of abnormal behavior.
    (3) Discussion of possible assistance to persons vulnerable to suicide, victims of rapes and other sex offenses, and recipients of death notifications.
    (4) Knowledge of agencies for referrals.

- Oral Communication

    (1) Recognition of the value and need of effective speaking by police officers.
    (2) Discussion of vocabulary, voice, pronunciation, friendliness, cheerfulness, and courtesy for good speaking.
    (3) Identification of dogmatism, lifelessness, nervousness, and lack of organization in speech as adverse factors affecting speech.

- Police Stress

    (1) Recognition of the factors causing job stress in policing including departmental stressors, family stressors, and community stressors.
    (2) Knowledge of the methods for dealing with stress with

emphasis on physical fitness, relaxation techniques, and nutrition.
(3) Information on agencies offering assistance.

MICHIGAN

- Interpersonal Relations

    (1) Knowledge of human relations skills such as sensitivity, proper language and gestures.
    (2) Development of skills which contribute positively to encounters between the police and citizens.
    (3) Study of the need of appropriate questioning, neutral and sensitive manner, objective attitudes and patient listening.

- Family Dispute Mediation

    (1) Knowledge of the need for full information, cautious manner, and watchful observation by police officers while handling domestic disputes.
    (2) Instruction on management of family disputes through psychological as well as legal means.

- Handling Abnormal Persons

    (1) Study of statutory provisions regarding handling of abnormal persons.
    (2) Recognition of the signs and symptoms of the mentally ill which may include strange behavior, peculiar loss of memory, extreme fright, and panic.
    (3) Knowledge of handling mentally disturbed persons in order to protect the public and the subject.
    (4) Awareness of the caution required in transporting mentally disturbed persons.

- Dealing With the Families of Juvenile

    (1) Police notification to parents and guardians regarding violation of traffic laws by children.
    (2) Discussion of the methods for conducting parent-juvenile interviews.
    (3) Instructions on how to conduct a successful conference with a probation officer.

MINNESOTA

- Police Ethics

    (1) Appreciation of the police need for high ethical and moral standards at all times.
    (2) Study of the primary provisions of the Law Enforcement Code of Ethics.

(3) Understanding of the relationship between ethics and professionalism in law enforcement.
(4) Sensitivity to ethical problem in an officer's nonenforcement
of the law due to personal reasons.
(5) Recognition of ethical dilemmas in acceptance of small gratuities such as coffee or price discounts.
(6) Awareness of misconduct involved in brutality, discourtesy,
false testimony, divulging confidential information, drinking
on duty, excessive off-duty drinking, extramarital affairs,
gambling, excessive indebtedness, and concealing unprofessional acts of fellow officers.

- Career Influences

(1) Identification of the sources of satisfactions and dissatisfactions
in a law enforcement career.
(2) Awareness of the positive influences of a law enforcement
career on an officer's family and personal life.

- Stress/Crisis Intervention

(1) Study of the psychological causes of stress, its manifestations,
and the effective ways of handling it.
(2) Understanding of crisis situations including recognition of
dangers in crisis intervention.
(3) Study of the characteristics of a crisis, typical reactions of
a person in crisis, and the importance of immediate response.
(4) Understanding of the qualifications needed for effective
handling of crisis situations.

- Conflict/Crisis Intervention

(1) Understanding of the underlying causes of conflict in interpersonal situations.
(2) Familiarity with symptoms and characteristics of verbal and
nonverbal conflicts.
(3) Knowledge of the effectiveness of a disinterested and impartial
third party in resolving conflicts.

- Emotional Stability

(1) Recognition of emotional stability and the lack of it in a police
officer.
(2) Knowledge of the importance of professionalism and emotional
detachment in handling human aberrations.

- Dealing With People

(1) Knowledge of the characteristics of persons suffering from
physical and mental abnormalities.
(2) Understanding of the causes of such abnormalities and the
ways of handling them.
(3) Discussion of psychopathic personality, chemical dependency,

sexual deviation, child abuse, hearing impairment and mental
retardation, etc.

- Crime Prevention

  (1) Knowledge of the need of citizens' involvement in crime pre-
      vention.
  (2) Study of the principles of crime prevention.

- Community Relations

  (1) Understanding of the difference between community relations
      and public relations.
  (2) Recognition of employment status, ethnic affiliation, education,
      wealth, mental state and police behavior, etc., on a person's
      attitude toward the police.

MISSISSIPPI

- Police Ethics

  (1) Understanding of the relationship between professionalism and
      ethics.
  (2) Familiarity with the Law Enforcement Code of Ethics.

- Human Relations

  (1) Appreciation of public perception of the police officer's job.
  (2) Knowledge of the role of attitude and prejudice on human be-
      havior.
  (3) Discussion of verbal and nonverbal communication, police
      stress, and cultural differences among people.
  (4) Recognition of police work as public service.
  (5) Awareness of the connection between a respect for the police
      and easier solution of problems faced by them.
  (6) Understanding of the spirit of the law.
  (7) Discussion of the means for combatting racial prejudice.
  (8) Understanding of the police as a part of, and not apart from,
      the community.

- Police Image

  (1) Understanding of the relationship between public attitude
      toward the police and their personal experience with individual
      officers.
  (2) Awareness of the damage possible to police image by thought-
      less, rude, haughty, and disrespectful officers.

- Crime Prevention

  (1) Understanding of the role of the aggressive police officer in
      crime prevention.

(2) Importance of enlisting community support in crime reduction and education of the public.

(3) Role of physical security as a means of reducing the opportunity to commit crime.

(4) Understanding of crime prevention as a task demanding knowledge of the people, surroundings, professional enthusiasm, and public involvement.

- Officer Survival and Crisis Intervention

   (1) Study of the key issues in police longevity and the techniques of officer survival.

   (2) Knowledge of the safety procedures required in domestic disturbances.

   (3) Knowledge of the legal provisions in the area of family disputes, and agencies for referrals.

MISSOURI

- Human Relations

   (1) Knowledge of the psychological and sociological factors affecting human behavior.

   (2) Understanding of the complexities in situations arising from conflict of behavior.

   (3) Role of the officer's own psychology in maintaining emotional self-discipline.

- Police and Minority Groups

   (1) Awareness of racial, religious, cultural, and ethnic backgrounds of various minority groups.

   (2) Recognition of the need for mutual respect and cooperation between minorities and the police.

   (3) Abilities to overcome prejudicial distractions in professional judgments.

- Public Relations

   (1) Awareness of the need for good will between the police and the public.

   (2) Importance of self-control, courtesy, fairness, and personal appearance in earning public good will.

- Police Ethics and Professionalization

   (1) Knowledge of the Code of Ethics as a guide to professional conduct.

   (2) Discussion of ethical and unethical conduct.

   (3) Identification of the need for proper selection, training, and continuing education for the development of law enforcement as a profession.

- Domestic Complaints

    (1) Knowledge of the difference between domestic disputes and civil problems.
    (2) Explanation of the techniques of mediation and control.
    (3) Knowledge of social agencies for referrals.

MONTANA

- Abnormal Behavior

    (1) Study of unhealthy personalities, psychosis, sub-normal intelligence and forensic psychology.
    (2) Instruction on the effective methods of handling abnormality.

- Crisis Intervention

    (1) Awareness of the need for thorough observation of a crisis scene.
    (2) Understanding of the ways which can create an impression of nonhostile authority.
    (3) Skills to calm an emotional individual through understanding, self-control, and reassurance.
    (4) Understanding of the need to encourage talking and avoidance of excessive force in subduing disputants.
    (5) Knowledge of mediation for helping disputants to find a solution to the problems at hand.
    (6) Knowledge of referral agencies.

- Effective Communication

    (1) Knowledge of nonverbal and verbal factors affecting response.
    (2) Skills for communicating with an audience.
    (3) Knowledge of public speaking and communication with the media.

- Officer Perception

    (1) Study of the difference between a casual observer and a perceptive officer.
    (2) Understanding of the effect of emotional condition, previous experience, prejudice and bias, etc., on perception.

- Police Stress

    (1) Knowledge of biological and psychological factors causing stress as well as recognition of the warning signs.
    (2) Discussion of stress-related phenomena like alcoholism, divorce, suicide, etc.
    (3) Knowledge of coping with stress through physical exercise, cognitive restructuring, relaxation techniques, and self-appraisal.

- Police Ethics

  (1) Importance of integrity, courage, responsibility, sacrifice and reputation in police work.
  (2) Study of consequences of prejudices as well as remedial measures.
  (3) Discussion of the Law Enforcement Code of Ethics.

- Crime Prevention

  (1) Knowledge of crime prevention as a cooperative venture between the police and the community.
  (2) Discussion of opportunity reduction, neighborhood watch, operation identification, business crime prevention and other concepts.
  (3) Study of Crimestopper Program in detail.

NEBRASKA

- Understanding of Human Behavior

  (1) Study of the impact of biological, sociological, psychological, and environmental factors in personality.
  (2) Understanding of culture, subculture, social roles, hierarchy of needs, motivations, etc., for better insights into human behavior.
  (3) Discussion of various stages of communication process and the principles of communication.
  (4) Definition of stress, identification of psychological and physiological effects of stress, and knowledge of coping mechanisms.
  (5) Recognition of behavior traits of the mentally ill and police responsibilities toward such people.
  (6) Knowledge of effective techniques and safety procedures in crisis intervention situations.

- Law Enforcement and the Community

  (1) Awareness of the importance of good police community relations.
  (2) Discussion of police professionalism.
  (3) Appreciation of the connection between professionalism, morale, self-image, and public image.
  (4) Recognition of the importance of police contacts with the public.
  (5) Awareness of the problems in accurately measuring successful community relations.
  (6) Study of the role of prejudice, rumor, hostility and discrimination, etc., in police community relations.
  (7) Knowledge of various issues in police relations with minorities.
  (8) Importance of police accountability to the public, wise use of power, sensitivity to public complaints, and compliance with the Law Enforcement Code of Ethics.

(9) Discussion of various types of programs for police training in community relations.

NEVADA

- Ethics and Professionalism
  (1) Understanding of the historical relationship between ethics and professionalism.
  (2) Recognition of integrity and professionalism as the most important elements of police image.
  (3) Knowledge of the Canons of Police Ethics.

- Mental Illness
  (1) Knowledge of the role of tact, caution, empathy, and understanding in handling of the mentally ill.
  (2) Skills to incapacitate a physically strong and violent mental patient.
  (3) Awareness of the need for caution before acting on a mentally ill call.

- Domestic Violence
  (1) Study of police responsibilities for restoration of order, investigation, and referrals.
  (2) Knowledge of the psychological characteristics of battered women and wife beaters.
  (3) Importance of safety precautions in handling domestic disputes.
  (4) Knowledge of the important steps such as control and assessment of situations, interview of the victims and assailants, and techniques of resolution including arrests and referrals.

- Crisis Intervention
  (1) Knowledge of the characteristics of a person in crisis.
  (2) Recognition of the ineffective coping mechanisms such as denial, rationalization, and displacement.
  (3) Knowledge of police objectives in a crisis situation which may include restoration of order, control of emotions and behavior, and appropriate legal steps.

NEW HAMPSHIRE

- Police Ethics and Unethical Behavior
  (1) Discussion of the need for the highest standards of ethical behavior for the police.
  (2) Recognition of unethical behavior and situations.
  (3) Awareness of the consequences of unethical behavior like false arrest, civil liability, and damaged public relations.

(4) Appreciation of the moral duty to report fellow officer's un-
    ethical conduct.
(5) Knowledge of corrupt practices undermining the basis of
    ethical and professional values.
(6) Awareness of the harmful effects of profanity, derogatory
    language, racist terminology, and police jargons.

- Police Community Relations

  (1) Acceptance of police functions as avenues for public service.
  (2) Understanding of the reasons why the public tends to berate
      the police.
  (3) Study of the relationships between crime prevention and pub-
      lic support.
  (4) Discussion of programs likely to create better relationships
      with the community.

- Mental Illness and Retardation

  (1) Knowledge of depression, psychosis, violence and their con-
      sequences.
  (2) Recognition of symptoms and characteristics of mental retarda-
      tion.
  (3) Identification of danger signs associated with mental retarda-
      tion.
  (4) Discussion of the psychological ways of handling the mentally
      disturbed persons.
  (5) Knowledge of agencies providing service for the mentally ill.

- Domestic Complaints

  (1) Importance of safety, effectiveness, legal propriety, and
      reasonableness in handling domestic disputes.
  (2) Awareness of the need for impartiality, tact, and responsive-
      ness in handling such disputes.
  (3) Knowledge of agencies providing service to victims of domestic
      violence.

- Stress

  (1) Knowledge of the causes of stress.
  (2) Identification of the physiological, mental, and psychological
      effects of stress.
  (3) Discussion of the techniques found useful in coping positively
      with stress.

NEW JERSEY

- Morals and Ethics

  (1) Appreciation of the need for the highest ethical and moral
      standards in law enforcement.

(2) Knowledge of the Law Enforcement Code of Ethics, Canons of Police Ethics, and peer pressure in corrupt police practices.

(3) Discussion of the methods for handling unethical conduct on the part of a fellow officer.

(4) Understanding of ethical impropriety involved in nonenforcement of laws due to personal reasons.

- Career Influences

  (1) Awareness of the negative consequences of policing.

  (2) Knowledge of the techniques for overcoming such consequences.

- Identification of Techniques for Dealing With Stress

  (1) Knowledge of the psychological and physiological sources of stress and the symptoms of stress.

  (2) Awareness of various stressful situations in daily lives of police officers.

  (3) Developing skills to combat the cumulative effects of stress.

- Police Responsibility to Provide Community Service

  (1) Identification of community service functions of the police.

  (2) Impact of school, the media, family, and peers on an individual's attitude toward the police.

  (3) Awareness of community expectations from the police.

  (4) Knowledge of the ways to promote positive community attitude toward the police.

- Community Relations/Crime Prevention

  (1) Knowledge of crime prevention techniques, including counseling of individuals and generating public consciousness.

  (2) Study of the need of sharing information with the public for getting them involved in crime prevention measures.

  (3) Discussion of the methods for encouraging popular participation in crime prevention.

- Community Relations/Referrals

  (1) Knowledge of agencies for referrals of individuals with special problems.

  (2) Knowledge of social service agencies in the community.

  (3) Identification of the avenues for improved utilization of community resources.

- Community Relations/Minority Subcultures

  (1) Awareness of varying perceptions of the police by different ethnic groups.

  (2) Study of prejudice and the process of becoming prejudiced.

(3) Knowledge of positive as well as negative consequences of police behavior on their relationship with minority community.

- Community Relations/Youths

  (1) Knowledge of important behavioral characteristics of adolescents including delinquent behavior.
  (2) Awareness of major responsibilities of patrol officers in dealing with juveniles.
  (3) Knowledge of measures for improving police-youth relations in order to prevent delinquency.
  (4) Discussion of the effects of positive police officer-youth contacts on the police officer, his or her department, the youth, the parents of the youth, and the community.

- Handling Persons With Special Needs

  (1) Awareness of the ethical responsibilities in handling persons with special needs.
  (2) Identification of the symptoms of neurotic, psychotic, character disordered, and suicidal individuals.
  (3) Knowledge of the criteria utilized for sending an individual for a short-term commitment for treatment.
  (4) Understanding of the methods for dealing with abnormal people.
  (5) Knowledge of agencies for referrals of persons with special needs.

- Community Relations/Crisis Intervention

  (1) Understanding of the police role in crisis intervention including prevention of harm, restoration of order, and referrals.
  (2) Awareness of personality and other factors contributing to agitated relations among people.
  (3) Identification of short-range and long-range goals of crisis intervention.

- Awareness of Emotional Reactions

  (1) Understanding of police officers' own emotional reactions to various types of individuals.
  (2) Importance of impartial enforcement of law by police officers.

- Telephone Communication

  (1) Importance of telephone conversation in promoting a positive police image and effective communication.
  (2) Instruction on prompt answering, appropriate greeting, accurate recording of information, demonstration of interest and sincerity, provision of service and information, and courteous termination of calls.

- Oral Communication

  (1) Recognition of the role of communication for effective police

service and improved community attitude toward the police.
(2) Identification of language and nonlanguage factors contributing to negative public response to the police.
(3) Lessons on controlling body and voice for effective police interactions with the public.
(4) Ability to communicate effectively with members of minority ethnic groups.

- Alcoholism As a Disease

  (1) Study of alcoholism as a disease.
  (2) Knowledge of treatment facilities available in the community.

- Dealing With Intoxicated Persons

  (1) Identification of alternatives available for handling public inebriates.
  (2) Knowledge of common injuries or illnesses which resemble drunkenness.
  (3) Recognition of danger signs associated with severe intoxication.
  (4) Skills in handling intoxicated or incapacitated persons.

- Observation and Perception

  (1) Identification of past experiences, mental condition, emotional involvement, and environmental conditions as factors affecting perception.
  (2) Importance of perception in police activities.
  (3) Instruction on the ways to improve observation and perception skills.

- Handling Disturbances, Disputes, Domestic Violence, and Child Abuse Complaints

  (1) Skills in handling disturbances, disputes, and violent domestic situations.
  (2) Instruction on handling domestic violence calls safely but effectively.
  (3) Recognition of the symptoms of child abuse and the police duty in handling abused, abandoned, and neglected children.
  (4) Identification of an officer's responsibilities at the scene of a disturbance, which include keeping the peace and ensuring security of persons and property.

- Handling Sick, Injured, and Distressed

  (1) Familiarity with agency policies and procedures for handling sick, injured, and deceased persons.

- Riot and Crowd Control

  (1) Identification of tactical principles of crowd and riot control.
  (2) Instruction on crowd and riot control formations.

- News Media Relations

  (1) Development of skills to deal effectively with the media for benefits of the police and the public.
  (2) Recognition of the legal rights of the media in regard to news.

NEW MEXICO[5]

- Ethics (Also Unethical Behavior)

  (1) Awareness of the need for the highest ethical and moral standards for police officers.
  (2) Understanding of the Law Enforcement Code of Ethics and the Canons of Police Ethics.
  (3) Appreciation of the problem created by an officer's acceptance of gratuities.
  (4) Realization of the obligation to take positive action against unethical conduct on the part of a fellow officer.

- Community Service Concept

  (1) Recognition of the police role as community service.
  (2) Acceptance of order maintenance, crime prevention, public education, service, and law enforcement as police responsibilities.

- Community Attitudes and Influences

  (1) Appreciation of the influence of school, the media, family, and peers in an individual's attitude toward the police.
  (2) Variation in expectations from the police in accordance with citizen status and police behavior.

- Citizen Evaluation

  (1) Awareness of the ways through which the police are evaluated by citizens.
  (2) Understanding of community expectations from the police.
  (3) Identification of the negative stereotypes about the police like unprofessional conduct, prejudicial acts, ineffectiveness, unethical behavior, and apathetic attitude.

- Crime Prevention

  (1) Understanding of the concepts of crime prevention.
  (2) Definition of crime prevention.
  (3) Identification of the areas of public-police cooperation in crime prevention.
  (4) Study of crime prevention methods like operation identification, neighborhood watch and crime stoppers programs, etc.
  (5) Knowledge of various security devices, as well as hazards, in residential structures.

- Stress Factors

  (1) Recognition of stress as the body's response to any excessive demand placed on it.
  (2) Identification of police activities like high-speed chase, shooting incidents, crisis intervention, and so on, which place demands on the body causing physiological changes.
  (3) Awareness of illnesses likely to be caused by constant physiological changes in the body.
  (4) Study of the techniques for physiological care including proper diet, exercise, change in activity, and muscle relaxation.

- Crime and the Elderly

  (1) Study of victimization of the elderly by examining the types, frequency, impact, and analysis of crime committed against them.

- Crisis Intervention/Interpersonal Relations

  (1) Recognition of the need for clear explanation of all police actions to affected persons.
  (2) Knowledge of the effect of education, training, media, family, peers, and so on, on one's verbal communication.
  (3) Awareness of negative public response to profanity, derogatory language, ethnically offensive terminology, and inappropriate use of jargon by police officers.
  (4) Knowledge of the scope of communication including verbal language, inflection of voice, symbols, body language, and good listening techniques.
  (5) Identification of some good listening techniques like eye contact, an open body position, appreciation of voice inflections, and empathic responses.
  (6) Instruction on the need of empathic response, appropriate body language, safety precaution, and other effective intervention techniques in handling family disputes.

- Mental Illness

  (1) Understanding of the need for minimal use of force, avoidance of threat, and putting everybody concerned at ease.
  (2) Importance of ignoring abusive language, avoidance of excitement, fair play, and alertness in handling the mentally disturbed.

NEW YORK

- Ethical Awareness

  (1) Understanding of the attitude and techniques of corrupt personnel, and the lack of dignity in corruption.
  (2) Awareness of various occupational temptations in police work.
  (3) Discussion of law enforcement ethics in general.

- Police and Minority Groups

  (1) Knowledge of racial, religious, and cultural backgrounds of minority groups.
  (2) Awareness of the methods conducive to controlling police prejudice.
  (3) Development of professional attitude for handling cultural differences with understanding.

- The Police and the Public

  (1) Acceptance of all aspects of police training as preparation for effective public relations.
  (2) Knowledge of the ways for building a positive and constructive environment of cooperation.

- News Media Relationship

  (1) The need of good relations between the police and the media for keeping the community informed of police activities.
  (2) Skills for providing information to the press without jeopardizing department's interest.
  (3) Study of the useful ways for reducing conflict between the police and the press.

- Domestic Violence

  (1) Study of domestic disputes as spouse abuse, child abuse, and abuse of the elderly.
  (2) Knowledge of the causes of and cures for such disputes.

- The Nature and Control of Civil Disorder

  (1) Consideration of various types of disorder, accompanying violence and damage, and dynamics of riot situations.
  (2) Study of situations necessitating use of force, and danger of overreaction.

- Intoxication

  (1) Definition of police responsibility in handling of public inebriates.
  (2) Discussion of effective techniques for dealing with publicly intoxicated persons.
  (3) Knowledge of sobering-up stations or similar facilities.

- Mental Illness

  (1) Knowledge of the symptoms of common types of mental illnesses.
  (2) Knowledge of handling the mentally ill without violation of legal provisions.
  (3) Discussion of emergency and routine cases as well as suicide attempts.

- Social Agency Services

  (1) Study of the scope of cooperation between social agencies and the police.
  (2) Knowledge of welfare, health, education, rehabilitation, and volunteer agencies.
  (3) Understanding of the impact of such agencies in community stability.

NORTH CAROLINA

- Civil Disorders

  (1) Study of the psychological aspects of crowd behavior.
  (2) Understanding of the abuses of the First Amendment rights.
  (3) Discussion of the ways to handle a wide range of group activities without jeopardizing life and property.

- Crisis Management

  (1) Discussion of the methods and techniques of handling disturbance calls.
  (2) Understanding of the differences between crisis and conflict.
  (3) Knowledge of intervention techniques including calming, brief interview, mediation, and referral.
  (4) Awareness of an officer's own safety and survival in crisis intervention.

- Deviant Behavior

  (1) Identification, evaluation, and effective control of persons displaying deviant behavior.
  (2) Discussion of the characteristics of deviant persons and the methods of handling such persons.

- Dealing With Victims and the Public

  (1) Appreciation of the need of knowledge, communication skills, and professional attitude to deal effectively with the public.
  (2) Emphasis on police community relations based on the principle that the police are a "part of," and not "apart from" the community.
  (3) Appreciation of the multiple and complex police role consisting of crime fighting, social work, order maintenance, and exercise of authority as government agents.
  (4) Knowledge of the role of attitude, ethical conduct, good communication skills, and knowledge (education, training) in professionalism.

- Observations and Perceptions

  (1) Discussion of observation and perception, and their importance in patrol work.

(2) Insights into psychology of observation and perception, as well as instruction on useful techniques of observation.

(3) Role of interest, emotions, and prejudice of individuals in observation and perception.

- High Incidents Calls for Service

  (1) Handling all requests for police assistance with seriousness and consideration.

  (2) Performance of house, bank, and store checks as a service to the public.

  (3) Intervention in neighborhood disputes, landlord-tenant conflicts, and similar events for community peace and harmony.

  (4) Instruction on providing assistance to the invalid, the elderly, missing and lost persons, and responding to emergencies like fire alarms.

- Crime Prevention Techniques

  (1) Study of crime prevention as a strategy demanding police knowledge, training, experience, and ability to deal with the community.

  (2) Study of history and philosophy of crime prevention as it originated with the Metropolitan Police in London.

  (3) Consideration of various crime control strategies like opportunity reduction, operation identification, neighborhood watch, target hardening, security devices, and so on.

NORTH DAKOTA

- Law Enforcement Ethics and Moral Issues

  (1) Identification of the reasons why law enforcement officers should exemplify the highest ethical and moral standards.

  (2) Study of the Law Enforcement Code of Ethics and the Canons of Police Ethics.

  (3) Critical response to unethical behavior and misconduct on the part of a fellow officer.

  (4) Discussion of abuse of discretion, acceptance of gratuities, and other unethical activities.

- Human Relations and Social Values

  (1) Recognition of changes in behavior, strange loss of memory, grand ideas about self and extreme fright, etc., as signs of mental illness.

  (2) Instruction on handling disturbed or violent people through dispassionate and nonabusive methods.

  (3) Awareness of the symptoms caused by physical ailments which can be wrongfully attributed to mental illness.

  (4) Development of contacts with citizens in order to strengthen community relations.

- Minority Relations
    - (1) Recognition of similarities between law enforcement officers and other minority groups.
    - (2) Awareness of the mechanisms of stereotyping and prejudice.
    - (3) Identification of police behavior found offensive by minority groups.

- Dealing With Variant Behavior
    - (1) Identification of the common symptoms of irrational behavior like denial of identity, one-sided conversations, hallucinations, unnatural gestures, and so on.
    - (2) Awareness of the need for understanding and encouragement of conversation, etc., for positive results.
    - (3) Avoidance of abuse, deception, anger, and the like while handling mentally ill persons.

- Crisis Intervention
    - (1) Insights into the psychological causes of human stress like fear, anger, compassion, and frustration.
    - (2) Identification of the symptoms of stress, the effective techniques of managing stress, and the physiological effects of stress.
    - (3) DIscussion of crisis intervention including the need for suitable attitude for handling crisis.
    - (4) Understanding of conflicts, verbal and nonverbal reactions to conflicts, and the techniques for resolution.
    - (5) Study of the ways a peace officer can improve human relations skills.

- Human Relations
    - (1) Appreciation of the complexities of police work and public demand for it.
    - (2) Discussion of the issues of training, education, and licensing in police professionalization.
    - (3) Importance of good public relations for all ranks.
    - (4) Knowledge of effects of the news media, public contacts with individual officers, and rumors on public attitude toward the police.
    - (5) Awareness of the importance of courtesy, tone, promptness, and other related matters in telephone communication.
    - (6) Impact of physical appearance, official behavior, choice of diction, and police efficiency on their public image.
    - (7) Sensitivity to negative consequences of police slovenliness, indifference, discourtesy, animosities, and lack of knowledge.
    - (8) Exemplary conduct of the police officer as a spouse, a parent, a neighbor, and a community leader.
    - (9) Explanation of humane relationship between subordinate officers and supervisors.

(10) Development of the art of getting along with others.
(11) Recognition of the harmful effect of police prejudice which
      may affect fairness and justice.
(12) Discussion of the ways to combat prejudice by being careful
      about police lack of objectivity.
(13) Study of the psychological, sociological, and economic reasons
      for racial antagonism.
(14) Recognition of social inequality, interference by the police,
      and eruption of pent-up emotions as reasons for riots.
(15) Understanding of the nature of crowds, police responsibility
      for peace, protection of life and property, and the need for
      discretion in handling protests.
(16) Importance of friendliness, courtesy, promptness and object-
      ivity in police contacts with the police.

OHIO[6]

• Human Relations

    (1) Knowledge of the characteristics of police work as a profes-
         sional endeavor.
    (2) Importance of good public relations to be cultivated by officers
         at all ranks.
    (3) Discussion of the useful hints and techniques to be practiced
         in telephone communications.
    (4) Awareness of the impact of deeds, manners and attitude of
         patrol officers on public image of the police.
    (5) Understanding the need of the police officer's setting a good
         example as a spouse, father, neighbor, community leader and
         public speaker.
    (6) Study of the importance of fruitful, rational, and humane
         command-subordinate relationship.
    (7) Instruction on the art of getting along.
    (8) Awareness of prejudice and the consequences of police pre-
         judice.
    (9) Recognition of the symptoms, consequences and remedies of
         racial antagonism.
    (10) Cultivation of proper attitudes and manners for meeting all
          kinds of encounters including labor trouble, protests and riots.

OKLAHOMA

• Police Community Relations

    (1) Awareness of the enormous demands of order maintenance and
         service functions on police officers' time.
    (2) Understanding of police human relations as a process of iden-
         tification and resolution of problems between the police and
         the community.

(3) Appreciation of the difference between public relations and community relations.

(4) Discussion of ways to improve community relations through frequent contacts with the public, avoidance of controversial conduct, and all officers' participation in police community relations programs.

- Crime Prevention

    (1) Discussion of the concept of crime prevention and the need for cooperation between police and citizens in crime prevention.

    (2) Study of opportunity reduction, operation identification, neighborhood watch, and security devices.

- Police Ethics

    (1) Definition of the term "ethics."

    (2) Understanding of the need for the highest ethical and moral standards for the police.

    (3) Appreciation of the problems associated with gratuities.

    (4) Understanding of the Code of Ethics.

    (5) Willingness of a police officer to take a stand against unethical practices of fellow officers.

- The Psychology of Human Relations

    (1) Study of motivation, self-interest and selfishness, and individual drives, urges, and needs.

    (2) Explanation of the functions of emotions.

    (3) Knowledge of the criteria governing normal social relations.

- Minority Relations

    (1) Recognition of police prejudice in their attitude towards minority.

    (2) Examination of prejudice as a frame of mind built on emotions, feelings of superiority, wrong attitudes, fear, and so on.

    (3) Understanding of the ways a person exhibits prejudice.

    (4) Understanding of undue physical force, verbal or psychological brutality, and systematic brutalization as manifestations of prejudice.

    (5) Study of minority complaints including inadequate police protection, lack of police service in inner-city neighborhoods, verbal and physical brutality, discrimination in police personnel practices, and so on.

- Interpersonal Communications

    (1) Understanding of all forms of communications, verbal and nonverbal.

    (2) Awareness of sarcasm, double-level communication, hint method, and avoidance of the use of a person's name as pitfalls in communication.

(3) Knowledge of four positions, namely, placater, blamer, computer, and distractor, that a person under stress may assume.

(4) Discussion of the ABC theory of communication, lead system, and violation of a person's body space.

- Crisis Intervention

    (1) Awareness of arrests, delinquency, divorce, demotion, loss of jobs etc., as capable of producing a crisis.

    (2) Discussion of domestic disputes, spouse abuse, and child abuse as the three most common crises encountered by law enforcement officers.

    (3) Understanding of the reasons why a wife continues to stay in an abusive situation.

    (4) Study of the progress of family violence which include tension-building stage, explosion stage, and kidness stage.

- Mentally Ill

    (1) Definition of the mentally ill according to the state law.

    (2) Knowledge of the reasons requiring the taking of a mentally ill person into protection custody.

    (3) Study of clerical steps involved in the processing of a mentally ill person.

OREGON

- Domestic Conflict Management

    (1) Knowledge of situations necessitating police intervention in domestic disputes.

    (2) Study of the need for objectivity, proper behavior, and restrained language in a crisis situation.

    (3) Knowledge of referral agencies and statutory obligations.

- Law Enforcement Profession

    (1) Discussion of assumptions, history, and means of improving police community relations.

    (2) Identification of the basic elements of professionalism.

    (3) Study of corruption, professionalism, and unethical conduct.

- Contemporary Society Awareness

    (1) Understanding of the societal changes related to crime.

    (2) Recognition of prejudice and discrimination as obstacles to police understanding of situations.

    (3) Study of the consequences of attaching labels to groups.

- Police Discretion

    (1) Knowledge of the proper uses of discretion in diverse situations.

(2) Study of the abuses of discretion including use of brutal force.

(3) Recognition of the advantages of discretion.

- Sexual Abuse and Child Neglect

    (1) Knowledge of the legal duties in child abuse and child neglect situations.

    (2) Understanding of the causes of child abuse.

    (3) Knowledge of agencies for referrals.

    (4) Identification of the needs of sexually abused children.

PENNSYLVANIA[7]

- Police Community Relations, Police Public Relations, and Police Ethics

    (1) Discussion of police community relations.

    (2) Appreciation of the importance of police citizen contacts.

    (3) Explanation of courtesy and public relations.

    (4) Knowledge of police ethics.

    (5) Study of police and the media relations as well as public speaking.

- Human Relations: Cultural Awareness

    (1) Understanding of ethnic, racial, and sexual differences.

    (2) Study of police socialization and stress.

- Mental Health Procedures Act--Crisis Intervention

    (1) Knowledge of handling emotionally disturbed persons and family crisis.

    (2) Study of the Mental Health Act.

    (3) Understanding of conflict management, resolution and referrals.

    (4) Instruction on riot control, handling of confrontations and hostage negotiations.

- Service Calls

    (1) Discussion of emergency and nonemergency calls.

    (2) Instruction on handling runaways and missing persons as part of service functions of the police.

RHODE ISLAND[8]

- Police Community Relations

    (1) Discussion of theories of personality formation and development.

    (2) Acquisition of the basic skills in interpersonal relations.

    (3) Study of the Code of Ethics and moral issues relevant to police work.

(4) Understanding of various dimensions of police community relations with particular emphasis on special groups.

- Domestic Violence

- Crime Prevention

- Police and the Media

- Police Ethics

- Police Stress Management

SOUTH CAROLINA

- Handling the Deaf
  (1) Study of the unique difficulties and problems of the deaf.
  (2) Knowledge of legal and constitutional rights of the deaf.

- Police Community Relations
  (1) Discussion of the need for trained attitude of police officers for successful community relations.
  (2) Importance of the basic values like loyalty, honor, and so on, for building a sound basis for police community relations.
  (3) Recognition of the need of mutual trust and faith for strong police community relations.

- Crowds and Mobs
  (1) Knowledge of casual, psychological, friendly, agitated, and hostile crowds.
  (2) Understanding of the process of degeneration of crowds into mobs.
  (3) Study of the characteristics of aggressive, escape, acquisitive, and expressive mobs.
  (4) Identification of various psychological factors like anonymity, force of numbers and novelty, etc., which help a mob to solidify.
  (5) Discussion of the destructiveness of crowds and mobs.
  (6) Study of the use of physical force, chemical agents, fire power, and so on, to control mobs.

- Crisis Intervention
  (1) Knowledge of the role the police play in domestic crisis.
  (2) Study of the causes and development of family disputes.
  (3) Understanding of the physical and psychological effects of stress and crisis.
  (4) Study of coping mechanism which may include calm reassurance, physical exercise, and the like.

(5) Skills for handling different stress situations such as death
notification, mental illness, suicide, or attempted suicide.

SOUTH DAKOTA

- Police Community Relations

  (1) Identification of the elements of professionalism such as well-
  defined sense of responsibility, motive of service, high stand-
  ard of self-criticism, and ethical code.
  (2) Inculcation of police professional values including protection
  of people, respect for all interests, restraints on the use of
  authority, purity of private conduct, fairness, spirit of service, avoidance of gratuities, awareness of civil rights, and
  concern for honest prosecution.

- Human Behavior

  (1) Study of human problems which lead to public contact with
  the police, methods of recognizing and dealing with such
  problems, and the scope of cooperation between law enforcement and other mental health services.
  (2) Knowledge of state hospitals, community centers, and special
  services connected with mental health system.
  (3) Discussion of alcohol- and drug-related outpatients, referral,
  consultation, and educational services.
  (4) Understanding of mental health problems relating to stress,
  excessive use of alcohol, and indulgence in drugs, which
  may also affect police officers.

- Domestic Violence

  (1) Definition of spouse abuse.
  (2) Knowledge of various factors peculiar to different stages of
  domestic violence.
  (3) Discussion of characteristics of batterers, battered wives, and
  battered children.
  (4) Study of the psychological issues involved in handling battered
  women like dealing with shock; information about legal, financial, medical, child care assistance; and helping battered
  women make positive choices.

- Crime Prevention

  (1) Familiarity with the history of London Metropolitan Police for
  a proper understanding of the concept of crime prevention.
  (2) Knowledge of target hardening, reduction of criminal opportunity and other crime prevention techniques.
  (3) Instruction on how to conduct security surveys.
  (4) Encouragement of citizen involvement in crime prevention efforts.

TENNESSEE

- Police Ethics

  (1) Discussion of the Law Enforcement Code of Ethics.

- Domestic Disturbances

  (1) Knowledge of the legal provisions and procedures in regard to domestic disturbances.
  (2) Study of the alternatives to criminal arrests in domestic disturbances.
  (3) Ability to prevent precipitation of conflicts.

- Recognizing and Handling Mentally Disturbed People

  (1) Understanding of the characteristics of the mentally retarded, psychoneurotic, paranoid and depressed individuals.
  (2) Knowledge of the effective police response suitable to each category.

- Stress Management

  (1) Understanding of the physical, mental, and emotional areas of stress.
  (2) Recognition of the early signs of people under severe stress.
  (3) Knowledge of ailments resulting from stress.
  (4) Instruction on the techniques for reduction of stress including study of its effects.

TEXAS

- Recognizing and Handling Abnormal Persons

  (1) Knowledge of the characteristics and symptoms of a mentally abnormal person.
  (2) Understanding of the psychological and behavioral considerations in handling abnormal persons.
  (3) DIscussion of the situations that call for physical restraints.
  (4) Study of the ways for handling a depressed person threatening or attempting suicide.
  (5) Understanding of the differences between certain physical conditions like diabetes, epilepsy and brain tumors, and mental disorders.
  (6) Discussion of a police officer's encounters with psychopathic persons.
  (7) Understanding of the peculiar characteristics of alcohol and drug addicts.
  (8) Knowledge of the various kinds of sexual offenses and the need for avoiding discussion of such incidents in the presence of children.
  (9) Understanding of the degrees of mental retardation, capabilities according to intelligence levels, and crime-proneness of

the mentally retarded.

(10) Knowledge of the psychological considerations necessary for handling such persons as well as their parents or guardians.

(11) Study of mental disorders and abnormal activities of old people.

(12) Understanding of the need for consideration, patience, and medical attention for persons suffering from old-age mental disorders.

• Crowd Control

(1) Discussion of casual, cohesive, expressive, and aggressive crowds.

(2) Study of aggressive, escape, and acquisitive mobs.

(3) Study of the impact of police language, behavior, excitement and the need for avoidance of confrontation while handling crowds and mobs.

• Crime Prevention and Public Service

(1) Discussion of crime prevention as a service to the public.

(2) Understanding of the need for cooperation between the police and the public in prevention of crime.

(3) Study of opportunity reduction, directed patrolling, security surveys, and so on, for an effective crime prevention program.

• The Peace Officer's Role in Society

(1) Understanding of interpersonal and intergroup adjustments, attitude, and prejudice for effective human relations.

(2) Discussion of the need for impartiality on the part of police officers, the characteristics of prejudiced persons, and the ways to combat prejudicial tendencies.

(3) Insights into the impact of police efficiency, courtesy, integrity, dress, equipment, and hygiene on the public perception of the police.

(4) Cultivation of objectivity, detachment, control of temper, and avoidance of judgments by officers.

UTAH

• Police Ethics and Professionalism

(1) Recognition of policing as a profession requiring ethics, skills, knowledge, education and training.

(2) Study of the consequences of nonenforcement because of personal reasons.

(3) Understanding of the relationship between professionalism and avoidance of corruption.

(4) Development of sensitivity toward unprofessional conduct of fellow officers.

- Police Community Relations

    (1) Recognition of the need for enlarging the area of common in-
         terests between the community and the police.
    (2) Study of the role of schools, the media, family, and peers
         in shaping public attitude toward the police.
    (3) Knowledge of the ways in which the community evaluates its
         police.
    (4) Discussion of crime prevention as a means of developing police
         community relations.
    (5) Perception of minority and ethnic subcultures, and the need
         for developing insights into other cultures.

- Personality Theory

    (1) Discussion of various aspects of human personality.
    (2) Understanding of motivation, perception, self-image, and be-
         havior.
    (3) Importance of observation in predicting own behavior as well
         as that of others.

- Abnormal Behavior

    (1) Knowledge of the nature and symptoms of the mentally dis-
         turbed and retarded.
    (2) Study of the psychological techniques of handling mentally
         ill or irrational persons.
    (3) Awareness of the need for avoidance of excitement, deception,
         unnecessary force, and aggressive response to verbal abuses
         from such persons.
    (4) Information about referral agencies in the community.
    (5) Discussion of neurotic, psychotic, psychopathic, suicidal,
         and retarded personalities.

- Crisis Intervention

    (1) Knowledge of psychological reasons for human stress including
         fear, anger, compassion, frustration, and conflict.
    (2) Appreciation of the physiological symptoms of stress and cri-
         sis.
    (3) Discussion of the methods for stress reduction including ex-
         ercise, diet, change of activity, and recreation.
    (4) Awareness of notification of death, molestation of a child,
         rape, accosting of an intruder by an elderly person, family
         disputes, serious accidents, and so on, which can cause
         severe stress.
    (5) Knowledge of various behavioral techniques for defusion of
         tense situations.
    (6) Study of the useful methods for assessment of violation, safety
         of person and property, as well as solution to problems.
    (7) Discussion of crisis involving repossession and landlord/tenant
         disputes.

- Officer Violator Relationship

  (1) Understanding of the psychology involved in the confrontation
      of traffic violators by officers.
  (2) Explanation of officious and oppressive manner, disrespectful
      attitude, officious tone of voice, and offensive body language
      which can cause conflicts.   '
  (3) Knowledge of profanity, derogatory language, ethnically of-
      fensive terminology, and inappropriate use of police jargons
      as negative factors in human relations.
  (4) Discussion of the need for professional demeanor and attention
      to personal safety.

- Decision Making (Police Discretion)

  (1) Understanding of the need for judicious and proper use of
      police power.
  (2) Need for balance between a police officer's concerns for the
      community and official authority.
  (3) Awareness of the role of police attitude in civil disorders.

- Interpersonal Communications

  (1) Knowledge of the importance of verbal and nonverbal communi-
      cations.
  (2) Understanding of the barriers to interpersonal communications.

VERMONT

- Dealing With Death

  (1) Study of the ways to make a death notification.
  (2) Knowledge of frequent emotional reactions in grieving process.
  (3) Instruction on practical handling of a death notification.

- Handling the Emotionally Disturbed

  (1) Understanding of the problems in handling psychotic and
      suicidal behavior.
  (2) Discussion of the most effective ways of dealing with these
      problems.
  (3) Information about available community resources.
  (4) Instruction on practical handling of emotionally disturbed in-
      dividuals.

- Interpersonal Communication

  (1) Knowledge of the techniques necessary for dealing with citi-
      zens as victims, violators, or citizens.

- Police Discretion

  (1) Understanding of the use of discretion in police work.

(2) Study of common practices, traditions, and techniques connected with the exercises of discretion.

- Police and the Press

    (1) Knowledge of the media role and discussion of the freedom of the press.
    (2) Skills and attitude for cooperative relationship with the press.

- Public Relations

    (1) Understanding of the community by the police.
    (2) Study of the role of communications in the police field.

- Domestic Crisis Intervention

    (1) Acquisition of special skills for dealing with persons involved in family fights, parent-child disputes, etc.

- Crowd Management

    (1) Knowledge of psychology of crowds, squad formation, and safe methods of dealing with strikes, riots, and demonstrations.

- Spouse Abuse

    (1) Study of the appropriate responses to domestic violence complaints.
    (2) Knowledge of the need for dealing with complaints after controlling violence.

- Stress Management

    (1) Awareness of police stress which arises because of life-threatening situations, fear of making serious mistakes, and so on.
    (2) Study of the nature and manifestations of stress.
    (3) Instruction on successful ways of coping with stress.

VIRGINIA

- Law Enforcement as a Profession

    (1) Study of the principles of professionalism.
    (2) Discussion of the "Law Enforcement Code of Ethics," and the Canons of Police Ethics.
    (3) Recognition of the need for police officers' adherence to high ethical and moral standards.
    (4) Development of proper attitude toward unethical and illegal conduct on the part of a fellow officer.
    (5) Discussion of the positive as well as negative aspects of discretionary enforcement of law.

(6) Awareness of the impact of law enforcement career on an officer's personal life.

- Communication

    (1) Identification of the negative nonlanguage factors in communication like officious and oppressive manner, disrespectful attitude, and the like.
    (2) Identification of the negative language factors like profanity, ethnically offensive terminology, and so on.
    (3) Understanding of the ways to communicate effectively with hostile, angry, hysterical, deranged, or other types of hypersensitive people.
    (4) Proper use of telephone for enhancing police image and effective and professional communication.

- Persuasion Techniques

    (1) Identification of a "good listener"; disadvantages of impersonal, passive, and indecisive approaches; and advantages of communication effectiveness.
    (2) Study of emotional control, good listening, impartiality, decisiveness, and salesmanship.

- Perception Techniques

    (1) Knowledge of experience, maturity, mental condition, emotional involvement, physical state, and environmental factors which affect perception.
    (2) Discussion of the techniques needed for effective handling of emotionally charged situations.

- Family Disputes

    (1) Instruction on effective handling of family disputes.
    (2) Identification of the inherent dangers to an officer intervening in a family dispute.

- Mentally Ill

    (1) Knowledge of the characteristics of intoxicated, paranoid, schizophrenic, epileptic, and diabetic persons.
    (2) Discussion of methods for handling various types of abnormal personality.
    (3) Study of the factors to be considered in handling mentally disturbed or irrational persons.

- Agency Referral

    (1) Information regarding private and public social service agencies.
    (2) Knowledge of the suitability of an agency to which a referral is made by a police officer.

- Crime Prevention

    (1) Identification of a practical crime prevention strategy.
    (2) Study of opportunity reduction, target hardening, security locking devices, and security hardware.

- Perception Techniques

    (1) Knowledge of experience, maturity, mental condition, emotional involvement, physical state, and environmental factors which affect perception.
    (2) Discussion of the techniques needed for effective handling of emotionally charged situations.

- Family Disputes

    (1) Instruction on effective handling of family disputes.
    (2) Identification of the inherent dangers to an officer intervening in a family dispute.

- Mentally Ill

    (1) Knowledge of the characteristics of intoxicated, paranoid, schizophrenic, epileptic, and diabetic persons.
    (2) Discussion of methods for handling various types of abnormal personality.
    (3) Study of the factors to be considered in handling mentally disturbed or irrational persons.

- Agency Referral

    (1) Information regarding private and public social service agencies.
    (2) Knowledge of the suitability of an agency to which a referral is made by a police officer.

- Crime Prevention

    (1) Identification of a practical crime prevention strategy.
    (2) Study of opportunity reduction, target hardening, security locking devices, and security hardware.
    (3) Understanding of crime prevention concepts.

WASHINGTON

- Ethics

    (1) Identification of the need for ethics in law enforcement.
    (2) Knowledge of the Law Enforcement Code of Ethics.
    (3) Sensitivity to unethical conduct with understanding of its consequences.

- Crime Prevention

    (1) Identification of the traditional approach to crime prevention

and benefits of crime prevention.
(2) Knowledge of commercial security and ability for making
    security recommendations to retailers.

- Crisis Intervention

  (1) Understanding of stress, its effect on individuals, and methods
      of dealing with it.
  (2) Knowledge of physical and emotional responses to stress as
      well as common sources of stress for the police.
  (3) Identification of reduction methods.
  (4) Knowledge of the symptoms of mental illness, abnormal per-
      sonality, as well as the techniques for handling the mentally
      ill.
  (5) Study of crisis and the techniques for dealing with it.
  (6) Study of conflicts and the police responsibility in conflict
      management.
  (7) Understanding of the need for calm, objectivity, accurate
      assessment, and suitable resolution of different situations.

- Miscellaneous Service Calls

  (1) Identification of the differences between mental illness, retar-
      dation, and senility.
  (2) Knowledge of handling the mentally ill in accordance with the
      Mental Health Treatment Act of 1973.
  (3) Understanding of the factors making suicide a serious health
      and social problem.
  (4) Knowledge of the proper procedures for responding to an
      investigating suicide calls.
  (5) Awareness of alcoholism, procedures in detoxification system,
      and the provisions of the Alcohol Treatment Act.
  (6) Discussion of disturbance calls and the options in handling
      noise disturbances.
  (7) Knowledge of the proper techniques for handling various types
      of service calls.

- Communication Skills

  (1) Understanding of the listening process for improving communi-
      cation skills.
  (2) Discussion of pleasant telephone manners.

- Use of Force

  (1) Understanding of the statutory provisions and other factors
      governing use of force.
  (2) Awareness of the typical problems leading to misuse of force.
  (3) Understanding of the legal, departmental, and psychological
      consequences of fatal force.

WEST VIRGINIA[9]

- Police Ethics

- Police Minority Relations

- Communication Skills

- Crisis Intervention

- Public Speaking

- Handling Abnormal Persons

WISCONSIN

- Human Relations
  (1) Understanding of the problems arising from behavior conflicts.
  (2) Explanation of the relationship between motivation and be-
      havior.
  (3) Development of insights by an officer for understanding and
      controlling own emotions.
  (4) Study of the causes of anti-authority feelings.

- Racial and Ethnical Differences
  (1) Understanding of the differences in backgrounds, customs,
      and basic beliefs of various ethnic and racial groups.
  (2) Study of the ways to function with objectivity and lack of
      prejudice while dealing with ethnic groups.

- Effective Verbal Communications
  (1) Study of skills to improve verbal ability in interpersonal com-
      munications.
  (2) Knowledge of the difference between fact, hearsay, and as-
      sumption.

- How to Recognize and Handle Emotionally Disturbed People
  (1) Understanding of the symptoms and unusual behavior of the
      mentally and emotionally disturbed.
  (2) Knowledge of the safety procedures in handling such cases.
  (3) Study of the mechanism for rendering assistance to the emo-
      tionally and mentally handicapped.
  (4) Knowledge of various legal provisions.
  (5) Information about referral agencies.

- Crisis Intervention Techniques
  (1) Understanding of the traumatic and emotional mental state of

a victim due to criminal incidents or other happenings.

(2) Knowledge of sympathetic treatment and other defusing techniques.

(3) Identification of the methods for prevention of repetition of such incidents.

- Police and Juveniles

  (1) Study of the ways that can help improve relationships between the police and juveniles.

  (2) Study of the causes which give rise to adverse opinions on both sides.

  (3) Discussion of the ways the police can prevent crime and recidivism among juveniles.

- Professional Ethics and Police Image

  (1) Understanding of the need for ethical conduct.

  (2) Awareness of the importance of police integrity.

  (3) Discussion of the police officer as an example to the community.

  (4) Knowledge of the Code of Ethics.

WYOMING

- Professional Orientation

  (1) Discussion of police professionalism and status of the police.

  (2) Understanding of the possible contradiction between policeman's concept of his role and public perception of it.

  (3) Discussion of the need for public assistance for the police and recognition of its importance.

  (4) Understanding of discretion and consequences of selective enforcement of law.

  (5) Knowledge of external and internal pressures giving rise to subculture.

  (6) Understanding of the need for police responsiveness toward community demands.

  (7) Knowledge of adverse public reaciton to police tendency to shield guilty colleagues.

  (8) Discussion of honesty, truthfulness, coercion, corruption, courtesy, and sensitivity to unethical conduct of fellow officers.

  (9) Understanding of communication, barriers to effective communication, and the relationship between officer's safety, and effective communication.

  (10) Discussion of police professionalism and the barriers to it.

- Professional Skills

  (1) Instruction on personal and interpersonal coping skills.

  (2) Discussion of various oral, written, behavioral methods, and

techniques for effective performance in interaction situations.
(3) Study of crisis intervention, stress management, and interpersonal communications as professional skills.

Notes

1. The courses titled Community Service Concept, Community
Attitudes and Influences, and Citizen Evaluation have not been discussed here since they are identical to the original California courses
analyzed later.

2. No descriptive material could be obtained in regard to the
course entitled, Special Communication--Deaf and Hearing Impaired.

3. In Hawaii, individual instructors are responsible for teaching the courses without guidelines from the POST commission.   Hence,
no guidelines were available at the Honolulu Police Department, which
supplied us with the course information.

4. The available descriptive material was very limited and,
therefore, the elements are brief.

5. The influence of California in New Mexico courses can be
observed clearly.

6. Within a comprehensive course extending over 16 hours,
police ethics, community relations, minority relations, and crowd behavior, etc., are taught.

7. According to Robert Nardi, Director, Bureau of Training
Education, Pennsylvania Police Academy, there are 22 certified school
in the state which are responsible for teaching the human relations
courses.   Hence, only brief outlines of the courses are maintained
by the POST commission in that state.

8. The details are not available in regard to these courses.

9. The course details are not available.

Appendix C:

LETTER TO POST COMMISSIONS

January 23, 1985

Dear   :

Based on my previous research, I am presently writing a book on police human relations which will be published by Scarecrow Press (Metuchen, New Jersey). Among other things, it will contain an account of state-mandated basic recruit training in human relations. I will attempt to present an accurate picture of your basic recruit program in this area with which I am generally familiar.

The purpose of this letter is to seek a little clarification needed in connection with the book and inform you of the new endeavor.

When I wrote to you in 1983, I mentioned that human relations training was likely to cover topics like these:

- Police Ethics
- Communication Skills
- Crowd Behavior
- Handling Stress

- Minority Relations
- Battered Women
- Police Role in Democracy
- Community or Citizen Relations

- Minority or Ethnic Subculture
- Crisis Intervention
- Perception Skills
- Dealing with Variant Behavior

In response, you sent me materials on many similar courses mandated in your state (please see enclosure). It is not, however, correct to assume that all these courses are actually included in your human relations block of instruction since some of these are also taught in other blocks of instruction. Also, I am not sure of the time allotted for each individual course. I need to determine precisely the offerings (subjects/topics) you view as human relations courses and the time allocated for each. Kindly insert the information in the enclosed table designed to minimize your time commitment, and mail it to me in the envelope provided. I do realize that your time is precious and your schedule heavy.

Hopefully, the proposed book will offer an informed analysis of state-mandated training and your pioneering efforts will be appreciated by a larger audience at national and international levels. Your assistance will be gratefully acknowledged in the book.

In case I can do anything for you, please do not hesitate to call me at (309) 298-1631 or 298-1038. I will be glad to assist you with your training program, particularly in regard to human relations. I have spent twenty years in policing which motivates me to work for the improvement of police training and hence, this enthusiasm.

Again, thank you for your support and cooperation. I look forward to hearing from you.

Yours sincerely,

Dilip K. Das, Ph.D.

cdg
enclosures

TABLE 1
HUMAN RELATIONS COURSES

Total hours of basic training required _____

Course Nomenclature	Time Allotted	Block of Instruction

Remarks:

Please return to: Dilip Das
                   Department of Law Enforcement Administration
                   Western Illinois University
                   Macomb, Illinois 61455

Appendix D:

ORIENTATION IN COURSES

NEW JERSEY

UNIT TITLE: Use of Force

4.21 UNIT GOAL: The trainee will understand when a police officer is justified under N.J.S.A. 2C in using force, including
deadly force, and will be aware of the consequences that
might result from the use of unlawful force.

PERFORMANCE OBJECTIVES:

4.21.1 The trainee will define each of the following terms and give
examples of each:

A. Force
B. Deadly Force
C. Unlawful force
D. Serious bodily harm
E. Minimal necessary force

4.21.2 The trainee will explain the general principle regarding the
use of force in law enforcement. The explanation will include
the limitations on the use of force, as specified in 2C.

4.12.3 The trainee will list circumstances when it is proper for a
police officer to use nondeadly force.

4.21.4 Given hypothetical situations where force may be necessary,
the trainee will state whether force is necessary in each
situation, and, if so, will identify the type of force that may
be used.

4.12.5 The trainee will list circumstances when it is proper for a
police officer to use deadly force.

4.21.6 The trainee will list the crimes for which a police officer may use deadly force to thwart commission or prevent escape after commission.

4.21.7 The trainee will list the considerations which a police officer must take into account when faced with a situation calling for the use of deadly force. These conditions will minimally include:

A. Type of crime and suspect involved
B. Threat to lives of innocent persons
C. Environment
D. Law
E. Officer's present capabilities
F. Capabilities of suspect's weapon(s)
G. Immediacy of threat

4.12.8 Given hypothetical situations where deadly force may be necessary, the trainee will state whether to shoot or not to shoot in each situation.

4.21.9 The trainee will describe his/her agency's policy concerning the use of warning shots.

4.21.10 The trainee will list five types of sanctions a police officer might face as a result of an improper use of force.

VIRGINIA

4.1   Laws on Use of Force

Learning Goal: The officer shall know the laws pertaining to the use of weapons and deadly force by law enforcement officers.

PERFORMANCE OBJECTIVES:

To meet the performance objective the officer shall:

4.1.1   Describe the fundamental elements of case law and statutory law pertaining to the justifiable use of deadly force by a law enforcement officer.

4.1.1.1. Define the elements of justifiable use of deadly force.

4.1.1.2 Explain the legal relationship between fear and the use of deadly force.

4.1.1.3 List and explain the factors and situations an officer must consider when faced with the use of deadly force.

4.1.1.4 Given audio-visual presentations or word-picture descriptions depicting situations where deadly force may be necessary, state (with each situation) whether deadly force is justified and reasonable.

4.1.1.5 Given audio-visual presentations or word-picture descriptions involving homicide by a law enforcement officer, identify when the homicide is justifiable.

WASHINGTON

12.1 USE OF FORCE

Learning Goal: The student will learn to identify the use of force and when it may be used by a police officer.

PERFORMANCE OBJECTIVES:

The student will:

12.1.1 Identify what is meant by the term "use of force."

12.1.2 Identify the "spectrum of force."

12.1.3 Identify and understand the statutory provisions (RCW) which allow an officer to use force.

12.1.4 Become familiar with other factors which affect use of force.

12.2 MISUSE OF FORCE

Learning Goal: The student will learn some of the causes and errors which result in misuse of force.

PERFORMANCE OBJECTIVES:

The student will:

12.2.1 Identify typical problems which cause misuse of force to occur.

12.2.2 Identify common errors by officers which increase the likelihood of misuse of force.

12.3 FATAL FORCE

Learning Goal: The student will learn the laws which allow, and the other factors which impact, the use of fatal force.

PERFORMANCE OBJECTIVES:

The student will:

12.3.1 Identify the laws which allow and define lawful use of fatal force by an officer.

12.3.2 Identify other factors which impact the use of fatal force.

12.4   EFFECTS OF FATAL FORCE

Learning Goal: The student will learn the different procedures and administrative actions that may take place after use of fatal force, as well as the personal changes that may occur.

PERFORMANCE OBJECTIVES:

The student will:

12.4.1 Identify typical department procedures which take place after use of fatal force.

12.4.2 Become familiar with typical firearms review board procedures.

12.4.3 Become familiar with the coroner's inquest process.

12.4.4 Identify personal changes which may take place in an officer who uses fatal force.

ADDITIONAL REFERENCES

COMMUNITY RELATIONS

Albrecht, S. L., & Green, M. (1977). Attitudes towards the police and the larger attitude complex: implications for police-community relations. Crimonology, 15(1), 67-86.

Baddely, F. (1977). Los Angeles police community relations department. International Criminal Police Review, p. 215-217.

Barret, C. T., Renner, K. E., & Moore, T. (1979-80). Problem interaction between the police and the public. Crime et/and Justice, 7-8(2), 113-118.

Brown, J., & Howes, G. (1975). The police and the community. Farnborough, Hants, (England): Saxon House.

Brown, W. P. (1975). Local policing--a three dimensional task analysis. Journal of Criminal Justice, 3(1), 1-15.

Carlson, H. M., & Sutton, M. S. (1979). Some factors in community evaluation of police street performance. American Journal of Community Psychology, 7(6), 583-591.

Charles, M. T. (1980). Utilization of attitude surveys in the police decision-making process. Journal of Police Science and Administration, 8(3), 294-303.

Coffey, A., Eldefonso, E., & Hartinger, W. (1971). Police-community relations. Englewood Cliffs, NJ: Prentice-Hall.

Cohn, A. W., & Viano, E. (Eds.). (1976). Police-community relations: images, roles, and realities. Philadelphia: Lippincott.

Cromwell, P. F. (1977). Issues in police-community relations. In D. T. Shanahan (Ed.), Administration of justice system--an introduction. Boston: Holbrook.

Decker, S. H. (1981). Citizen attitudes toward the police--a review of past findings and suggestions for future police. Journal of Police Science and Administration, 9(1), 80-87.

Decker, S. H., Smith, R. L., & Uhlman, T. M. (1979). Does anything work? An evaluation of urban police innovations. In R.
Baker & F. A. Meyer, Jr. (Eds.), Evaluating alternative law enforcement policies. Lexington, MA: Heath.

Earle, H. H. (1980). Police community relations--a crisis in our
time. Springfield, IL: Charles C. Thomas.

Farmer, R. E., & Kowalewski, V. A. (1976). Law enforcement and
community relations. Reston, VA: Reston Publishing.

Garbor, I. R., & Low, C. (1973). The police role in the community.
Criminology, 10(4), 383-409.

Goldsmith, J., & Goldsmith, S. S. (1974). Police community--
dimensions of an occupational subculture. Pacific Palisades, CA:
Palisades Publishers.

Hewitt, W. H., & Newman, C. L. (eds.). (1970). Police-community
relations: an anthology and bibliography. Mineola, NY: Foundation
Press, 1970.

Kelly, J. A. (1973). An appraisal of the attitudes of police officers
toward the concept of police-community relations. Journal of Police
Science and Administration, 1(2), 224-231.

Kersetter, W. A. (1981). Patrol decentralization--An assessment.
Journal of Police Science and Administration, 9(1), 48-60.

Klyman, F. I., & Kruckenberg, J. (1979). A national survey of
police community relations training. Journal of Police Science and
Administration, 7(1), 72-79.

Mayhall, P. D. (1979). Community relations and administration of
justice. New York: Wiley.

Radelet, L. A. (1980). Police and the community. Encino, CA:
Glencoe.

Reddy, W. B., & Lansky, L. M. (1975). Nothing but the facts--and
some observations on norms and values. Journal of Social Issues,
31(1), 123-138.

Sherman, L. W. (1977). Law enforcement in a democracy: a review
of policing a free society. Criminal Law Bulletin, 13, 401-409.

Tobias, J. J. (1972). Police and public in the United Kingdom.
Journal of Contemporary History. 7(1-2), 201-220.

Wagner, A. E. (1980). Complaints against the police--the complaint.
Journal of Police Science and Administration, 8(3), 247-252.

Wasikhongo, J. M. N. (1976). The role and character of police in
    Africa and Western Countries: a comparative approach to police
    isolation. International Journal of Crimonology and Penology, 4(4),
    383-396.

Watson, N. A. (1966). Police community relations. Gaithersburg, MD:
    International Association of Chiefs of Police Research & Develop-
    ment Division.

_____. (ed). (1965). Police and the changing community:
    selected readings. Washington, DC: International Association of
    Chiefs of Police.

_____. (1980). Police service and police-community relations.
    International Criminal Police Review, 35(335), 42-58.

White, M. F., & Menke, B. A. (1982). On assessing the mood of
    the public toward the police: some conceptual issues. Journal of
    Criminal Justice, 10(3) 211-230.

Whitehouse, J. E. (1978). Historical perspectives on the police com-
    munity service functions. In P. F. Cromwell, Jr., & G. Keefer
    (eds.), Police-Community relations St. Paul, MN: West.

CRIME PREVENTION

Brody, J. P. (1981). Towards a popular Justice in the United
    States--the dialectics of community action. Contemporary Crisis,
    5(2), 155-192.

Campbell, D. C. (1984). Youth and crime prevention: an untapped
    resource. The Police Chief, 51(2), 28-29.

Formby, W. A., & Smykla, J. O. (1981). Citizen awareness in crime
    prevention: do they really get involved? Journal of Police Science
    and Administration, 9(4), 398-403.

Goldstein, H. Police response to urban crises. Public Administration
    Review, 28(5), 417-423.

Kelling, G. L. (1978). Police field services and crime. Crime and
    Delinquency, 24(2), 173-184.

Strangler, J., & Beedle, S. (1981). Institutionalization--a survey of
    community attitudes toward crime prevention. Portland, OR: Port-
    land Bureau of Police Crime Prevention Division.

_____, & _____. (1981). Evaluation of the residential security
    survey program. Portland, OR: Portland Bureau of Police Crime
    Prevention Division.

U.S. National Advisory Commission on Criminal Justice Standards and Goals. (1973). A national strategy to reduce crime. Washington, DC: U.S. Government Printing Office.

DOMESTIC VIOLENCE/CRISIS/CONFLICTS

Adelman, C. S. (1977). Teaching police crisis intervention techniques. Victimology, 2(1), 123-126.

Arthur, G. L., Sisson, P. J., & McClung, C. E. (1977). Domestic disturbances--a major police dilemma, and how one major city is handling the problem. Journal of Police Science and Administration, 5(4), 421-429.

Axelberd, M., & Valle, J. (1978). Development of the behavioral scale for measuring police effectiveness in domestic disputes. Crisis intervention, 9(2), 69-80.

_____, & _____. (1979). Effects of family crisis intervention training on police behavior. Crisis Intervention, 10(1), 18-27.

Bae, R. P. (1981). Ineffective crisis intervention techniques--the case of the police. In S. T. Letman, (ed.), Journal of Crime and Justice, 4, 61-82.

Bard, M. (1969). Family intervention police teams as a community mental health resource. Journal of Criminal Law, Criminology, and Police Science, 60(2), 247-250.

_____. (1970). Training police as specialists in family crisis intervention. Washington, DC: U. S. Government Printing Office.

_____. (1976). Issues in law enforcement: essays and case studies. Reston, VA: Reston Publishing.

_____. (1976). Role of law enforcement in the helping system. In J. Monahan (ed.), Community mental health and the criminal justice system. Elmsford, NY: Pergamon.

_____. (1979). The crime victim's book. New York: Basic Books.

_____. (1980). Functions of the police and justice system in family violence. In M. R. Green (ed.), Violence and the family. Boulder, CO: Westview.

_____, & Connolly, H. (1978). Police and family violence--policy and practice. In Battered Women--issues of public policy. Rockville, MD: National Institute of Justice/National Criminal Justice Reference Service Microfiche Program.

_____, & Zacker, J. (1976). Police and interpersonal conflict--
third-party intervention approaches, Washington, DC: Police
Foundation.

_____, & _____. (1978). How police handle explosive squabbles.
In D. E. J. MacNamara (ed.) Readings in Criminal Justice, 1978-
1979. Guilford, CT: Dushkin.

Bell, Daniel J. (1984). The police response to domestic violence:
an exploratory study. Police Studies, 7(1), 23-30.

Berk, S. F., & Loseke, D. R. (1981). Handling family violence--
situational determinants of police arrest in domestic disturbances.
Law and Society Review, 15(2), 317-346.

Breslin, W. J. (1978). Police intervention in domestic confrontations.
Journal of Police Science and Administration, 6(3), 293-302.

Cesnick, B. I., Puls, M., & Pierce, N. (1977). Law enforcement
and crisis intervention services--a critical relationship. Suicide
and Life-threatening behavior, 7(4), 211-215.

Coffey, A. (1974). Police intervention into family crisis: the role
of law enforcement in family problems. Santa Cruz, CA: Davis.

Danish, S. J., & Ferguson, N. (1973). Training police to intervene
in human conflict. In J. R. Snibbe, et al. (eds.), Urban policeman in transition--a psychological and sociological review. Springfield, IL: Charles C. Thomas.

Day, L. E. (1978). Technical assistance project--domestic violence
survey-report. Chicago: Illinois Law Enforcement Commission
Statistical Analysis Center.

Dow, M. (1976). Police involvement. In M. Borland (ed.), Violence
in the family. Atlantic Highlands, NJ: Humanities Press.

Driscoll, J. M., Meyer, R. G., & Schanie, C. F. (1976). Training
police in family crisis intervention. In J. Monahan (ed.), Community mental health and the criminal justice system. New York:
Pergamon.

Dutton, D. G. (1980). Social-psychological research and relevant
speculation on the issue of domestic violence. In C. T. Griffiths
& M. Nance (eds.), Female offender, Burnaby, B.C.: Simon
Fraser University Criminology Research Centre.

_____. (1981). Training police officers to intervene in domestic
violence. In R. B. Stuart (ed.), Violent Behavior, pp. 173-202.
New York: Brunner/Mazel.

Ellison, K. W., Cross, J. P., & Genz, J. L. (1980). Training in stress management--a comprehensive program aimed at command staff, first line supervisors, officers, and recruits. Police Chief, 67(9), 27-31.

Erez, E. (1986). Intimacy, violence, and the police. Human Relations, 39(3), 265-281.

Fleming, J. (1978). Family violence--a look at the criminal justice system. In Domestic Violence, 1978. Washington, DC: U. S. Congress House Committee on Education and Labor.

Goldstein, A. P., Monti, P. J., Sardino, T. J., & Green, D. J. (1979). Police crisis intervention. Elmsford, NY: Pergamon.

Green, M. R. (1980). Violence and the family, Boulder, CO: Westview.

Hendricks, J. E. (1984). Death notification--the theory and practice of informing survivors. Journal of Police Science and Administration, 12(1), 109-116.

Hicks, R. D., & Dolphin, G. (1979). Avoiding family violence--the nonverbal behavior of police intervention at family fights. Police Chief, 46(3), 50-55.

Jaffee, P. E. (1974). Family Crisis intervention, etc. Unpublished doctoral dissertation, University of Florida.

Jolin, A. (1983). Domestic violence legislation--an impact assessment. Journal of Police Science and Administration, 11(4), 451-456.

Kennedy, D. B., & Homant, R. J. (1984). Battered women's evaluation of the police response. Victimology, 9(1), 174-179.

Keogh, James. (1980). Crisis intervention, a practical approach. The Police Chief, 47(1), 56-57.

Langley, R., Levy, R. C. Wife abuse and the police response. Washington, DC: U.S. Department of Justice Federal Bureau of Investigation.

Lerman, L. G. (1982). Elements and standards for criminal justice programs on domestic violence. Response, 5(6), 9-14.

Liebman, D. A., & Schwartz, J. A. (1973). Police programs in domestic crisis intervention--a review. In J. R. Snibbe et al. (eds.), Urban policeman in transition--a psychological and sociological review. Springfield, IL: Charles C. Thomas.

Loving, N. (1981). Spouse abuse--a curriculum guide for police trainers. Washington, DC: Police Executive Research Forum.

Martin, J. P. (1978). Violence and the family. New York: Wiley.

Maynard, P. Maynard, N, McCubbin, H. I., & Shao, D. (1980). Family life and the police profession--coping patterns wives employ in managing job stress and the family environment. Family Relations, 29(4), 495-501.

Mulvey, E. P., Reppucci, N. D. (1981). Police crisis intervention training--an empirical investigation. American Journal of Community Psychology, 9(5), 527-546.

Murphy, R. B., McKay, E., Schwartz, J. A., & Liebman, D. A. (1976). Training patrolmen as crisis intervention instructors. Gaithersburg, MD: International Association of Chiefs of Police. Reprinted from Police Chief.

Nemetz, W. C. (1977). Crisis intervention. The Police Chief, 44 (4), 16, 70.

Pagelow, M. D. (1981). Secondary battering and alternatives of female victims to spouse abuse. In Lee H. Bowker (ed.), Women and crime in America. Riverside, NJ: Macmillan.

Parnas, R. L. (1967). Police response to the domestic disturbance. Wisconsin Law Review, 914.

Pearce, J. B., & Snortum, J. R. (1983). Police effectiveness in handling disturbance calls--an evaluation of crisis intervention training. Criminal Justice and Behavior, 10(1), 71-92.

Roy, M. (ed.). (1982). An analysis of domestic battering. New York: Van Nostrand Reinhold.

Schreiber, F. B. (1978). Domestic disturbances--officer safety and calming techniques, Northbrook, IL: MTI.

Schudson, C. B. (1978). Criminal justice system as family--trying the impossible for battered women. In Domestic Violence, 1978. Washington, DC: U. S. Congress House Committee on Education and Labor.

Scott, J. F. (1976). Police authority and the low-income Black family--an area of needed research. In L. E. Gary & L. P. Brown (eds.), Crime and its impact on the black community. Washington, DC: Howard University Institute for Urban Affairs and Research.

Sherman, L. W., & Berk, R. A. (1981). Police responses to domestic assault--preliminary findings. Washington, DC: Police Foundation.

Stratton, John. (1976). Law enforcement's participation in crisis
counseling for rape victims. The Police Chief, 43(3), 46-49.

Walter, J. D. (1981). Police in the middle--a study of small city
policy intervention in domestic disputes. Journal of Police Science
and Administration, 9(3), 243-260.

Wilt, G. M., Bannon, J. D., Breedlove, R. K., Sandker, D. M.,
Michaelson, S., Fox, P. B., & Keenish, J. W. (1977). Domestic
violence and the police--studies in Detroit and Kansas City.
Washington, DC: Police Foundation.

Zlotnick, J. (1979). Victimology and crisis intervention training
with police. Crisis Intervention, 10(1), 2-17.

EDUCATION FOR THE POLICE

Bell, D. J. (1979). Police role and higher education. Journal of
Police Science and Administration, 20(10), 467-475.

Bennett, R. R. (1978). Effects of education on police values and
performance--a multivariate analysis of an exploratory model. In
C. Wellford (ed.), Qualitative Studies in Criminology. Beverly
Hills, CA: Sage Publications.

Berg, B. L., True, E. J., & Gertz, M. G. (1984). Police, riots and
alienation. Journal of Police Science and Administration, 12(2), 186-
190.

Finckenauer, J. D. (1975). Higher Education and police discretion.
Journal of Police Science and Administration, 3(4), 450-457.

Germann, A. C. (1971). Changing the police--the impossible dream.
The Journal of Criminal Law, Criminology, and Police Science,
62(3), 416-421.

Germann, A. C. (1976). Law enforcement; a look into the future.
The Police Chief, 43(11), 24-26, 28.

Gilbert, J. N. (1974). From the street to the classroom. Police
Chief, 41(8), 26-27.

Hart, W. (1979). Ph.D.'s as police--eggheads or experts. Police
Magazine, 2(2), 20-23.

Hoover, L. T. (1975). Police educational characteristics and curricula. Washington, DC: Government Printing Office.

Kuldan, V. D. (1974). Education--punishment or reward. Police
Chief, 41(8), 25-26.

Lynch, G. W. (1976). Criminal Justice Higher Education--some perspectives. Police Chief, 43(8), 63-65.

_____. (1976). The contributions of higher educaiton in ethical behavior in law enforcement. Journal of Criminal Justice, 4(4), 285-290.

Nelson, C. (1980). The third force--an international police association scholarship report. Police Journal, 53(2), 138-146.

Sanderson, B. E. (1976). Police officers--the relationship of college education to job performance. Unpublished master's thesis, California State University.

Santarelli, D. E. (1974). Education for concepts--training for skills. Police Chief, 41(8), 20 & 76.

Shanahan, D. T. (1977). Education for police service. In D. T. Shanahan (ed.), Administration of Justice System. Boston: Holbrook.

Sherman, L. W. (1978). College education for police--the reform that failed? Police Studies, 1(4) 32-38.

HISTORICAL ROOTS OF AMERICAN POLICE

Amidon, H. T. (1977). Law enforcement from the beginning to the English bobby. Journal of Police Science and Administration, 5(3), 355-367.

Carte, G. E. (1976). Technology versus personnel--notes on the history of police personnel reform. Journal of Police Science and Administration, 4(3), 285-297.

Carte, G. E., & Carte, E. H. (1975). Police reform in the United States. Berkeley: University of California.

Douthit, N. (1975). Enforcement and nonenforcement roles in policing: A historical inquiry. Journal of Police Science and Administration, 3(3), 336-345.

Haller, M. H. (1971). Civic reforms and police leadership, Chicago, 1905-1935. In H. Hahn (ed.), Police in urban society. Beverly Hills, CA: Sage Publications.

Haller, M. (1976). Historical roots of police behavior, Chicago, 1890-1925. Law and Society Review, 10(1), 303-324.

Lyman, J. L. The metropolitan police act of 1829: an analysis of certain events influencing the passage and character of the Metropolitan Police Act in England. The Journal of Criminal Law, Criminology, and Police Science, 55(1), 141-154.

Miller, W. R. (1976). Cops and bobbies: police authority in New York and London, 1930-1970. Chicago: University of Chicago.

Monkkonen, E. H. (1981). Police in urban America 1860-1920. Cambridge, New York: Cambridge University Press.

Murphy, P. V. (1976). Development of the urban police. Current History, 70(417), 245-248.

Reith, C. (1952). The blind eye of history: a study of origins of the present police era. London: Faber and Faber.

_____. (1938). The police idea: its history and evolution in England in the 18th century and after. London: Oxford University Press.

_____. (1943). British police and the democratic ideal. London: Oxford University Press.

Richardson, J. F. (1970). The New York police: colonial times to 1901. New York: Oxford University Press.

_____. (1974). Urban police in the United States. Port Washington, NY: Kennikat Press.

Walker, S. (1977). Critical history of police reform. Lexington, MA: Heath.

HUMAN RELATIONS

Adams, H. J., & Spicer, C. A. (1983). Humanism as repression--counselors training police. Counselor Education and Supervision, 21(3), 181-186.

Alderson, J. C. (1979). New philosophy for police. Police Review, 87(4498), 532-534, 536, & 538-539.

Bard, M. Role of law enforcement in the helping system. Community Mental Health Journal, 7(2), 151-160.

_____, & Zacker, J. (1976). The police and interpersonal conflict: Third-party intervention approaches. Washington, DC: Police Foundation.

Blumberg, S. K. (1979). Humanistic guidelines for the law enforcement profession. The Police Chief, 46(3), 46.

Boer, B. L., & McIver, B. C. (1973). Human relations training--laboratories and team policing. Journal of Police Science and Administration, 7(2), 162-167.

Coffey, A., Eldefonso, E., & Hartinger, W. (1976). Human relations--law enforcement in a changing community (2nd ed). Englewood Cliffs, NJ: Prentice-Hall.

Danish, S., & Brodsky, S. (1973). Illinois-state police--police human relations training. Carbondale: Southern Illinois University Center for Study of Crime, Delinquency, and Corrections.

Davis, Philip. (1983). Toward a philosophy of law enforcement education. The Police Chief, 50(2), 48-49.

Edelwich, J., & Brodsky, A. (1980). Burn-out-stages of disillusionment in the helping professional. New York: Human Sciences.

Fischer, J., & Gochros, H. L. (1975). Human relations training. Police Law Quarterly, 5(1), 15-22.

Fitzpatrick, C. (1982). Audiovisual role play helps overcome problems in police human relations training. Training Aid Digest, 7 (2), 1 & 3.

Gazda, G. M. et al. (1977). Human relations development: a manual for educators. Boston: Allyn and Bacon.

Hall, E. T. (1978). Human relations training in local police department: Implications for program development. Dissertation Abstracts International, 39/11-B, 5555.

Henderson, G. (1974). Human relations: from theory to practice. Norman: University of Oklahoma Press.

_____. (1981). Police human relations. Springfield, IL: C. C. Thomas.

Kroeker, L. L., Forsyth, D. R., & Haase, R. F. (1974). Evaluation of a police-youth human relations program (EN). Professional Psychology, 5(2), 140-154.

MacGuire, R. J. (1979). Human dimension in urban policing--dealing with stress in the 1980s. Police Chief, 46(11), 26-27.

Maier, N. R. F. (1952). Principles of human relations. New York: Wiley.

Manella, F. L. (1971). Humanism in police training. Police Chief, 38(2), 26-28.

Miller, L. S., & Braswell, M. C. (1983). Human relations and police work. Waveland.

Reiser, M., & Steinberg, J. L. (1972). Police, 16(12), 12-16.

Russell, H. E., & Beigel, A. (1982). Understanding human behavior for effective police work--second edition. New York: Basic Books.

Siegel, A. I. (1963). Professional police human relations training. Springfield, IL: C. C. Thomas.

Silver, I. (1980). Humanistic training of the police: some preliminary reflections. Police Studies, 2(4), 3-11.

Sisson, P. J., Arthur, G. L., & Gazda, G. M. (1981). Human relations for criminal justice personnel. Boston: Allyn and Bacon.

Somers, A. (1982). Improving human relations between the Hispanic community and law enforcement. The Police Chief, 49(3), 32-33.

Stead, P. J. (1974). Humanism of command. Police Journal, 47(4), 283-289.

Watson, N. A. (1973). Issues in human relations. Gaithersburg, MD: International Association of Chiefs of Police.

NEGATIVE CONSEQUENCES OF POLICING

Bennett, R. R., & Corrigan, R. S. (1980). Police occupational solidarity--probing a determinant in the deterioration of police-citizen relations. Journal of Criminal Justice, 8(2), 111-122.

Conser, J. A. (1980). Literary review of the police subculture--its characteristics, impact, and policy implicaitons. Police Studies, 2(4), 46-54.

Dash, J., & Reiser, M. (1978). Suicide among police in urban law enforcement agencies. Journal of Police Science and Administration, 6(1), 18-21.

Farmer, R. E., & Lynn, H. M. (1980). The prevention model for stress reduction: a concept paper. Journal of Police Science and Administration, 8,(1), 54-60.

Holzman, H. R. (1977). Violence and dissent: a comparative analysis of police control of protest demonstrations in Japan and in the U.S. Abstracts on Police Science, 5(6), 337-351.

Johnson, D. L., & Luxenburg, J. (1983). Personality type and job stress. The Police Chief, 51(1), 52-53.

Keller, P. A. (1978). A psychological view of the police officer paradox. The Police Chief, 45(4), 24-25.

Kroes, W. H., Margolis, B. L., & French, J. R. P., Jr. (1974). Social support, occupational stress, and health. Journal of Police Science and Administration, 2(2), 145-155.

_____. (1980). Society's victim--the policeman: An analysis of job stress in policing. Springfield, IL: C. C. Thomas.

Lawrence, R. A. (1984). Police stress and personality factors. Journal of Criminal Justice, 12(3), 247-263.

Leitner, L. A., Posner, I., & Lester, D. (1983). Stress, mood, and job satisfaction in police chiefs. The Police Chief, 50(1), 54-55.

Lester, D., Leitner, L. A., & Posner, I. (1983). Stress and its management for police officers. Police Journal, 56(4), 324-329.

Malloy, T. E., & Mays, G. L. (1984). Police stress hypothesis--a critical evaluation. Criminal Justice and Behavior, 11(2), 197-224.

Maslach, C., & Jackson, S. E. (1979). Burned-out cops and their families. Psychology Today, 12(12), 58-62.

Miller, J., & Fry, L. J. (1977). Work-related consequences of influence, respect, and solidarity in two law enforcement agencies. Sociology of Work and Occupations, 4(4), 451-478.

Milton, C. H., Halleck, J. W., Lardner, J., & Albrecht, G. L. (1981). In H. W. More, Jr. (ed.), Police use of deadly force. Cincinnati, OH: Andersen.

Muir, W. K., Jr. (1980). Power attracts violence. Annals of the American Academy of Political and Social Science, 48-52.

O'Neil, M. W., Hanewicz, W. B., Franway, L. M., & Cassidy-Riske, C. (1982). Stress inoculation training and job performance. Journal of Police Science and Administration, 10(4), 388-397.

Regoli, R. M., Poole, E. D., & Hewitt, J. D. (1979). Exploring the empirical relationship between police cynicism and work alienation. Journal of Police Science and Administration, 7(3), 336-339.

Scharf, P., & Binder, A. (1983). The badge and the bullet: police use of deadly force. New York: Praeger.

Scharf, P., Lenninger, R., and Marrero, D. (1979). Use of legal deadly force by police officers in a democratic society. In F. A.

Meyer & R. Baker (eds.), Determinants of law enforcement policies. Lexington, MA: Heath.

Sherman, L. W. (1980). Police and violence. Annals of the American Academy of Political and Social Science. 452, 1-12.

Shook, H. C. (1978). Pitfalls in policing. The Police Chief, 45(4), 8.

Spielberger, C. D., et al. (1981). The police stress survey: sources of stress in law enforcement. Washington, DC: U. S. Department of Justice.

Stratton, J. G. (1978). Police stress: an overview. Police Chief, 45, 58-62.

Swanton, B. (1981). Social isolation of police--structural determinants and remedies. Police Studies, 3(4), 14-21.

Territo, L., & Vetter, H. (1981). Stress and police personnel. Boston: Allyn and Bacon.

Terry, W. C., III. (1983). Police stress. In C. B. Klockars (ed.), Thinking about police: contemporary readings. New York: McGraw Hill.

Terry, W. C., III. (1983). Police stress, etc. Journal of Police Science and Administration, 11(2), 156-165.

Tifft, L. L. (1975). Control systems, social bases of power, and power exercise in police organizations. Journal of Police Science and Administration, 3(1), 66-76.

Tobias, J. J. (1980). Hazards beyond the hazards. Police Chief, 47(6), 48-51.

Toch, H. (1980). Mobilizing police expertise. Annals of the American Academy of Political and Social Science, 452, 53-62.

Violanti, J. M. (1983). Stress patterns in police work. Journal of Police Science and Administration, 11(2), 211-216.

_____, & Marshall, J. R. (1983). The police stress process. Journal of Police Science and Administration, 11(4), 389-394.

Westley, W. A. (1970). Violence and the police: a sociological study of law, custom, and morality. Cambridge, MA: MIT Press.

White, S. E., & Marino, K. E. (1983). Job attitudes and police stress. Journal of Police Science and Administration, 11(3), 264-274.

Wiechman, J. D. (1979). Police cynicism toward the judicial process. Journal of Police Science and Administration, 7(3), 340-345.

POLICE AND LAW

Adams, T. F. Law enforcement--an introduction to the police role in the criminal justice system (2nd ed.). Englewood Cliffs, NJ: Prentice-Hall.

Brandstatter, A. F., & Hyman, A. A. (1971). Fundamentals of law enforcement. Beverly Hills, CA: Glencoe Press.

Coffey, A., Eldefonso, E., & Grace, R. C. (1982). Principles of law enforcement: an overview of the justice system. New York: Wiley.

Eldefonso, E., & Coffey, A. (1981). Criminal law--history, philosophy, and enforcement. New York: Harper & Row.

Hepburn, J. R. (1981). Crime control, due process, and the measurement of police performance. Journal of Police Science and Administration, 9(1), 88-98.

Goldstein, H. (1968). Trial judges and the police. Crime and Delinquency, 14(1), 14-25.

Hall, J. (1953). Police and law in democratic society. Indiana Law Journal, 28(2), 133-177.

Kenney, J. P., & More, H. W., Jr. (1979). Principles of investigation. St. Paul, MN: West.

Marx, G. T. (1982). Who really gets stung: Some issues raised by the new police undercover work. Crime & Delinquency, 28(2), 165-193.

Murphy, P. V. (1976). Development of the urban police. Current History, 70(417), 245-248.

Ostrom, E. (1975). On righteousness, evidence, and reform: the police story. Urban Affairs Quarterly, 10, 464-486.

Park, A. J. (1981). Teaching the constitution. The Police Chief, 47(7), 60-64.

Perry, M. J. (1976). Abortion, public morals, and police power--ethical function of substantive due process. UCLA Law Review, 23(4), 689-736.

Sherman, L. W. (1980). Execution without trial--police homicide and the constitution. Vanderbilt Law Review, 33(71), 71-100.

Sherwin, S., & Renner, K. E. (1979). Respect for persons in a study of the use of force by police officers. Clinical Research, 27(1), 19-22.

Skolnick, J. H. (1982). Deception by police. Criminal Justice Ethics, 1(2), 40-54.

Tapp, J. L., & Levine, F. L. (1977). Law, justice, and the individual in society: psychological and legal issues. New York: Holt, Rinehart, and Winston.

Wiechman, D. J. (1979). Police cynicism toward the judicial process. Journal of Police Science and Administration, 7(3), 340-345.

Zalman, M. (1980). Future of criminal justice administration and its impact on civil liberties. Journal of Criminal Justice, 8(5), 275-286.

Zimring, F. E., & Frase, R. S. (1980). Criminal Justice system--materials on the administration and reform of the criminal law. Boston: Little Brown.

POLICE AND POLITICS

Baldwin, R., & Kinsey, R. (1982). Police, powers, and politics. London: Quarter Books.

Bruce, J. (1976). Taking care of labor: police in American politics. Theory and Society, 3, 89-117.

Marenin, O. (1982). Parking tickets and class repression: the concept of policing in critical theories of criminal justice. Contemporary Crises, 6, 241-266.

Meyer, F. A., Jr., & Baker, R. J. (1979). Determinants of law enforcement policies. Lexington, MA: Lexington Books.

Platt, A., & Cooper, L. (eds.). (1974). Policing America. Englewood Cliffs, NJ: Prentice-Hall.

Spitzer, S. The political economy of policing. In D. F. Greenberg (ed.) (1981). Crime and capitalism. Palo Alto, CA: Mayfield.

Sayre, W. S. & Kautman, H. (1960). Governing New York City politics on the metropolis. New York: Russell Sage Foundation.

POLICE BEHAVIOR

Brent, E. E., Jr., & Sykes, R. E. (1979). Mathematical model of symbolic interaction between police and suspects. Behavioral Science, 24(6), 388-402.

Collins, E. D. (1979). Methods of handling complaints against the police an annotated bibliography. Chicago: Council of Planning Librarians Bibliographies.

Ferdinand, T. N. (1980). Police attitudes and police organization: some interdepartmental and cross-cultural comparisons. Police Studies, 3(3), 46-60.

Friedrich, R. J. (1977). Impact of organizational individual, and situational factors on police behavior. Unpublished doctoral dissertation, University of Michigan, Ann Arbor.

Grewirtz, D., Parker, L. C., & York, M. W. (1977). Self-disclosure among police and college students. Psychological Reports, 41(1), 935-941.

Leonard, V. A. (1980). Fundamentals of law enforcement. St. Paul, MN: West.

Lovitt, R. (1976). Psychological consultation to a police training academy--problems and opportunities. Community Mental Health Journal, 12(3), 313-319.

Nash, P. W. Trait study of police officers by education level. Unpublished doctoral dissertation, Florida Atlantic University.

Philips, J. E. D. (1976). Sociological analysis of occupational stress and job satisfaction of police in selected rural and urban perishes in Louisiana. Unpublished doctoral dissertation, Louisiana State University.

Poole, E. D., & Regoli, R. M. (1979). Examination of the effects of professionalism on cynicism. Social Science Journal, 6(3), 59-66.

Primeau, C. C., Helton, J. A., Baxter, J. C., & Rozelle, R. M. (1975). Examination of the concept of police officer held by several social groups. Journal of Police Science and Administration, 3(2), 189-196.

Rokeach, M., Miller, M. G., & Snyder, J. A. (1977). Value gap between police and policed. In J. L. Tapp & F. J. Levine (eds.), Law, justice, and the individual in society. New York: Holt, Rinehart, & Winston.

Swank, C. J. (1978). Dogmatic and authoritarian personality relationships between the police, the campus, and the community.
Abstracts on Police Science, 6(3), 123-131.

Sykes, R. E., & Brent, E. E. (1980). Regulation of interaction by
police--a systems view of taking charge. Criminology, 18(2),
182-197.

Terris, B. J. (1967). The role of the police. Annals of the American Academy of Political and Social Science, 374, 58-69.

POLICE ETHICS

Bayley, D. H. (1978). Police corruption in Britain and America.
Police Studies, iv(4), 16-23.

Carlson, H. M., & Sutton, M. S. (1975). Effects of different police
roles on attitudes and values. Journal of Psychology, 91(1),
57-64.

Clement, R. C. (1976). The police, the media, and ethics. The
Police Chief, 43(3), 8.

Cochrane, R., Butler, & Anthony, J. P. (1980). The values of
police officers, recruits, and civilians in England. Journal of
Police Science and Administration, 8(2), 205-211.

Doucet, R. J. (1978). Training: a proactive approach towards
corruption and integrity problems. The Police Chief, 45(1), 32-
33.

Eastman, G. D. (1981). Education, professionalism, and law enforcement in historical perspective. Journal of Police Science and
Administration, 9(2), 119-130.

Felkenes, G. T. (1984). Attitudes of police officers toward their
professional ethics. Journal of Criminal Justice, 12(3), 211-220.

Flammang, C. J. (1975). Let's stop talking ethics. Police Chief,
42(1), 66-69.

Gardner, J. D. (1976). Our ethical future ... condoned or con-
demned. The Police Chief, 43(11), 32-33.

Goldstein, H. (1975). Police corruption: a perspective on its nature
and control. Washington, DC: Police Foundation.

Hansen, D. A. (1973). Police Ethics. Springfield, IL: C. C.
Thomas.

Heffernan, W. C. (1982). Two approaches to police ethics. Criminal Justice Review. 7(1), 28-35.

_____. (1981). Criminal justice ethics: an emerging discipline. Police Studies, 4(3), 24-28.

Kooken, D. L. (1957). Ethics in police service. Springfield, IL: C. C. Thomas.

Kornblum, A. N. (1976). The moral hazards: Police strategy for honesty and ethical behavior. Lexington, MA: Lexington Books.

Moore, M. D. (1975). Law enforcement code of ethics--a guide to police/community relations. Police Chief, 42(3), 56.

Muscari, P. G. (1984). Police corruption and organizational structures: An ethicist's view. Journal of Criminal Justice, 12(3), 235-245.

Olivet, G. D. (1976). Ethical philosophy in police training. Police Chief, 43(8), 48 & 50.

Potts, L. W. (1981). Higher education, ethics, and the police. Journal of Police Science and Administration, 9(2), 131-134.

Sherman, L. W. (1978). Controlling police corruption--the effects of reform policies--summary report. Washington, DC: Superintendent of Documents, GPO.

Sherman, L. (1982). Learning police ethics. Criminal Justice Ethics, 1(1), 10-19.

Sherwin, S., & Renner, K. E. (1979). Respect for persons in a study of the use of force by police officers. Clinical Research, 27(1), 19-22.

Skolnick, J. H. (1982). Deception by Police. Criminal Justice Ethics. 1(2), 40-54.

Stefanic, M. D. (1981). Police ethics in changing society--fundamental beliefs and concepts of right and wrong should not change. Police Chief, 48(5), 62-64.

Teevan, J. J., Jr., & Dolnick, B. (1973). Values of the police--a reconsideration and interpretation. Journal of Police Science and Administration, 1(3), 366-369.

Watkinson, J. (1979). A declaration on the police. The Police Journal, 52(2), 126-139.

POLICE TRAINING

Berkeley, G. (1969). The European police: challenge and change. Public Administration Review, 28(5), 407-416.

Campbell, J. M., & Formby, W. A. (1977). Law enforcement training and education--a job-related approach. Journal of Police Science and Administration, 5(4), 469-473.

Craig, R. L., & Bittel, L. R. (eds.). (1967). Training and development handbook. New York: McGraw-Hill.

Doig, J. W. (1968). Police problems, proposals, and strategies for change. Public Administration Review, 28(5), 393-406.

Earl, H. H. (1973). Police recruit training. Springfield, IL: C. C. Thomas.

Engle, C. D. (1974). Police training in noncrime function. The Police Chief (41(6), 61-65).

Gardner, J. M., & Veno, A. (1976). Community psychology approach to policing training. Professional Psychology, 7(4), 437-441.

_____. (1969). Police response to urban crisis. Public Administration Review, 18(5), 407-416.

Harlick, R. J. (1966). Report of the President's Commission on Crime in the district of Columbia. Washington, DC: Government Printing Office.

_____. (1968). Police recruit training. In Municipal Yearbook, (1968). Chicago: International City Manager's Associaiton.

Harris, R. N. (1973). The police academy: an inside view. New York: Wiley.

Kirkpatrick, D. L. (1977). Evaluating training programs: evidence v. proof. Training and Development Journal, 11, 9-12.

Lester, R. L. (1973). Training research: identification of training need. Personnel Journal, 52(3).

Parker, T. C. (1973). Evaluation: the forgotten finale of training. Personnel Journal, 50(6), 59-63.

Preiss, J. J., & Ehrlich, H. J. (1966). An examination of the role theory: the case of the state police. Lincoln: University of Nebraska Press.

Regoli, R. M., Poole, E. D., & Walls, W. L. (1980). Assessing the effect of education on police officer attitudes toward the police agency and its supervisors. Police Science Abstracts, 8(6), 335-341.

Reith, C. (1952). The blind eye of history: a study of the origins of the present police era. London: Faber and Faber.

Roberts, A. R. (1978). Training police social workers--a neglected area of social work educaiton. Journal of Education for Social Work, 14(2), 98-103.

Sherrid, S. D. (1979). Changing police values. In C. D. Spielberger (ed.), Police selection and evaluation. Washington, DC: Hemisphere.

Stratton, J., & Knowles, G. (1978). Police department Psychologist. International Criminal Police Review, 33(320), 210-212.

U. S. President's Commission on Law Enforcement. (1967). Task force report: the police. Washington, DC: U.S. Government Printing Office.

Wasserman, R., & Couper, D. (1974). Training and education. In O. E. Stahl & R. A. Stauffenberger (eds.), Police Personnel Administration. North Scituate, MA: Duxbury.

Wilson, J. Q. (1963). Police and their problems--a theory. Public Policy, 1-19.

PROFESSIONALISM

Adams, R. (1981). Education as a component of law enforcement professionalism: The concept and its measurement. Southern Journal of Criminal Justice, 6(2), 22-38.

Auten, J. H. (1981). The paramilitary model of police and police professionalism. Police Studies, 4(2), 67-78.

Ayres, R. M. (1975). Police Unions--a step toward professionalism. Journal of Poice Science and Administration, 3(4), 400-404.

Baker, R., Meyer, F. A., Jr., & Rudoni, D. (1979). Police professionalism--the need for clarity. In R. Baker & F. A. Meyer, Jr. (eds.), Evaluating alternative law-enforcement policies. Lexington, MA: Heath.

Bopp, W. J. (1977). On professionalization. In D. T. Shanahan (ed.) Administration of Justice System. Boston: Holbrook.

_____. (1978). O. W. Wilson and the search for police profession. New York: Kennikat.

Brown, G. E. (1979). Professionalism of police--proceed with caution. Police Chief, 46(11), 22-24.

Brown, S. E., & Vogel, R. E. (1983). Police professionalism. Journal of Crime and Justice, 6, 17-37.

Chackenian, R. (1977). Police professionalism and citizen evaluations--a preliminary look. In J. Munro (ed.) Classes, Conflict and Control--Studies in Criminal Justice Management. Cincinnati, OH: Anderson Publishing.

Clement, R. C. (1976). Education and training: The foundations of professionalism. (Book review). The Police Chief, 43(8), 8.

Cliff, R. E. (1974). Toward a professional police. Santa Cruz, CA: Davis.

Daniel, E. D. (1977). Political pressure, integrity, and professional police administration. Police Chief, 44(5), 24-25.

Decottis, T. A., & Kochan, T. A. (1978). Professionalism and unions in law enforcement. In P. F. Cromwell, Jr., & G. Keefer (eds.), Police community relations. St. Paul, MN: West.

Douthit, N. (1975). August Vollmer: Berkeley's first Chief of Police and the emergence of police professionalism. California Historical Quarterly, 54, 100-124.

Duignan, John F. (1978). Education's role in the quest for professionalism. The Police Chief, 45(1), 32-33.

Feville, P., & Juris, H. A. (1976). Police professionalization and police unions. Sociology of Work and Occupations, 3(1), 88-113.

Gazell, J. A., Parker, W. H. (1976). Police professionalization and the public: an assessment. Journal of Police Science and Administration, 4(10, 28-37.

Grossman, J. H., & Kohnke, W. R. (1976). Police professionalism--an attitudinal approach. Law and Order, 24(4), 20, 21, & 24.

Hanley, D. M. (1976). Police professionalism: A view from the middle. The Police Chief, 43(11), 34, 50, 52.

Huber, R. A. (1977). Police work--profession or trade. International Review of Criminal Police, (33), 17-22.

Keil, T., & Ekstrom, C. (1978). Police Chief professionalism. Sociology of Work and Occupation, 5(4), 470-486.

Lotz, R., & Regoli, R. M. (1977). Police cynicism and professionalism. Human Relations, 30(2), 175-186.

Mecum, R. V. (1979). Professionalism: A new look at an old topic. The Police Chief, 46(8), 46-49.

Miller, J., & Fry, L. (1976). Measuring professionalism in law enforcement. Criminology, 14(3), 401-412.

Miller, J., & Fry, L. (1976). Reexamining assumptions about education and professionalism in law enforcement. Journal of Police Science and Administration, 4(2), 187-196.

Narduli, P. F., & Stonecash, J. M. (1981). Politics, professionalism and urban services. Social Science Quarterly, 64(1), 206-207.

Poole, E. D., & Regoli, R. M. (1979). Examination of the effects of professionalism on cynicism among police. Social Science Journal, 16(3), 59-66.

_____, & _____. (1979). Assessing the effects of police professionalism on role conflict. Abstracts on Police Science, 7(3), 137-143.

_____, & _____. (1979). Police professionalism and cynicism-- an empirical assessment. Criminal Justice and Behavior, 6(2), 201-206.

_____, _____, & Lotz, R. (1978). Linkages between professionalism, work alienation, and cynicism in large and small police departments. Social Science Quarterly, 59(3), 525-534.

Potts, Lee W. (1982). Police professionalization: Elusive or illusory, Criminal Justice Review, 7(2), 51-57.

Price, B. R. (1977). Police professionalism. Lexington, MA: D. C. Heath.

_____. (1979). Integrated professionalism. Journal of Police Science and Administration, 7(1), 93-97.

_____. (1976). Police administrators' ambivalence toward professionalism. Criminal Justice Review, 1(2), 13-20.

Regoli, R. M., & Poole, E. D. (1980). Police professionalism and role conflict--a comparison of rural and urban departments. Human Relations, 33(4), 241-252.

Reinke, R. W. (1974). Police professionalism--a national certification program. Public Management, 56(7), 18-19.

Rudoni, D., Baker, R., & Meyer, F. A., Jr. (1978). Police professionalism--emerging trends. Policy Studies Journal, 7, 454-460.

Sapp, A. D. (1978). Issues and trends in police professionalism. Criminal Justice Monograph, 8(5), 20-28.

Schubert, F. A. (1983). Police professionalism and public interest. Police Chief, 50(5), 14-15.

Sherman, L. W. (1974). Sociology and the social reform of the American police, 1950-1973. Journal of Police Science and Administration, 2(3), 255-262.

Smith, D. C. (1978). Dangers of police professionalism--an empirical analysis. Journal of Criminal Justice, 6(3), 199-216.

Staufenberger, R. A. (1977). Professionalization of police--efforts and obstacles. Public Administration Review, 37(6), 678-685.

Stinchcombe, J. B. (1980). Beyond bureaucracy--a reconstruction of the "professional" police. Police Studies, 3(1), 49-61.

Walder, S. (1976). Police professionalism--another look at issues. Journal of Sociology and Social Welfare, 3(6), 701-711.

Walker, S. (1979). Professionalism at the crossroads--police administration in the 1980s. In R. G. Iacovetta & Dae H. Chang (eds.), Critical issues in criminal justice. Durham, NC: Carolina Academic Press.

_____. (1977). Critical history of police reform--emergence of police professionalism. Review by Richardson, J. R. (1980). Journal of Urban History, (2), 231-246.)

_____. (1977). A critical history of police reform: The emergence of professionalism. Lexington, MA: Lexington.

Webster, William H. (1982). Professionalism in law enforcement. The Police Chief, 49(4), 8.

Welty, G. (1975). Professions, the police and the future. In E. C. Viano & J. H. Reiman (eds.), Police in Society. Lexington: Heath.

Yerger, M. G., & Brown, W. P. (1978). Police professionalism and corruption control. Journal of Police Science and Administration, 6(3), 273-282.

RELATIONSHIPS WITH SPECIAL GROUPS

Altschull, J. H. (1975). Press and the police--news flow and ideology. Journal of Police Science and Administration, 3(4), 425-433.

Bayley, D. H., & Mendelsohn, H. (1969). Minorities and the police. New York: Free Press.

Berkman, D. J. (1979). Preliminary national assessment of child abuse and neglect and the juvenile justice system: the shadows of distress, Sacramento, CA: American Justice Institute National Juvenile Justice System Assessment Center.

Binder, A. and Scharf, P. (1980). Violent police-citizen encounters. Annals of the American Academy of Political and Social Science, 452, 111-121.

Brooks, W. D., & Friedrich, G. W. (1970). Police Image--an exploratory study. Journal of communication, 20(4), 370-374.

Brostoff, P. M. (1976). Police connection--a new way to get information and referral services to the elderly. In J. Goldsmith & S. S. Goldsmith (eds.), Crime and the Elderly. Lexington, MA: Heath.

Clements, C. B. (1975). School relations bureau--a program of police intervention. Criminal Justice and Behavior, 2(4), 358-371.

Cooper, J. L. (1980). Police and the Ghetto. Port Washington, NY: Kennikat.

Decker, S. H. (1981). Citizen attitude toward the police--a review of past findings and suggestions for future police. Journal of Police Science and Administration, 9(1), 80-87.

_____, & Smith, R. L. (1980). Police minority recruitment-a note on its effectiveness in improving black evaluations of the police. Journal of Criminal Justice, 8(6), 387-393.

Frawley, W. J. (1981). Buffalo community youth officer program-- final report. Buffalo, NY: Buffalo Police Department, New York State Division of Criminal Justice Services.

Goldstein, A. P. (ed.). (1979). Police and the elderly. Elmford, NY: Pergamon.

Grange, J. (1974). Understanding conflict--experience and behavior. Police Chief, 41(7), 36-37, 38.

Greer, E. (1978). Class nature of the urban police during the period of black municipal power. Crime and Social Justice, 9, 49-61.

Hamel, R. (1979). Assisting the elderly victim. In A. P. Goldstein et al. (eds)., Police and the elderly. Elmsford, NY: Pergamon.

Hepburn, J. R. (1977). Impact of police intervention upon juvenile delinquents. Criminology, 15(2), 235-262.

Hockstedler, Ellen. (1984). Impediments to hiring minorities in public police agencies. Journal of Police Science and Administration, 12(2), 227-240.

Johnson, W., & Thompson, J. (1978). Child abuse--the policeman's rule--an innovative approach. In J. M. Eekelaar & S. N. Katz (eds.), Family Violence, Sacremento: California Commission on Peace Officer Standards and Training.

Lazin, F. A. (1980). How the police view the press. Journal of Police Science and Administration, 8(2), 148-159.

McGowan, R. H. (1977). Our senior citizens--now a way to help. Police Chief, 44(2), 54-55.

Miranda, A. (1980). Fear of crime and fear of the police in a Chicano community. Sociology and Social Research, 64(4), 528-541.

Moretz, W. J., Jr. (1980). Kids to cops--"We think you are important, we're not sure we understand you." Journal of Police Science and Administration, 8(2), 220-224.

Schack, S., Grisson, G., & Wax, S. B. (1980). Police service delivery to the elderly. Washington, DC: University City Science Center.

Skoog, D., Roberts, L. W., & Boldt, E. D. (1980). Native attitude toward the police. Canadian Journal of Criminology, 22(3), 354-359.

Smith, D. (1981). Upsurge of police repression--an analysis. Black Scholar, 12(1), 35-57.

Solomayor, M. (1979). Juvenile delinquency--a community perspective. Agenda, 9(3), 15-19.

Stratton, J. G. (1975). Effects of crisis intervention counseling on predelinquent and misdemeanor juvenile offenders. Juvenile Justice, 26(4), 7-18.

Wilson, B., & Cooper, J. L. (1979). Ghetto reflections and the role of the police officer. Journal of Police Science and Administration, 7(1), 28-35.

SOCIAL SERVICE

Aaronson, D. E., Dienes, C. T., & Mushend, M. C. (1977). Policing public inebriates in decriminalized cities: A summary of
methods. Contemporary Drug Problems, 6(4), 607-627.

Bard, M. (1971). The role of law enforcement in the helping system.
Community Mental Health Journal, 7, 151-160.

_____. (1975). Role of law enforcement in the helping profession.
In A. R. Coffey & V. E. Renner (eds.), Criminal Justice as a
system. Englewood Cliffs, NJ: Prentice-Hall.

_____, & Zacker, J. (1976). Police and interpersonal conflict-
third party intervention approaches. Washington, DC: Police
Foundation.

Barocas, H. A. (1973). Urban policeman: crisis mediators or crisis
creators. American Journal of Orthopsychiatry, 43, 633-634.

Bayley, D. H. (1980). Ironies of American law enforcement. Public
Interest, (59), 45-56.

Bittner, E. (1967). Police discretion in emergency apprehension of
mentally ill persons. Social Problems, 14, 278-292.

_____. (1976). Police on skid row--a study of peacekeeping.
In W. B. Sanders & H. C. Daudistel (eds.), Criminal Justice
Process. New York: Praeger.

Bonovitz, J. C., & Bonovitz, J. S. (1981). Diverson of the mentally ill into the criminal justice system: the police intervention
perspective. American Journal of Psychiatry, 138(7), 973-976.

Brandt, A. (1975). Reality police: The experience of insanity in
America. New York: Morrow.

Brown, D., & Iles, S. Community constables: a study of a policing
initiative (Home Office Research and Planning Unit Paper #30).
London: Home Office.

Burnett, B. B., Carr, J. J., Sinapi, J., & Taylor, R. (1976).
Police and social worker in a community outreach program. Social
Casework, 57, 41-46.

Carr, J. J. (1979). Administrative retrospective on police crisis
teams. Social Casework, 60(7), 416-422.

Clark, D. B. (1981). Death in the family--providing consultation to
the police on the psychological aspects of suicide and accidental
death. Death Education, 5(2), 143-155.

Cohn, A. W., & Ward, B. (1980). Improving management in criminal justice. Beverly Hills, CA: Sage Publications.

Colbach, E. M., & Fosterling, C. D. (1976). Police social work. Springfield, IL: C. C. Thomas.

Cooke, G. (1979). Training police officers to handle suicidal persons. Journal of forensic sciences, 24(1), 227-233.

Curran, James T., & Ward, Richard H. (1975). Police and law enforcement. New York: AMC.

Dunford, F. W. (1977). Police diversion: an illusion. Criminology, 15, 335-352.

Euler, J., et al. (1974). The police social worker--a community broker. The Police Chief, 41, 28-32.

Green, R. (1976). Police as social service workers? Journal of Sociology and Social Welfare, 3(6), 691-700.

Gregory, S. Fremont (California) police department victim services project final report. Fremont, CA: Fremont Police Department.

Hall, M. N. (1982). Law enforcement officers and death notification--a plea for relevant education. Journal of Police Science and Administration, 10(2), 189-193.

Handberg, R., & Pilchick, S. (1980). Police handling of mental patients: crisis intervention requirements and police behavior. Criminal Justice Review, 5(2), 66-73.

Hanley, D. M. (1976). Police professionalism--a view from the middle. Police Chief, 43(11), 50 & 52.

Henderson, H. E. (1976). Helping families in crisis--police and social-work intervention. Social Work in Health Care, 21(4), 314-316.

Hipple, J. L., & Hipple, L. (1976). Training law enforcement officers. Social Work, 21(4), 316-317.

Kowaleski, V. A. Police and social service agencies: Breaking the barriers. Police Chief, 42(10), 259-262.

Lovrich, N. P., Jr., & Pachon H. (1977). The consolidation of urban public services: a focus on the police. Public Administration Review, 37, 38-47.

Lowenstein, L. F. (1976). The schism between the law and social
  worker. The Police Journal, 49(2), 82-86.

McKenna, J. S., Breuer, M., & Singer, R. B. (1980). Police Social
  Services--The 1st decade. Police Chief, 47(7), 38-43.

Mennig, J. C., & Eastman, W. E. (1977). Delivery of services to
  the community. In D. T. Shanahan (ed.), Administration of Justice. Boston: Holbrook.

Minitz, E., & Sandler, G. B. (1974). Instituting a full-service
  orientation to policing. Police Chief, 41(6), 44-45, 48-50.

Nielsen, E. Social Work and the Police. Social Work, 27(3), 287.

Parkinson, G. C. (1980). Cooperation between police and social
  workers--hidden issues. Social Work, 25(1), 12-18.

Pogrebin, M. (1980). Service and law enforcement. Police Chief,
  47(11), 48-59, 69.

Price, B. R. (1976). Police administrator's ambivalence towards
  professionalism. Criminal Justice Review, 1(2). 13-20.

Punch, M. (1979). Secret social service. In S. Holdaway (ed.),
  British police. Beverly Hills, CA: Sage Publications.

_____, & Naylor, T. (1973). The police: a social service. New
  Society, 24, 358-361.

Reid, T. A., Garner, P. W., & Tondo, T. R. (1977). Hamden
  juvenile evaluation, etc. Journal of Clinical Child Psychology, 6
  (3), 98-101.

_____. (1981). Report from the national Hispanic conference on
  law enforcement and criminal justice, July 29-30, 1980, Washington,
  DC: Interamerica Research Associates.

Roberts, A. R. (1976). Police social workers--a history. Social
  Work, 21(4), 294-299.

_____. (1978). Training police social-workers--neglected area of
  social-work education. Journal of Education for social work, 14
  (2), 98-103.

Schaffer, Evelyn, B. (1976). A new approach to delinquency pre-
  vention--the Illinois police/social service project. The Police
  Journal, 49(1), 35-41.

Schonborn, K. (1976). Police and social workers as members of new
  crisis-management teams. Journal of Sociology and social welfare,
  3(6), 679-688.

Scott, E. J. (1980). Innovations in South Carolina Law Enforcement, 1980. Columbia: University of South Carolina College of Criminal Justice.

_____. (1981). Calls for service--citizen demand and initial police response. Washington, DC: U. S. Department of Justice, National Institute of Justice.

Moore, A. (1981). Patterns of police--referral agency interaction. Washington, DC: U. S. Department of Justice, National Institute of Justice.

_____. (1981). Police referral in Metropolitan Areas--Summary Report. Washington, DC: U. S. Department of Justice, National Institute of Justice.

Treger, H. (1976). Wheaton-Hiles and Maywood Police-Social service projects-comparative impressions. Federal Probation, 40(3), 33-39.

_____. (1976). Social work in the police agency--implications for education and practice. Journal of Education and Social Work, 12(2), 43-50.

_____. (1981). Police-social work cooperation. Journal of Contemporary Social work, 62(7), 426-433.

_____, Thomson, D., & Jaeck, G. S. (1974). Police-social work team model--some preliminary findings and implications for system change. Crime and Delinquency, 20(3), 281-290.

_____. (1975). The police-social work team. Springfield, IL: C. C. Thomas.

Woolf, D. A., & Rudman, M. (1977). Police-social-service cooperative program. Social Work, 22(1), 62-63.

SUBJECTS OF GENERAL INTEREST

Alderson, J. C., & Stead, P. J. (eds.). (1973). The police we deserve. London: Wolfe.

Atulman, M. A. (1976). Social psychological approach to the study of police corruption. Journal of Criminal Justice, 4(4), 323-332.

Baker, R., & Meyer, F. A., Jr. (1979). Evaluating alternative law-enforcement policies, Lexington, MA: Lexington.

Banton, M. (1964). The policeman in the community. New York: Basic Books.

Bennett, T. (ed.). (1983). The future of policing. Cambridge, Eng.: Cambridge University, Institute of Criminology.

Berkeley, G. (1969). The European police: challenge and change. Public Administration Review, 28(5), 423-430.

Broderick, J. J. Police in a time of change. Morristown, NJ: General Learning.

Doig, J. W. (1968). Police problems, proposals, and strategies for change. Public Administration Review, 28(5), 393-406.

Drummond, D. S. (1976). Police Culture, Beverly Hills, CA: Sage Publications.

Ericson, R. V. (1982). Reproducing order: a study of police patrol work. Toronto: University of Toronto Press.

Fell, R. D., Richard, W. C., & Wallace, W. L. (1980). Psychological job stress and the police officer. Journal of Police Science and Administration, 8(2), 139-147.

Goldstein, H. (1969). Police response to urban crisis. Public Administration Review, 28(5), 417-423.

Holdaway, S. (1983). Inside the British police: a force at work. Oxford: Blackwell.

Johnson, T. A., Misner, G. E., & Brown, L. P. (1981). Police and society--an environment for collaboration and confrontation. Englewood Cliffs, NJ: Prentice-Hall.

Kirkham, G. L., & Woolan, L. A., Jr. (1980). Introduction to law enforcement. New York: Harper & Row.

Moore, M. D. (1977). Police--In search of direction. In L. Gaines & T. A. Ricks (eds.), Managing the police organization. St. Paul, MN: West.

Niederhoffer, A. (1974). Behind the shield--the police in urban society. New York: Doubleday.

Pogrebin, M., & Atkins, B. (1976). Probable causes for police corruption: some theories. Journal of Criminal Justice, 4(1), 9-16.

Reiser, M. (1972). The police department psychologist. Springfield, IL: C. C. Thomas.

_____. (1973). Practical psychology for police officers. Springfield, IL: C. C. Thomas

_____. (1982). Police psychology--collected papers. Los Angeles: Lehi.

Rudas, G. (1977). Changing role, responsibilities and activities of the police in a developed society. International Review of Criminal Police, (33), 11-16.

Sherman, L. W. (1977). City police, police administrators, and corruption control. New York: John Jay.

_____. (ed). (1974). Police corruption: a sociological perspective. Garden City, NJ: Anchor.

Skolnick, J. H., & Gray, T. C. (1975). Police in America, Boston: Little, Brown.

_____, & Schwartz, R. D. (eds.). (1970). Society and legal order: cases and materials in the sociology of law. New York: Basic Books.

Taylor, W., Bank, W., & Braswell, M. (1978). Issues in police and criminal psychology. Lanham, MD: University Press of America.

Terris, B. J. (1967). The role of the police. Annals of the American Academy of Political and Social Science, 374, 58-69.

_____. (1970). The role of the police. In A. Niederhoffer & A. S. Blumberg (eds.), The ambivalent force. Hinsdale, Ill.: The Dryden Press.

Wilson, J. Q. (1969). What makes a better policeman. The Atlantic, 223(3), 129-135.

_____. (1969). Dilemmas of police administration. Public Administration Review, 28(5), 407-416.